Ruinair

How to be treated like shite in 15 different
countries … and still quite like it

Paul Kilduff

Collins

*Playa Mar
Puerto Pollensa
May 2011*

*Flight ABZ
Buckie*

Collins
An imprint of HarperCollins Publishers
77-85 Fulham Palace Road
www.collins.co.uk

First published in 2008 by Gill & Macmillan Ltd

This edition published in 2009 by Collins

© Paul Kilduff 2008

ISBN: 9780007306152

Typography design by Make Communication
Print origination by TypeIT, Dublin
Printed by Clays Ltd, St Ives, plc

A CIP catalogue record for this book is available from the British Library.

Mixed Sources
Product group from well-managed
forests and other controlled sources
www.fsc.org Cert no. SW-COC-1806
© 1996 Forest Stewardship Council

FSC is a non-profit international organisation established to promote the
responsible management of the world's forests. Products carrying the FSC
label are independently certified to assure consumers that they come
from forests that are managed to meet the social, economic and
ecological needs of present and future generations.

Find out more about HarperCollins and the environment at
www.harpercollins.co.uk/green

Ruinair

How to be treated like shite in 15 different countries
… and still quite like it

'For years flying has been the preserve of rich
fuckers. Now everyone can afford to fly.'
MICK O'LEERY, CHIEF EXECUTIVE
RUINAIR HOLDINGS PLC

Contents

Prologue

Is that Mick? I stare ahead at the check-in queue for London Stansted. Others spot him too and peer over. It looks like Mick. He wears faded denim jeans and a creased check shirt, with buttons undone and sleeves rolled up. He is active and agitated. So it must be Mick. I have never stood so close to a man worth six hundred million euro who doesn't possess a tie, nor apparently an iron. Mick is the closest thing we have to a real cult in Ireland.

I wonder why he bothers to stand in a queue, five or six people ahead of me, taking another flight to his Mecca. He could have jumped the line; instead he joins the *Great Unwashed*. I'm vaguely impressed. I wonder if he really purchased a ticket like I did, how long ago he booked it and if it's as cheap as my flight.

There's no sign of Mick when I reach the departure gate so he must be in the VIP area. But suddenly he stands up like a Messiah in our midst and assists his staff to take our boarding cards. I purposefully join his personal queue and he rips my boarding card in two with a practised ease. Mick doesn't look at me. We don't bond.

I have an aisle seat in the centre of the B-737. Mick sits a few rows ahead, reads an *Irish Times* at speed, then grazes some business papers. He chats to a colleague who sits opposite. The crew are on their very best behaviour today. So is their boss. He hasn't sworn at anyone yet, us passengers included. I wonder where it all went wrong. We both attended private schools in Ireland favoured by the cream of the country: rich and thick. We were at university in Dublin at the same time. We joined large accounting firms in Dublin. He almost qualified as an accountant, but I did. He left the profession to buy a few corner shops in Dublin, but I took a proper day job. One of us is now a multi-millionaire and one of us writes books.

How does he do it? There isn't a spare seat on the flight. I paid a teeny ten euro return fare for the trip. It's cheaper than parking a car at the airport, cheaper than the books on sale in the terminal, cheaper than the sandwich and coffee available on board, cheaper than the train to civilisation at the other end. The taxes, fees and charges are still a mystery to me. I paid forty penal euros. Mick had the gall to charge me a €6 credit card handling fee, yet I did it all online. I mean, who ever handled my credit card but myself?

Today we fly to a place to the north-east of London called Stansted, which is *Connex*ted by rail to Liverpool Street. This modern accessible airport is an essential component of this airline's strategy. Experience shows that passengers will fly from somewhere to nowhere, but will not fly from nowhere to nowhere. I stalk Mick along the corridors on our communal route march towards Arrivals. I spy a row of five middle-aged men in grey suits wearing shiny British Airport Authority ID badges. They are on bended knee as they shake his hand. Mick delivers 60 per cent of all passengers arriving at their airport. It's like a visit from the Pope.

The new world order is in the concourse. Ruinair have half the floor space. EzJet have the rest. Herr Berlin is the latest upstart. Buzz were badly stung. DebonAir went out of fashion. Go are long gone. The walls of the terminal are adorned with Ruinair's smiley bulbous aircraft, their route map cobweb and must-see website address. The latter is the most searched travel website in Europe and the world's most searched airline brand according to Google. Ruinair is the world's largest international scheduled airline by passenger numbers, ahead of Lufthansa, Air France and British Airways, and is the third most valuable airline in the world, surpassed only by Southwest Airlines and Singapore Airlines. Even with its millions of passengers, Ruinair only enjoys an 8 per cent market share of the 600 million people who fly annually within Europe.

We are the Ruinair generation who take flights abroad in the same way our parents took bus trips into town. Ruinair takes us from A to somewhere remotely near B; from Aarhus to Zaragoza (Pyrenees). They fly to every hamlet in Europe: Altenburg, Billund, Brno, Lamezia, Pau, Vaxjo (which sounds like a toilet cleaner), Weeze, Zadar; places that I doubt even exist. *RuinWhere?* They fly to the vague destination of Karlsruhe Baden-Baden (Stuttgart), so Bad they named it twice. They fly to Balaton in Hungary, which is not a city, but a lake. Fifty million passengers travel annually on 550 routes between 26 countries on our own *Eireflot*.

This is no longer a little Irish airline. It's an epidemic of biblical proportions. As I study the Ruinair route map, I am reminded of their Spanish routes. I decide I will book another flight, this time to Malaga. I am confident the fare will be as low, and the experience as painless, as today. Surely Mick and his very cheap airline couldn't ruin my precious summer holiday.

Spain ... not quite

Ruinair Flight FR7043 – Saturday @ 2.10pm – DUB-AGP-DUB

Fare €300 plus taxes, fees and charges €40

The first sign of terminal trouble is the subtle inactivity at the Malaga departure gate. Our scheduled boarding time passes quite uneventfully. Growing mumblings of discontent and half-truths circulate like gossip. A lady with us has a daughter who works for this airline, such an admission to make, think of the public shame and humiliation, but she telephones her daughter. There is an aircraft outside so there's hope, but she learns it has technical problems. The screens show '*Retrasado*'. This is Spanish for '*Your Aircraft Is Fucked*'. We wait in a void of passenger information and customer service. Every Ruinair flight number has an FR prefix. If the R stands for Ruinair, someone tell me please, what does the F stand for?

One brave passenger walks up to the desk and comes back with his hands outstretched, holding up ten fingers in full view to us. We will board in ten minutes time? He announces: 'Delayed until ten o'clock tonight.' Eight hours late. An engineer is flying out on another aircraft to rescue us from our fate. I recall Mick's statement: '*If a plane is cancelled will we put you up in a hotel overnight? Absolutely not. If a plane is delayed, will we give you a voucher for a restaurant? Absolutely not.*' I paid an arm and a leg for this trip, not to mention other essential body parts. Three hundred euros plus taxes, twenty euros less than our green national flag carrier Aer Lingus. And if Aer Lingus will now fly me from Dublin to London for one euro, does that make them a low fares airline? Ruinair is not a low fares airline. It's only a *lower* fares airline.

My fellow passengers are middle-aged couples returning from their place in the sun with a tan to demonstrate that they're loaded, glamorous leathery mothers and svelte daughters swapping copies of chick-lit and *Hello*, and gangs of forty-something businessmen still dressed in their garish checked golfing gear, all owning their little piece of Marbella or Puerto Banus. There is utter incredulity from four Americans who have lost all faith in European air travel. Airline credibility is like virginity. You can only lose it once. There are two Spaniards who can go home, eat, sleep, shop, clean, procreate and still return in time to depart. We sit near the screens showing departure times. In the past I have looked at these screens and gained much amusement from various charter airlines' delays of, not hours, but days or weeks. Our flight is top of the list with a now nine-hour delay. Others pass by and smile over at us. Today the joke is on us.

I find a girl from Iberia; that's the airline, not the peninsula. She checks her screens and tells me my flight has now completely disappeared and she doesn't know what gate it might leave from. She is baffled because she says she used to work with the little Irish airline but she left. Wise woman. Somehow I survive nine hours in the terminal. You can only read the small print on the reverse side of your boarding card so many times. I visit every shop ten times, doze, read all known English language newspapers, down fries and Cokes, but still there are eons to kill until departure. At a time like this I harp back to Mick and his wise words: *'An airplane is nothing more than a bus with wings on. Are we are trying to blow up the notion that flying is some kind of orgasmic experience rather than a glorified bus service? Yes, we are.'* Success.

We are drawn to the gate like moths to a flame as midnight approaches. A few Irish guys are drunk and enter the *Ladies* by mistake. Inside naked sunburnt babies are bathed in the hand basins by irate mothers. Passengers lie on the airport floor, their energy levels as depleted as their mobile telephone batteries. We prepare to board but there is mass confusion. Some of us have yellow fluorescent pen 'P's hand-written on our boarding cards. We think it means *Priority*. Others behind in the scrum ask if anyone has a yellow pen they can use. The Americans ask what the 'P' means. I tell them it stands for *Pissed Off*.

On board it's clear some passengers are well and truly hammered, having spent nine hours in the airport bar knocking back rounds of San Miguel. 'Same again.' A guy sitting in the emergency exit aisle is swapped by Gavin the cabin supervisor with another passenger, because he's too drunk to do anything in the event of an emergency, save a burp, stagger or a *Ralph and Huey*. He carries a plastic beaker of beer with him as he rises to move seats. The crew say nothing. Apparently you can now bring your own alcohol on board. He takes the proffered seat and asks Gavin for a Heineken. Gavin tells him to wait until we are airborne.

We get a vague explanation from the pilot as to the technical problem. It's something to do with the 'data management' system. So that's okay. It's not like it's important or anything, like a wheel, an engine or a wing. The pilot is female, called Carole somebody. She introduces her colleague on the flight deck, another female. The Americans look at each other and become very non-PC. 'Two women pilots?'

Our aircraft is one of those pre-historic 23-year-old Boeing 737s, one evidently previously owned by Lufthansa because all the warning signs are in a language I don't immediately understand. *Schwimmweste unter Ihrem Sitz. Nicht Rauchen. Ausgang.* I start looking for old pre-WWII signs like *Gott im Himmel* and *Hände Hoch*. The aircraft is so old that there's a receptacle in the WC for the disposal of used lethal razor blades. I sit in one of those tired sunken velour seats where I worry my butt will become permanently wedged and I won't ever be able to get up, and I might have to spend the rest of my life going back and forth on this aircraft, never getting any help from the crew, what with their fast turnaround times. As Mick says about this unique low fares travel experience: '*You want luxury? Go somewhere else.*'

The in-flight service is uneventful save for the resentment of the Americans. When it is announced there are drinks and snacks *available for purchase*, they exclaim to Gavin, 'You're kidding. Ten hours on the ground and you don't even give us a goddamn cup of water?' They have not heard Mick's proclamation: *'No, we shouldn't give you a bloody cup of coffee. We only charge 19 euros for the ticket.'* One of the Americans is creative and asks the crew, 'Do you have ice cubes? Can you give me a cup of ice? You don't charge for ice?' She denies his request. The American isn't beaten. 'Can we drink the water from the taps in the toilets?' he perseveres. She stares back blankly. 'That is forbidden.' Later the crew come past with plastic bags and one girl says to me 'Rubbish?' and I wonder if she's asking for my opinion about this airline.

Flights which depart late often arrive on time because airlines brazenly lie about journey times. Not this time. We land in Dublin at 1am local time on the next day. When I checked in thirteen hours ago I was clean-shaven but after this journey of *Palinesque* proportions, I now have a beard like Santa's. We had religious education classes at school where a Holy Ghost priest educated us on the concept of eternity. He told us to think of time as a grain of sand and then add all the grains in the world together to gain a concept of eternity. Now I know I need to additionally include the delay on this flight to fully comprehend eternity.

I am still seething days later but consider myself fortunate to have escaped from Malaga. I mean, I could still be there today. My Ruinair experience demonstrates that sometimes it can be better to arrive than to travel. I crave a feeble revenge of sorts. I don't hold out much hope but I craft a stroppy letter.

Customer Service
Ruinair Ltd
Dublin Airport

Dear Sirs,

I had the great misfortune to travel on FR7043 from Malaga to Dublin where our departure time was delayed by a record-breaking ten hours. In these circumstances can you firstly advise me of the exact reason for this delay since at the time all we got was the usual vague explanation?

Can you explain why no information was given to us at any

time by any of your staff and why do you have zero staff located at Malaga airport? Why was it necessary to fly an engineer all the way out from Dublin when surely you could use local contractors to do maintenance work? Can you confirm the defective aircraft in question, a Boeing 737, is twenty-three years old, and if so, isn't this three years longer than the useful life of twenty years as recommended by the makers?

Can you explain the utterly chaotic boarding process where some of us had handwritten 'P's on our boarding cards, which some thought meant 'Priority', and if so why was this not used when boarding as opposed to the ugly scrum we endured?

Can you advise why drunk passengers were allowed to board the flight after ten hours spent in the airport bar; one male passenger being moved by the cabin supervisor from a seat in the emergency exit row since he was too inebriated to do anything in the event of an emergency save barfing, and when moved he had a plastic beaker of beer in his hand; and do you now allow passengers to bring their own alcoholic drinks on board direct from the terminal bar?

Lastly please confirm you will reimburse me for my evening meal in the airport and the extra day's car parking at the airport when a seven-day holiday became an eight-day human endurance test. If I had paid ten euros for this return flight I wouldn't bother with this letter, but I paid a whopping €300 which isn't so wonderfully low fares after all.

Yours etc,
Disgusted of Dublin

I am amazed to receive a reply the very next day by email. It must be all the practice they get.

Dear Mr Kilduff,

Thank you for your letter received today. We regret any inconvenience caused due to the delay to your flight FR7043. Regrettably on the day in question your flight developed a technical fault on arrival at Malaga. Unfortunately the local engineer, after a detailed inspection, advised that a part was required for the aircraft and therefore it was necessary to transport the part from our service centre in Dublin. Despite our rigorous maintenance standards, technical problems occasionally arise and may cause delays.

I do sincerely regret that our sequential boarding policy was not adhered to by the agents at Malaga. We have clearly instructed all airports and handling agents to board all flights by boarding card number sequence and please be assured that this lapse in policy will be taken up with our agents at Malaga.

We have strict guidelines for the carriage of passengers who are under the influence of alcohol. Our in-flight personnel are particularly vigilant and tactful in relation to passengers who, although creating no disturbance, may have being drinking prior to departure and in this regard such passengers are monitored throughout the flight. I do assure you, had it been visible to the crew that any passengers were consuming their own alcohol on board it would have been confiscated by the crew.

As you may appreciate, we are a very efficient low fare airline and whilst we pride ourselves upon not charging extortionate fares that many of our competitors do, equally our low fares do not permit us to meet consequential expenses of passengers who may on rare occasions be inconvenienced. In this regard, I regret that we are not in a position to accede to your request for reimbursement. This should be claimed from your travel insurers.

I do hope that despite your dissatisfaction on this occasion, you will afford us the opportunity of welcoming you on board a flight in the near future and providing you with our normal friendly and efficient service, this time without interruption.

Yours sincerely

For and on Behalf of

RUINAIR LIMITED

Mick knows how best to describe this carefully worded, cut and pasted, utterly useless reply since he has coined a choice expletive to be used by his airline in one-to-one print media interviews to describe any simple procedure which other airlines claim to be complex. Mick's word is *Bolloxology*.

Mick's Plane Speaking

On low fares: *'People ask how we can have such low fares. I tell them our pilots work for nothing.'*

On destination airports: *'Sometimes there is not even a road to the airports we fly to.'*

On flying gangs of lager louts on stag weekends: *'We call them the Chianti louts heading to villas in Tuscany and the South of France.'*

On competition: *'Any idiot can paint a plane and start out offering low fares. It's about sustainability. We've been profitable now for twenty years. Nobody else can compete with us. They're all screwed.'*

On in-flight gambling: *'A lot of people are, frankly, bored on flights. We believe they have a high propensity to get involved in all sorts of games. We might have the pilot calling out the bingo numbers.'*

On how his airline might fail: *'Nuclear war in Europe, a major accident or believing our own bullshit. In any airline there is always a strong possibility of management stupidity. The biggest threat we face is a management fuckup.'*

On future fares: *'I have a vision in the future that we will be flying everyone for free, but I'm damned if I'm going to pay for them to fly.'*

On future travel: '*We may not be even flying in 2030. We may be all beamed about like Star Trek.*'

On opening new routes: '*We never want to be the explorers, they always get their heads shot off.*'

On trains: '*Trains are incredibly over-subsidised and don't service people's needs. The trains were fine in Victorian times when if you didn't have a stable you walked, but no one needs to use them now.*'

On politics: '*I think the most influential person in Europe in the last twenty to thirty years has without doubt been Margaret Thatcher, who has left a lasting legacy that has driven us towards lower taxes and greater efficiency. And without her we'd all be living in some bloody inefficient unemployed French republic.*'

On women: '*I generally get on very well with women, but I used to work seven days a week and usually sixteen-hour days. I had no time for girlfriends. I didn't have girlfriends for ten or fifteen years.*'

On fatherhood: '*I want to spend more time at the office. I am staying in the guest room and I don't plan to re-emerge until my son is at least two years old and ready to take instructions. I'm taking the company approach to it: I am subcontracting everything.*'

On retirement: '*It will be some time after we have established world domination, then it will be time for me to go. I will leave the airline when it's not growing rapidly and when it's getting dull and boring. I won't be gone in three or five years' time. But I have promised my wife that I will be.*'

On succession: '*In the future the company will need a chief executive who is different than I am. As the biggest carrier in Europe, they would have no use for someone who runs around in jeans and calls politicians idiots and says that the EU Commission is made up of Communists. I'm good at doing the loud-mouth and fighting everyone but it will be inappropriate to have somebody here shouting, swearing, abusing the competition. We will need more professional management than me.*'

On regrets: '*I don't look back at all. I'm forty-seven and I'm not going to be sitting here pulling wool out of my navel wishing I had done something differently. This is the most fun you can have with your clothes on.*'

On personal popularity: *'I don't give a shite if nobody likes me. I am not a cloud bunny, I am not an aerosexual. I don't like aeroplanes. I never wanted to be a pilot like those other platoons of goons who populate the airline industry. I'm probably just an obnoxious little bollocks. Who cares? The purpose is not to be loved. The purpose is to have the passengers on board.'*

France

Ruinair Flight FR42 – Sunday @ 7.55am – DUB-BVA-DUB

Fare €2 plus taxes, fees and charges €33

I plan to exact my revenge, to beat them at their low fares game and see *all* fifteen countries in Western Europe for the price of my ruined trip to Spain. And if I can purchase some cheap flights then gradually I will single-handedly reduce their average revenue per seat. My idea might fly but I am not sure if I can do it. I'm not certain if anyone cheap flies to Liechtenstein.

Mick approves of cheap flying. '*We gave away 15 per cent of our seats last year for free. If we didn't give them away, they'd be empty, but this way we have got the chance to sell car hire, a sandwich or a cup of tea. We're working on the multiplex cinema model — they make most of their money from the sale of popcorn, drinks and sweets, not cinema tickets. It is our ultimate ambition to get to a stage where the fare is free.*'

So I am doing something I've never done before: travelling to a place I never knew I wanted to go to, which is probably not quite where I think it is, and I am not sure what I will do once I get there. My ticket was purchased in one of those unlimited 'limited offers', the sort of special fares promotion that they only have on the front page of their website every single week. It was the Irish comedian Dara O'Briain who first noted that when you search for the Ruinair website address on the internet, you are first taken to a nearby website, from where you can catch a bus to get to the intended website address. The fare is two teeny euros. I have lost more through a hole in my pocket or put more into the collection plate at Sunday mass. These low fares are advertised in the media but often garner free publicity, such as the time Ruinair was criticised by the UK's Advertising Standards Authority for using offensive language in an advertisement. Published before Bonfire Night, the advertisement had depicted fireworks with the headline *'Fawking great offers'*. Even worse was the reaction to their advertisement showing the soles of a pair of feet on top of another pair of feet, with a 'fare for 2' of £69, and the slogan above *'Blow me, these fares are hard to swallow!'* How low.

It's good to fly to France for lunch. I could have taken the 46A bus into Dublin city centre for a bite instead but the bus fare into town is €1.90 each way, so it's much cheaper to travel to France for one euro each way. Mick likes these low prices: *'Our strategy is like Wal-Mart and Dell. We pile it high and sell it cheap. If anyone beats us on price, we will lower ours. We are the Tesco of the airline industry.'* This is cheaper than staying at home for two days. Forget the fact that the taxes, fees and charges are 1,650 per cent of the fare. The only things cheaper are the 'free' Christmas cards I receive annually from the Disabled Artists Association.

I am certain that it's costing this airline more than one euro in aviation fuel to move my butt six hundred miles eastwards towards France. I agree with Sir Bob Geldof's opinion on low air fares to unknown destinations: *'If I can get a £7 flight to somewhere within two hundred miles of Venice, you know, destination unknown, magical mystery tour, well, I'll take it. Seven quid, I don't care where I fucking go.'*

Flying is now all about queuing. We queue at the check-in to receive a boarding card, we queue at security to show the boarding card and we queue at the gate while they take back a piece of the boarding card they gave us earlier. After twenty years of flying from Dublin, Ruinair's boarding cards still show a space for *Seat Number*, albeit unused. With fifty minutes to go to the scheduled departure time, some passengers are already standing around at the gate. These are the passengers classified by this airline at an Investors' Day presentation as 'well-trained passengers'. More specifically, airline pilots officially refer to us passengers as 'SLF' (self-loading freight). There are signs and lines to queue but Irish people as a rule don't queue. The same guy who put the chocks under the nose-wheel asks us to form two orderly queues. 'Jaysuswha'didhesay?' I hear.

This airline has inadvertently created two classes of travel: early class and late class, much like business class and economy class in the old days. If you are late for check-in, you are doomed, and Mick agrees. *'We don't care if you don't show up.'* Many of my fellow passengers have evidently passed the *Advanced Masters Degree in Queue-Jumping.* This airline formerly used the same policy as on the *Titanic* when they used to invite passengers with children to go first. It was almost worth borrowing a child for the day. Now, like everything else on this airline, they charge passengers to stand in a queue. If you are a parent and you wish to be sure of a seat alongside your child, then that will be three euros each. I don't know what the mad rush is for anyway. I mean, we're all going to get seats. It's not like some of us will be left sitting on the cabin crew's knees or on the toilet seats if we are the last to clamber on board.

Or maybe we will. A few years ago Ruinair flew from Girona in Spain to Stansted with people seated in the aircraft's toilets. The airline, which was reported to the regulator following the incident, acknowledged that the flight was overcrowded and that it should not have happened. 'Ruinair does not overbook its flights,' a spokesman said. 'We are taking it very seriously and it is the subject of an internal investigation.' The passengers seated on the toilets for the duration of the flight were Ruinair staff. Other staff not on duty on the particular flight sat in jump-seats in the passenger cabin. Ruinair said the incident occurred because too many off-duty staff were allowed on board. This is what's known as a Loo Fares Airline.

Today the arriving passengers are still deplaning as we begin to get ready to board. Someday soon we will rush them at the two doors, like on the Tube. In fact this airline reminds me of the London Underground in many respects, but without the sense of personal space I enjoy on the Tube. Boarding is monitored in a simple manner. None of this new-fangled computer or electronic rubbish, as used by other airlines, is required. A staff member sits at a desk with an A4 page of numbers 1 to 189 and uses a highlighter marker to cross off our sequence number as we board. When a few of us have passed him by I expect him to leap up with joy, show us his completed fluorescent grid of work and shout *Full House*.

Getting onto the plane is by the scrum method. Two packs of burly passengers line up in opposite directions, wait for the signal and charge. '*Crouch ... touch ... hold ... engage.*' Like the Six Nations. We don't depart the terminal, rather we escape in a circuitous double-pronged pincer movement. Obstacles such as passing freight traffic, abandoned electrical machinery and lethal rotating jet engines don't matter because we want to get the best fucking seat. It's such a race that it seems other passengers genuinely do not believe there will be seats for all. I'm on the inside and past the departure gate, but a girl cuts through the walkway and comes up fast on my rear, so without indicating left or right, I move ahead and speed to the rear steps, until the girl breaks into a fast stride last seen in that ludicrous Olympic walking race and makes towards the same rear steps, so I edge her off at the steps with a shoulder charge and we board the aircraft with myself in pole position to find ... there are lots of vacant seats so we're both gutted. I wonder if we boarded only by the rear steps, could the arriving passengers exit by the front steps simultaneously and save time?

My preference is to use the rear steps to board. There's no point using the front steps unless you're the pilot. It's also proven to be safer to sit at the rear because you never hear of aircraft reversing into mountains. Also the 'Black Box' flight recorder is located in the tail and even when jets plunge into the Florida Everglades or the Amazonian rainforest, they always find the 'Black Box' intact, so that's encouraging. It's great to choose your own seat on board to avoid sitting beside large, loud or drunk people, teary babies or beardy loonies. I rarely sit in the emergency row with the extra leg room. Firstly you will spend the next two hours sitting ten feet away from the noisiest mother of all jet engines. And if that over-wing door blows out, you're hoovered.

The tray tables of the seats in a few of the back rows of the aircraft are down and have tatty photo-copied multi-lingual notices advising we cannot sit there. I don't know why. Maybe the crew dine there? I try to sit in one of these blocked seats but the cabin crew are having none of it and propel me along the aisle. This certainly undermines their treasured principle that we can sit anywhere we like when we board. *'I think we certainly have democratised flight, in that there's no curtains anymore, there's no business class anymore, you're not made to feel, you know, two inches tall, like, "Here you go, down with the poor people at the back." Everybody is the same on Ruinair,'* says Mick.

I take a row of seats only to find others before me had a food fight here and I'm sitting on their bread and crisps. The new B737-800 aircraft sports a nausea-inducing puce-yellow interior. This is the only airline in the world who employ an interior designer suffering from colour blindness. It's the same colour they use in McDonalds restaurants. Yellow is inviting and instantly warming but once you're sitting for ten minutes you want to vacate your seat and leave. This is not so easily done at 500 mph and at 32,000 feet.

A fellow passenger holds her boarding card towards me. 'Where is the seat number, please?'

'You can sit anywhere,' I advise helpfully. She is a veritable virgin. So rare these days.

Getting the optimal seat is a priority and it's not easy because there is some excellent top-notch competition out there these days, so practice and discipline are essential. It's important because the average elbow is wider than the seat's armrest and the middle seats create a war zone on two fronts. I am entitled to the entire armrest, and that means both of them. When selecting an aisle or window seat, do so depending on your strongest arm. I prefer an aisle seat. We all wish to establish our personal comfort zone with no one sitting next to us. Years of research by Boeing's head of aircraft seating found that one single factor most powerfully affects perceived passenger in-flight comfort: whether or not the seat next to you is empty. Even if the aircraft only has one free seat, then that free seat needs to be right beside me. Today I take an aisle seat where the window seat is already occupied by another solo flyer.

We nod in an unspoken agreement and pile everything we own in this world into the empty middle seat: coats, newspapers, books, food, bags, scarves, the kitchen sink and a few dead rabid dogs. It usually works. The seat remains empty.

More extreme strategies are required to keep an entire row of three seats all to yourself. First take the aisle seat to block easy access for others. The Bag technique is where I take a sick bag and hold it over my mouth and as people come past I heave into the bag and make eye contact with my tired teary eyes looking for sympathy. The Zombie technique is where I sit tall in the seat, eyes wide and staring straight ahead and from that position I bounce my head back and forth until I am dizzy. The Busy technique is where I put down all the trays in the row, spread out my papers, lunch, water, mobile telephone, briefcase, pens, books and whatever else I can muster and look too busy and annoyed to move anything for anyone who dares ask me if the seats are free. The One-Liner technique includes saying to any would-be neighbour, 'It sure feels good to be out of prison.' Another technique which works only for men is the Love technique where I grab an aisle seat and as passengers walk past, I boldly look them up and down, smile at them and occasionally give them a nice stare. Women think I am trying to pull them and men don't really want to know what I am thinking. If someone makes a move for the two seats I reach over and pat the seats and wink. This latter technique never fails. Either way, I am sitting on my own in an empty row.

Today there are lucky latecomers. The penultimate passengers are two flustered red-faced Dublin girls. 'Jaysus, we wus sittin' at the right gate but lookin' at the wrong screen. I don't know wha'. We're the ones hirin' a car when we get there. How are we gonna find our way around northern France when we can't find our way outta the bleedin' terminal building?' The very last passengers to board don't seem bothered at all as they stand around like a bunch of eejits in the aisles. They are all French. *Naturellement.* The aircraft is about 85 per cent full, which is typical for this airline. I am convinced they would achieve their average load factor of 85 per cent if they commenced a new daily service with one cent fares from Dublin to Timbuktu (South).

I wind my watch forward by one hour because France is one hour ahead of Ireland, plus about ten years. It was the Irish writer and Nobel prize-winner George Bernard Shaw who said that Ireland is the safest place to be on earth during an earthquake, since everything happens here forty years later. The pilot announces there will be a delay in departing. He says there is fog in France. All Ruinair pilots graduate with highest honours from the *Aviation School of Expectation Management*. We are advised we will sit in the aircraft going nowhere for one hour. We get another explanation. 'We were also a bit delayed here earlier with all the planes moving about at this hour of the morning. We had to get the plane from the hangar.' So that's where they keep them. I have seen them tow many aircraft to gates at 7am, as if they manufacture them around the corner. We groan and curse, anger rising. He announces later it's only a thirty-minute delay and we all smile. We take off thirty minutes late but somehow we all feel ecstatically happy about it. One excited child becomes vocal before the take-off: 'We're leaving. Quick. Put something in your mouth.' The same child will later utter upon our planned descent: 'We're going down. Watch out. Mind the road.'

On board there are unending announcements made at foghorn volume about smoking, the lavatories or asking us to buy things. I know why they make so many announcements. Because they cost nothing. What's wrong with putting a sign up somewhere and letting us rest in peace? When I get on a train, no one stands in the aisle each time to announce I can't use the lavatory when the train is in a station. They put up a sign instead. And I just know it. We all do. The safety announcements are unintelligible since they are delivered in a language unique to this airline, referred to as *Spanglish*. A gentleman behind mutters under his breath, 'Sure, I'd understand it better if she spoke it all in Spanish.' The girl has such a heavy Spanish accent that I doubt even a genuine Spanish passenger could understand her chesty pronouncements.

One part of the safety announcement always grates. '*In the event that we land on water, life vests are located under your seat.*' I'm not sure that if we do land on water this will be the first matter on my mind. More distracting matters such as staring at the fish outside the windows may take precedence. A life vest? Who's going to need a life vest? I would rather have scuba diving equipment under my seat. But the most annoying aspect is when they ask us to read the safety card stuck on the back of the seat and some guy across the aisle leans forward and starts reading it intently. We are all experienced, nonchalant, big-time travellers so no one dares to follow suit and read the instructions, but we all sit there and worry that if we hit a mountain, he will appear on the RTE News to explain how he alone survived and watched us perish at Mach One. 'The safety card I read made it clear what I should do in the event of plunging into a mountain.'

The cabin crew are vaguely good-looking in a lost, vacant sort of way. The lights are on but there's no one on board. Some might be Eastern European since they don't have much English. All they can utter is 'Any drinks or snacks to buy?' These are the people who will save us in the event of an emergency. They joined this airline to see all of Europe but now they only get to spend 25 minutes (maximum) in a range of ex-military airbases, where one of them draws the short straw to go face us passengers in the terminal.

There's something fairly awful about these blue staff uniforms. The female crew are either very tall or very short, or are very thin or very not-so-thin but they all wear the same size uniform. I don't know if Ruinair would consider doing uniform fittings for their staff? A small sum spent on what people would call uniform rules would go a long way to raising personal pride and corporate appearance. Grown men with bad haircuts wearing stained jackets and grubby off-white shirts try to sell us scratch cards, then tickets and telephone cards and Baggies of neat alcohol (and if we drink too many Baggies they will sell us a Lifeline 'hangover preventer' cure for three euros) and then perfumes and toys on this flying hypermarket.

The secret of success of this airline is that the seats are free but everything else costs us big-time, including checking in, boarding, luggage, food, drinks and even wheelchairs. They operate like Gillette where razors are cheap but blades are expensive; or like Vodafone where mobile telephones are cheap but minutes cost. Ruinair management don't think like other airline management, they think like supermarket retailers. No passenger purchases a scratch card so evidently we're not as stupid as we may appear. Mick has a view on selling scratch cards and so much more to passengers. *'They're for morons. On board our flights we don't allow anybody to sleep because we are too busy selling them products.'*

The coffee on sale on board is Fairtrade coffee but not for the right reasons. Mick says: *'The fact that our tea and coffee supplier is a Fairtrade brand is a welcome bonus, but the decision was based on lowering costs. We'd change to a non-Fairtrade brand in the morning if it was cheaper.'* I never purchase their tea on board on principle. Ruinair charge €2.75 for a cup of tea. Last time I was in Tesco, 80 Lyons tea bags cost €2.78. Once they sell the first cup, Ruinair are making a profit. But I am thirsty.

'Can I have a bottle of water please?' I ask.

'Still?'

'Yes, I still want it.'

I always carefully read the description on the label of the bottle. A few years ago this airline's highly profitable brand of bottled water did not come from a pure mountain stream or a rocky highland spring. It was mere tap water. Ruinair's Blue Rock water, which cost £1.85 for a 500 ml bottle, was supplied by Britvic Soft Drinks in the UK. While the label did not claim the water to be genuine spring water, neither did it make it clear that it was tap water. The same product was pumped into thousands of homes by Thames Water at a cost to consumers of only 0.06p per litre. This is what is known as a L'eau Fares Airline.

It's an inevitable fact of aviation that when people are stuck in a small metal tube for several hours with not much to do, one of the few distractions open to them to pass the time is to look at the cabin crew. The cashiers and shelf-stackers who double as flight attendants have exotic European makey-up unisex names such as Rosalba, Vaida, Danija (email me!), Edyna and Lorana but blondie Beata still remains the happiest crew member I will meet on my extensive travels. Most of the cabin crew appear to still be of schoolgoing age and are bunking off from lessons by having these day jobs. Their job description is to make *really* sure we don't want anything to eat or drink. I buy something else for the one-hour flight but the girl leaves me twenty cents short in change. I assume she'll return with the change but she doesn't remember or care. I don't bother asking. Twenty cents from each of their 50 million passengers will add an extra €10 million to their profit. Never in the field of human transportation was so much owed by so few to so many. Before we land we pass any of our rubbish to the crew, thereby becoming the world's first self-cleaning aircraft.

There is a programme on BBC where the actor Tony Robinson looks at *The Worst Jobs in History*. He's included jobs like *Public Executioner, Rat Catcher, Sewer Cleaner* and *Collector of Bodies during the Bubonic Plague*. In the next series he's looking at working as cabin crew for this airline. This is in contrast to the best jobs in the world, such as coach to the Swedish women's soccer team or Chief Taster for the Guinness quality assurance team with responsibility for all pubs in the greater Dublin area, who drive vans around Dublin on which locals have handwritten on the side: *Emergency Response Unit*. Or indeed the easiest jobs in the world, e.g. weather forecaster in southern Spain (*er ... tomorrow it's going to be hot*).

However, never dare to confront a member of the Ruinair crew. They might be armed and dangerous. Ruinair once sacked an air hostess who admitted keeping an illegal stun gun at her Strabane home. Sinead McDermott had worked for the airline for four years and was dismissed for gross misconduct and bringing the company into disrepute. The stun gun, which was shown in court, was capable of discharging 500,000 volts and could incapacitate somebody causing localised pain for up to five minutes. The brunette, who appeared in court wearing a low-cut top, skirt and boots, received a 200 hour community service order. McDermott listed the reasons for having the stun gun, saying she had received nuisance phone calls, her car had been burned, she had been followed and she feared for her safety. The resident magistrate said he took into account the fact McDermott had pleaded guilty at the first opportunity, which showed an element of remorse, her clear record and the fact she had lost a 'good job' as Ruinair cabin crew.

France is a country with the same population as the UK and has

double the land mass of the UK, yet there is not a single domestic
French low fares airline, thanks to the state-sponsored monopoly
of Air France. In a war amongst low fares carriers, providing cheap
flights to all five corners of France is the last remaining battle yet
to be fought. The French countryside is a *clichéd* patchwork of
manicured fields and dense forests but, as widely rumoured,
Beauvais airport terminal is a tent. The Departures end has white
metal walls and a canvas top which flutters nicely in the soft
breeze. This may be the only airport in the world at risk of being
closed in the event of high winds, not because aircraft are unable
to land, but because the airport blew away. The runway is so basic
that the pilot has to execute a U-turn and come back the same way,
only to stop as a tiny two-seater Piper aircraft comes across in
front. We disembark as the ground staff place a sign saying *Dublin*
on the tarmac for those taking the return trip. It's unnecessary
because there are only two aircraft in the entire airport and all 189
passengers are not going to fit into that Piper. Twenty paces later
and we are inside the terminal. Ten more paces and through
passport control. Ten more paces to the WC or the baggage
carousel, whichever is deemed more urgent. Ten paces to outside.
Paris Beauvais airport is closer to the city of Amiens than it is to
the French capital, but who would fly to Amiens?

Paris is the world's top destination for tourists but it ranks as
only the world's 53rd friendliest city. I admit I have never warmed
to the Parisians. They are so annoyingly arrogant about everything. Most locals in any European capital will take the chance to
speak a few words of English but Parisians wouldn't lower
themselves. If you have dinner in Paris, the locals excel. They
instantly recognise the best dishes on the menu and ask the
sommelier if he knows which side of the hill the *Pinot Noir* grapes
were grown on. As you dine on the finest food, they will find
something to criticise. And all this from a nation who gladly dine
on horses, snails and frogs. And every two years we dare to visit
them at *Stade de France* when their brutal rugby team administers
a regular thrashing to our brave boys in green (we have won once
in 35 years). The only redeeming feature about the French in
general is that they cannot manufacture a decent motor car for

love or money. P.G. Wodehouse conceded that the French invented the only known cure for dandruff, called the *Guillotine.*

There is a bus to Paris but the fare costs more than the flight and the duration of the bus journey is longer than the duration of the flight. I could hire a car today but I have seen too much of Parisian driving skills to risk that option. When you buy a new car in Paris you must go out on the first day with a claw hammer and knock lots of dents and holes in the side of the car, because if you don't, some other lunatic driver will do it for you in a 2cv the next day. I enquire at the airport information desk about taking a local bus into the town.

One of the girls points outside. '*Voila, ze bus.*'

I almost get on the bus but I check first. 'To Beauvais?'

She shakes her head. '*Non. A Paris.*'

I stand my ground. 'I want to go to Beauvais.'

She turns to her colleague. '*Il veut aller a Beauvais.*' Incredulity. They stare as if I'm on day release.

I persevere. 'The bus?'

Much shaking of heads. '*No bus. Rien.*'

I'm sure there's a bus. 'Not on a Sunday?' I ask.

'*Jamais, jamais. Taxi.*'

Beauvais is the capital of the Oise region of Picardy and has 60,000 inhabitants. The *Hotel le Chenal* is in the town centre. It's not a three-star hotel, it's *the* three-star hotel. I once stayed in a two-star hotel but I broke out into a rash at the lack of stars, and I once stayed in a hotel where the maid did not fold the toilet roll into a nice point daily so I checked out immediately. This hotel offers typical French hospitality. It takes me ten minutes to convince the duty manager I *have* a reservation, not that I want to make one. He fumes behind the counter and utters his first words of a genuine French welcome. 'You pay me eighty euro now.' It's fairly quiet here. If ten more guests check in, that'll make eleven in all.

The manager asks me if I want breakfast. I tell him that it's the most important meal of the day and of course I do, since I have paid for it, but then I realise he's only determining if he needs to employ a chef. My room overlooks the train station. There are exotic lights outside which change from red to amber to green and back. The bath is diamond-shaped, too big for one. I saw the same bath in a documentary I was forced to watch on a brothel in the Nevada desert. I accidentally stumble upon filth on the TV. Channel 17 features Priscilla upon a chaise longue, who has a compulsion to slowly undress. I am shocked. This sort of stuff should only be shown on pay TV. After her comes Natalia. Then Eva. Olga. Maria. Claudia. Etc.

The history of Beauvais is as potted as shrimps. In 1357 a peasant revolt began here, the *Jacquerie*. History shows me that the peasants are always revolting: poor dental hygiene, inappropriate dress sense and a lack of proper table manners are endemic. Beauvais's main products are blankets, carpets, ceramic tiles, brushes, bricks, chemicals, felt and tractors. Beauvais's only famous citizen is a lady named Jeanne Hachette. In 1472 the Duke of Burgundy laid siege to the town and all was lost until Jeanne killed an enemy soldier with an axe, tore down his Burgundy flag and rallied the troops. Her statue lies in the main town square and she is good-looking and well-built, in a bronze-casting sort of way. Her achievements are celebrated every October with a procession through the town where the women take precedence over the men. This day must be especially difficult for the French male.

The city centre was destroyed by WWII bombardments so the buildings are new but still ugly. I stroll along the main street, *Rue Carnot*, where there are estate agents who have perfected the pricing of houses to an amazing science, their windows displaying exact prices such as €183,564 and €242,973. I immediately stick out in the streets because I am the only person not carrying a huge baguette as if I plan to mug someone with it. I use my excellent command of French to buy my own baguette for lunch, and also largely for self-protection. A few people stop me to ask me questions. Do I look like I know about metered car parking and the one-way system?

The Cathedral of Saint-Pierre is a spectacular disaster. It was begun in 1225 and was to be the largest cathedral in Europe but its vaults collapsed in 1272. The French builders had another go soon after and built a 128-metre spire but this collapsed in 1284. Today it's a stub of a cathedral, having a chapel, a choir and a transept, and there's another church where the nave should be located. The cathedral's astronomical clock required the co-ordinated assembly in the 1860s of 90,000 different parts, surely a feat only equalled by the average irate IKEA flat-pack customer. If this clock had been assembled in Ireland, we would have many pieces left, surplus to requirements. These would be discarded on the sly as a workman looks at his trusty Casio watch and announces, 'Sure, it's keeping good time, like.' I stare at the clock for some time and realise it's completely useless. I cannot tell the time by looking at the face.

There is a *Son et Lumiére* show but there's quite a crowd here so I buy a ticket in good time. There are 100 chairs with headsets in front of the clock and I get a great seat in the front. The crowds thin as the show starts. No one else bought a ticket. The lights go up and people walk over to gawk but the area is roped off to stop freeloaders. They see me sitting on my own and maybe they can see a corner of the clock. The narrator in my headset begins an explanation, in much detail, of the first of the fifty-two different clock faces. The onlookers start taking photographs, the oldies with cameras and the young with mobile phones. I don't know whether they photograph me or the clock but they send the photograph back to their mates. *'This is the one guy who bought the ticket to watch that crap clock show in that half-built church.'* Towards the end of the show various wooden religious figures repeatedly move around the clock on wooden runners but, like BBC chat show hosts, there are few moving parts. The angels wave their arms about a bit and Jesus gives me a nod and a wink a few times. I'm not that impressed. I bet this happens every time.

I am not a huge fan of museums, especially the Imperial War Museum in London, which contains the three worst words in the English language, but the National Tapestry Museum is a top attraction. The huge carpets should be underfoot rather than on walls. Some of the tapestries took five years to make. My mother used to have a *Singer* like that. I walk the town in the evening but fail to find anything happening in any bars or restaurants. I slowly realise that by merely being here, I am in grave danger of *becoming* the nightlife. I return in despair to the hotel at 8.30pm. The manager prematurely wishes me *Bon nuit*. He knows nothing happens here. I am aghast to find Channel 17 has shut down for the night so I retire for a long soak in my brothel bath.

I always look forward to a large hotel breakfast, avoiding only melon balls on principle, what with the awful suffering caused to the poor melons. Today there's a buzz of sombre conversation at the front bar where locals perch on bar stools as they down espressos, but they glare back. The manager waves me away as if I'm a beggar on the take. '*Petit déjeuner. Ze back room.*' I sit at one of only two place settings, have cornflakes from one of two bowls, take oj in one of the two glasses and eat two of the last four croissants. It would not be unreasonable for me to assume that one remaining guest has yet to dine.

Before I check out, I surf the TV and accidentally stumble upon Channel 17. I get twenty seconds of Olga on the same chaise longue until the broadcast ends precisely at 10am. I wait ten polite minutes to check out but the manager gives me that knowing look. '*That porno channel just finished, eh?*' Upon my polite enquiry the manager shows me the timetable of the bus from the *Gare* to the airport. One bus leaves at 8.04am and the next leaves at 11.50am. I have missed the first bus and the second is too late for me. There are four hours between buses. They don't use a bus timetable around here, they use a calendar.

I arrive by taxi at Beauvais terminal one nano-second after the Paris bus deposits ninety ginger Irish passengers plus bags. I stand in line out the door, drag my bag across bare concrete and check in by the building site hoardings. The overhead screens have twee pictures of little thatched cottages because all Irish houses still look this. Past security I wait inside the tent, which upon close inspection is a marquee in need of a party. One moment the apron is deserted and the next there's 210 million dollars of Boeing's finest hardware; all three aircrafts sporting the angelic harp on the tail with the tricolour and the EI aircraft number on the fuselage. The aircraft are bound for Dublin, Shannon and Milan.

Who ever thought a Paddy airline could fly Italians from an airport 80 km from Paris to near Milan for one euro? I enjoy a swirl of national pride. I want to strut my stuff inside the tent and tell everyone that those shiny aircraft are ours. Sure, it's all we have as a nation: Guinness, Waterford Crystal (now made in Poland), Bono and the lads, Boyzone, Westlife, Saint Bob, the baldy girl who did the Prince cover, Terry Wogan, the ex-James Bond actor, St Paddy's Day, Riverdance, the shamrock, the *craic* and this airline. Plus literary chaps like Joyce, Shaw, Yeats, Beckett, Swift and meself, and also the Corrs, particularly Andrea. And not forgetting Sharon of the RTE News, Noodles Carey from the weather and Lisa who does the weather forecast on Sky News.

Mick shares my patriotic enthusiasm. '*They don't call us the fighting Irish for nothing. We have been the travel innovators of Europe. We built the roads and laid the rails. Now it's the airlines. I'm Irish and we don't have to prove anything. We are God's own children. We bow down to nobody. The airline industry is full of bullshitters, liars and drunks and we excel at all three in Ireland. We will be the world's biggest airline. There is no shortage of ambition here. We'll stuff every one of them in Europe, we won't be second or third and saying, "Didn't we do well?" We are a small Irish company, out there stuffing it to the biggest airlines all over Europe, and of course that feels good.*'

Customer Service
Ruinair Ltd
Dublin Airport

Dear Sirs,

I wish to complain about my recent flight from Dublin to Beauvais.

I boarded early to get a good seat at the rear of the aircraft. I remind you that your website states the following: 'We operate a free seating policy, so seats cannot be pre-booked. However, we operate a priority boarding system which allows you to choose your own seat on board.' There were seats vacant in rows at the rear but when I went to sit there a cabin crew girl told me I could not sit in these rows. When I asked her why not, she replied, 'Balance.' I said I was fine and I hadn't touched a drop of hard liquor all day. When I asked her what she meant, she did

*not know, but kept saying 'For balance.' Clearly she was
repeating something she had been told without fully
understanding it. I have travelled on many other airlines and
have seen passengers sit in these rows and we all lived to tell the
tale to our loved ones. Now I am worried that if I sit ever again
in these rows on any aircraft I may single-handedly cause the
aircraft to topple over and plunge to mother earth, and all
because of very little old me. I might add there were some rather
large Americans on board who sat randomly all over the aircraft
and they were a far greater danger to the 'balance' of the aircraft, since I am only a mere 12 stone and they were humungous.*

　　*My complaint is that although you state passengers can
choose their own seat on board, clearly this is not the case. I look
forward to your detailed and 'balanced' reply.*

　　Yours etc,
　　Disgusted of Dublin

Four days later ...

Dear Mr Kilduff,

　　I acknowledge receipt of your letter.

　　*I apologise for any inconvenience caused by not being able to
sit in certain rows on your flight with us.*

　　*Whilst we do operate a free seating policy, on recommenda-
tion from the manufacturers Boeing, we are advised when an
aircraft is not filled to a certain capacity it is necessary to cordon
off three rows of seats. This is for weight and balance purposes.*

　　*Once again I apologise for any inconvenience caused and
hope that the above is sufficient information.*

　　Yours sincerely
　　For and on Behalf of
　　RUINAIR LIMITED

More *bolloxology*. And here's why. A few months later I read in
the newspaper of a former Ruinair cabin crew member sacked for
allegedly falling asleep on the job who was 'delighted' that a
tribunal has found she was unfairly dismissed. One Ms Vanessa

Redmond was fired after a passenger complained she had blocked off rows of seats and fallen asleep while reading a novel on a Dublin to Durham flight. The passenger, who was married to a Ruinair manager, said he believed he saw Ms Redmond fall asleep. Ms Redmond denied all the charges apart from blocking off a row of seats, which her Ruinair colleagues testified was common practice because they didn't want passengers 'in their faces'. Balance, me arse.

How to Build Your Own Five Billion Euro Airline

Incorporate your new airline in the Republic of Ireland on 28 November with £1 of share capital '*to carry on the business of general carriers and forwarding agents and to use machines of all kinds capable of being flown in the air,*' as if there's much choice other than using aircraft. Seriously consider calling your airline *Trans Tipperary Air* but then decide to name it after yourself. You know that one in ten new airlines succeed.

The late Tony Ruin was born in Thurles in 1936, worked as a clerk with Aer Lingus in Shannon, ran the Aer Lingus operation in New York's JFK, dabbled in aircraft leasing and set up Guinness Peat Aviation with Aer Lingus and a City of London bank, hanging on to a 10 per cent personal stake in a fledgling enterprise ultimately worth millions years later. Tony once told a senior manager, '*The world is made up of fuckers and fuckees and in our relationship, you are my fuckee.*' On an Aer Lingus flight from London to Dublin Tony once encountered a senior Aer Lingus executive who publicly ridiculed him for flying on his arch rival, to which Tony replied: '*I had to fly on your airline — all our Ruinair flights are full today.*' Tony once admitted to being happiest when stepping either on or off an airplane, much like myself.

Start your airline by flying from Waterford to London Gatwick,

Waterford being ninety miles from Dublin and shortly to be renamed Dublin South International. Use a single turbo-prop fifteen-seater Bandeirante aircraft which today would not hold all your management team. Hire only cabin crew smaller than 5 foot 2 inches to operate in the tiny cabin. Employ 51 people and fly 5,000 passengers between Britain and Ireland.

1986

Launch a second route: Dublin to London Lootin'. Charge £99 for a flight (which seems steep now but was half the price charged by the two flag carriers). Run press advertising campaigns which ask 'Do you want to pay £100 for breakfast?' Use two 46-seater BAE-748 aircraft. Launch a Knock to Lootin' route, Knock being a village in the west of Ireland where the Virgin Mary allegedly appeared and granted favours, much like the Holy Stone of Clonrickett as seen in Father Ted. Employ 151 people and fly 82,000 passengers.

1987

Lease three bac1-11 aircraft from Tarom, the Romanian state airline. The planes come with Romanian pilots and crew, making for challenging cabin announcements. Increase the number of routes to fifteen, all between Ireland and the uk. Lose £3 million. Employ 212 people and fly 322,000 passengers.

1988

Lease three more aircraft from Tarom, making six in all. Launch the first routes to Europe: Dublin to Brussels (not Charleroi) and Munich (not Friedrichshafen). Launch a business class service and a frequent flyer club, neither of which endure. Incur more losses. All is gloom and doom. Employ 379 people and fly 592,000 passengers. Appoint an assistant to Mr Ruin called Mick O'Leery: born 20 March 1961, son of Timothy and Gerarda originally from Co. Cork, the eldest boy of six children, educated at St Mary's national school and the Christian Bothers in Mullingar, and Clongowes Wood College in Co. Kildare, a graduate of Economics & Social Studies from Trinity College Dublin and formerly a trainee tax accountant for eighteen months with KPMG Stokes Kennedy Crowley Dublin (where he assisted Mr Ruin with his tax affairs) and a successful former owner of three corner newsagent shops in Walkinstown, Terenure and Crumlin.

1989

Lose more money hand over fist. Employ 477 people and fly 644,000 passengers. The new guy called Mick tells you to shut down the airline due to the huge and accumulating losses, his first and only mistake.

1990

Realise you have lost £20 million due to intense competition from BA and Aer Lingus. Tell the government you are going to shut down and will lay off the workforce unless you get rights to fly to London's newest out of town airport, Stansted. Invest £20 million additional cash when no one believes your airline can fly. Send the chap called Mick to Southwest Airlines in Texas, USA: a low fares airline flying only one type of plane to out of the way airports with quick turnaround times and high flight frequency and where passengers find their own seats on board and pay for drinks and food. Allow Mick to nick all Southwest's best ideas as he returns to Dublin to implement a new and identical business model. Employ 493 staff and fly 745,000 passengers.

1991

Commence Dublin to Stansted flights. The Gulf War causes traffic to plummet as passengers prefer to stay at home and watch tanks guarding Heathrow on their TV. Move your main UK base from Lootin' to Stansted. Watch Dan Air go bust. Agree with Mick privately that he will be paid 25 per cent of the annual profits of the airline in excess of £2 million. Employ 477 staff and fly 651,000 passengers, the only year of such a decrease, but for the first time ever make an annual profit of a mere £293,000.

1992

Reduce routes from nineteen to six between Ireland and the UK. Employ 507 staff and fly 945,000 passengers.

1993

Buy six second-hand Boeing 737s from Britannia. Employ 503 staff and fly 1,120,000 passengers.

1994

Appoint Mick as Chief Executive Officer. Chuck out the old BAC planes and use only Boeing 737s. Employ 523 staff and fly 1,666,000 passengers.

1995

Overtake BA and Aer Lingus to become the biggest passenger carrier on the Dublin to London route, the busiest international air route in Europe, largely due to the water, making train travel difficult and driving even more hazardous. Open your first UK domestic route, flying from Stansted to Glasgow Prestwick. Celebrate your tenth anniversary in business. Buy four Boeings from Dutch airline Transavia bringing the fleet size to eleven 737s. Employ 523 staff and fly 2,260,000 passengers.

1996

Open new routes to Leeds, Bradford, Cardiff and the Bournemouth Riviera. Buy eight more 'slightly used with one careful owner' Boeings from Lufthansa. The EU completes the *Open Skies* deregulation of airlines in Europe allowing free competition on all internal routes. Cancel Mick's lucrative profit-sharing deal and give him 22 per cent of the airline instead. Employ 605 staff and fly 2,950,000 passengers.

1997

Jet off to the continent and start four new routes to Stockholm, Oslo, Paris and Brussels, or at least within sixty miles of these cities. Buy two more 737s bringing the fleet to 21 aircraft. Float your company on the Dublin and New York NASDAQ Stock Exchanges and watch the airline's share price double on the first day of trading, valuing the company at €300 million. Employ 659 staff and fly 3,730,000 passengers.

1998

Open new routes to Malmo, St Etienne, Carcassonne (where?), Venice (or close), Pisa and Rimini. Order 45 new Boeings for two billion US dollars, being 25 firm orders and 20 options, an option being a sort of Irish aircraft order — *sure we might buy the planes or we might not, but sure they're only seventy million bucks a shot so sure we'll let you know either way later on … like.* Employ 892 staff and fly 4,629,000 passengers.

1999

Go mad and open new routes to Frankfurt (close), Biarritz, Ostend (where now?), Ancona, Genoa, Turin, Derry and Aarhus. Employ 1,094 staff and fly 5,358,000 passengers.

2000

Launch an online flight booking facility which garners 50,000 bookings per week. Live with the eternal shame of one of your cabin crew named Brian Dowling winning *Big Brother.* Sponsor the Sky News weather forecast to raise your profile. Employ 1,262 staff and fly 7,002,000 passengers using 26 aircraft.

2001

Fly Tony Blair and family to their holidays in Carcassonne in France and milk the resultant publicity for all it is worth. Post 9/11 watch other airlines panic and oil prices soar but immediately order 100 new Boeings plus options on 50 more, the biggest aircraft order of the year. Open your first continental base at Brussels Charleroi and drive Belgium's Sabena Airlines livid (an airline that only made a profit in one of the prior forty years and thus soon to be bankrupt and whose name stands for Such A Bad Experience, Never Again). Employ 1,467 staff and fly 9,355,000 passengers using 36 aircraft.

2002

Open your second continental base in the small peasant village of Hahn, seventy miles from Frankfurt. Start flying on 26 new routes in all. Become Europe's number one airline in terms of punctuality, fewest cancellations and least lost luggage. Employ 1,547 staff and fly 13,419,000 passengers using 41 aircraft.

2003

Buy out a competitor, Buzz, from KLM for 24 million euros and relaunch their routes for half the fares. Become the largest airline operating at London Stansted. Open new continental bases in Milan (or Bergamo) and Stockholm (or Skavsta). Another Gulf War. Mount a mock invasion of Lootin' airport in a tank for the publicity. Launch 73 new routes. Overtake British Airways for the first time by carrying more passengers in a month in Europe. Employ 1,746 staff and fly 19,490,000 passengers using 54 aircraft.

2004

Become the most searched airline on the web as ranked by the teenage billionaire gurus at Google. Open bases near Rome and Barcelona. Warn of a 'bloodbath' on fares in the winter months and consequently watch your own share price nosedive in a freefall. Watch the European Union expand eastwards and salivate at the prospect of all those potential passengers. Employ 2,288 staff and fly 24,635,000 passengers using 72 aircraft.

2005

Fly ten UK Conservative Party officials to their annual conference at Blackpool for a fare of one penny. Mick turns down an offer from the BBC to play the Alan Sugar role in the hit TV series *The Apprentice*. Open new bases at Liverpool, Pisa, East Midlands, Cork and Shannon. Order another 70 Boeings just for the heck of it but tell Boeing to skip the window shades, reclining seats and seat pockets to save a few euros. Note that you can squeeze 59 more seats into a new Boeing 737-800 than in an old Boeing 737-200. Carry more passengers in August than British Airways on their entire worldwide network, and thus claim to be 'The World's Favourite Airline' (despite the fact that Southwest Airlines in the US carry twice as many passengers). Go on at length always about a 'no fuel surcharge ever' guarantee as oil prices soar. Employ 2,700 staff and fly 30,946,000 passengers using 87 aircraft.

2006

Open bases in Bremen, Madrid and Marseilles. Accept the delivery of your hundredth shiny new Boeing 737. Fly for the first time outside Europe by opening new routes to Morocco. Launch an online check-in service which was free but now, like everything else, costs money. Make an all-cash offer for Aer Lingus and refer to it as a 'small regional airline' despite the fact that Aer Lingus flies to the US and Middle East and your airline doesn't. Employ 4,200 staff (of 25 different nationalities but 24 of them being Eastern European) and fly 42,500,000 passengers using 103 aircraft.

2007

Open bases in Alicante, Valencia, Belfast, Bristol and Dusseldorf Weeze. For the first time sell seats for one cent *including* taxes, fees and charges and watch your bookings website grind to a halt with four million hits on a single day. Launch 'BING' which delivers fare specials direct to customers' computers. Discuss the possibility of a future low fares airline flying between Europe and the USA with fares from ten euros and consider calling it RuinAtlantic or Ego Air. Mourn the passing of Tony Ruin, accede to his last request and fly one Ruinair Boeing 737 aircraft over his funeral in County Kildare in a not so silent final tribute. Employ 4,500 staff and fly 50,000,000 passengers using 133 aircraft.

2008

Open bases in Birmingham and Bournemouth. Announce that the possible new low fares airline to the USA will have 'beds and blowjobs' in Business Class and see the related press conference video 'climax' on YouTube. Watch helplessly as the price of a barrel of oil goes to $148. Take the cheap option and park your excess aircraft at airports in the wintertime. Be sued by President Nicolas Sarkozy over a press advertisement featuring his wife-to-be. See XL Airways go bust. Continue to criticise the BAA'Britain's Awful Airports'. Maintain an average fare of €44. Employ 5,200 staff and fly 58,000,000 passengers using 163 aircraft.

2009 etc.

More of the same. See above, ad nauseum. Specifically, annoy the hell out of everyone else. Retire.

The Low Fares Airline (1)

THE IN-LAW FARES AIRLINE

Rod Stewart may be about to pledge 'for richer for poorer' as he weds Penny Lancaster. But the famously skinflint rocker, 62, isn't about to let costs go sky-high — as he has made his kids take a no-frills budget flight to the bash in Italy. Daughter Ruby, 20, joked as they boarded the Ruinair jet at Stansted: 'We should all take it in turns to stand up at the end of the wedding and say my dad's really cheap!'

THE MIRROR

THE LAW FARES AIRLINE

Ruinair is the choice of actor Jude Law, who was heading for an Easter holiday break with his kids. A few months ago he claimed he was broke after a pricey divorce settlement with his ex-wife Sadie Frost. 'I lost everything in order to get the right to visit my children. My bank account is therefore almost always empty.'

WWW.CELEBRITY-GOSSIP.NET

THE LOW BLAIRS AIRLINE

Tony Blair gave budget travellers a shock when he boarded their low-cost flight back to London at the end of a week-long Italian holiday.

Blair and a seven-member entourage flew from Rome on a commercial flight with no-frills carrier Ruinair, according to Rome's Ciampino airport. The prime minister has drawn unwelcome attention from British newspapers in the past for using more costly state flights for holiday trips abroad. Ruinair's press office could not immediately say how much Blair paid for his ticket. After all other passengers boarding the Stansted-bound Boeing 737 had been double-checked by security, Mr Blair's party was ushered to specially-reserved seats at the front of the plane. The flight left the Rome airport 25 minutes late following the additional security checks. Showing his thirst for budget travel had its limits, Blair was met on the London airstrip by a limousine. A passenger said. 'We only paid £49 for our tickets so, assuming he did the same, he must have saved the country a fortune.'

REUTERS

United Kingdom

Ruinair Flight FR206 – Tuesday @ 8.30am – DUB-STN-DUB

Fare €2 plus taxes, fees and charges €42

Ruinair have a proud history of stopping passengers. In 2003 they refused boarding to 'IT girl' and *Bollinger* babe Tara Palmer Tomkinson because she did not have a required passport, despite travelling on an internal flight within the UK. She forgot IT. Apparently she retorted, 'Do you know who I am?' She was lucky not to suffer the fate of a US domestic passenger who once shrieked the same riposte, before a check-in agent used a public address system to speak to the entire Departures terminal: *'May I have your attention please. We have a passenger here who does not know who he is. If anyone can help him find his identity, please step forward to this counter.'* Also in 2003 they refused boarding to Jeremy Beadle, much to the relief of the other passengers on the flight. They stopped Marian Finucane, one of Ireland's best known media personalities, because she had no ID. They refused boarding to a John O'Donoghue on a flight from Cork to Dublin because he did not have any picture ID and he was the Irish government's Minister for Tourism. They stopped *'Iron Mike'* Tyson from boarding a Gatwick to Dublin flight because he arrived late. The brutal, aggressive yet floored Tyson was quoted as saying, 'As long as I am not too late, then it's okay.'

But I am not truly convinced. Ruinair flew the oldest football in the world from Glasgow Prestwick to Hamburg Lubeck to take pride of place at a World Cup exhibition in Hamburg. Checking in under the name of Mr A. Football, the sixteenth-century pig's bladder, reputed to have been kicked about by Mary Queen of Scots at her weekly five-a-side game in Linlithgow, travelled in a specially designed box, had its own seat and I am told selected a pizza and Bovril from the in-flight menu. I am sure that ball had no passport. I always heed Mick's advice. *'On the photo identification, we are sorry for the old people who do not have a passport, although it only applies between Ireland and the United Kingdom, but our handling people are in an impossible position. We cannot include old age pension books as a form of identification when we are dealing with sixteen different countries coming through Stansted. The handling people on the ground simply cannot handle it. It has to be very simple, which is the reason we require a passport, driving licence or the international student card. We do not want the university student card or the Blockbuster video card.'*

Never engage Ruinair check-in staff in voluntary conversation for fear they find an obscure reason to deny boarding. *'Sorry sir, that couldn't possibly be you in that awful passport photograph.'* Today is not the day to naively ask for a good window seat near the front and see their reaction. Be conscious of the small print they put on page 173 of their standard email confirmation. This states the following. *'Look mate, no matter what happens at any stage in this flight, it's your own fault not ours, so don't ever try to mess with us.'* I worry they will get me soon at check-in. They get us all eventually. I will be late. I will have no ID. I will forget the email confirmation. The check-in queue will be too long. I will not have shaved. They won't like my jumper. Some braver folk dice with death and bring a Post-it note with their confirmation reference. But I always bring along my emailed itinerary so I can show the check-in girl that I only paid one euro.

Ruinair weigh passenger checked luggage as carefully as the US Department of the Treasury weigh gold bars leaving the Fort Knox Bullion Depository in Kentucky. I watch other passengers on their knees on the floor, opening suitcases and dividing their life's possessions into heavy items and not-so-heavy items, all being somewhat reminiscent of that U2 song 'All That You Can't Leave

Behind'. Someone spots an unused check-in desk with a weighing scales so others check the weight of their baggage with fingers crossed, but the cashiers who double as check-in agents are not happy that the rabble are using the scales. A reading of 15 kg on the red display is joy; 16 kg is despair. 'She wants to charge me for one feckin' kilo over.' The guy ahead with a huge suitcase is about to be badly screwed until the cashier asks him to weigh his backpack which is a tiny 2 kg. He moves about 5 kg of dirty laundry from suitcase to backpack and so avoids excess baggage charges but holds us up for ages and all his baggage is still going in the aircraft, whether it's in the hold or the overhead bin, and all their petty baggage rules suddenly seem so pointless.

I heard a rumour that Ruinair may introduce charges for customers who travel with *emotional* baggage, in an attempt to avoid delays caused by family arguments at check-in and at boarding. They will have a strict rule of 'maximum of one divorce case per passenger' with no pooling of cases allowed. So if a mother turns up at the airport with her children from a first marriage, and she is still not talking to her second husband, the check-in girl will ask her a series of questions about the divorce and all the suppressed anger and guilt felt by the family, and Ruinair will charge her an extra ten euros. If the mother complains that this money-grabbing reminds her of the absent father who just took, took, took and left her nothing in his will, Ruinair will add another five euros.

What do you think Mick? *'People are overly obsessed with charges. They complain we are charging for check-in, but people who use web check-in and only have carry-on luggage are getting even cheaper fares. We are absolutely upfront about charges and the baggage charges and the check-in charges will rise. We will keep raising them until we can persuade the 40% to 50% of passengers who travel with us for one or two days to bring just one carry-on bag. I can go away for two weeks with just my overnight bag. Instead of packing a hairdryer, why not buy one when you get there?'*

I have long since tired of playing their checked baggage game. It's easier to pay the checked baggage fee of when booking a trip of any longer than a few days. So on the day of travel I can put the baggage in the hold or else carry it on and I have found that once you pay the fee they never bother to look at your carry-on baggage and I can take as much as I can carry with me on board so they don't lose my baggage. This arrangement suits both parties since they have their blood money and I can do what I want with my luggage. A few euros to transport a suitcase to Europe is a steal in every sense. I mean, FedEx or DHL would charge me a hundred euros or more and they would not be as quick.

Check-in is fairly ugly with many long queues snaking around the Departures area but no clue as to which desks they lead to. Lost Ruinair staff with less than perfect English stand and look at us. There's a queue beside me for a flight to Bournemouth and I'm not sure why. Maybe Bournemouth is close to somewhere more exciting. Near the check-in queue are a gang of teenage Nike Hoodie boys, apparently wearing legitimate tracksuits emblazoned with the names of various Dublin boxing clubs. A gent asks where they are going. One of the freckled shaven-head terriers clenches up a fist. 'We're off to kill the feckin' English.'

This airline, like any multi-million Boeing, is a well-oiled machine. Their operating system is simple. Each aircraft departs from its base on the first wave of flights early in the day (much like when the Japanese set off *en masse* early one morning for Pearl Harbour), and by the end of the operating day at midnight all crew and aircraft are back home. There is no scheduled over-nighting away from base, so there are no nasty hotel bills to pay. Each aircraft usually makes eight flights per day, from 6am to midnight. I saw a programme on RTE where their pilots said the 'earlies' are getting earlier, they don't get a break for nine hours and cannot even get off the plane to buy a sandwich because they must supervise the refuelling. Landing and taking off many times per day is a more stressful job than flying intercontinental long haul. But on the upside Ruinair pilots do not have to fly to congested hubs like Heathrow and Schiphol.

One cabin crew team works the first four flights, or sectors, then another cabin crew takes the last four flights. Sometimes the pilots can fly a six-sector day which involves three return flights from Ireland to the UK. This airline rosters pilots on a pattern of five early-start days and two days off, followed by five late-start days and two days off, known as 5/2/5/2, which some crews like because of the predictability. But many of their pilots fly so much that they reach the 900-hour annual maximum limit specified by Europe's aviation regulations before the year is over, and as the airline runs the same rostering year for everyone from 1 April to 31 March, this can lead to a crew crisis and lack of pilots at the end of every March when the pilots can sit around for weeks with their feet up since it would be illegal for them to take to the air.

Some of the pilots feel overworked so they set up a covert website for the Ruinair European Pilots Association called www.repaweb.org in order to communicate privately with each other. Ruinair do not approve but the Irish High Court dismissed an application by Ruinair seeking disclosure of the identities of pilots using the website. Ruinair contended that some of their pilots had been intimidated by postings by anonymous individuals using code names including 'I hate Ruinair' and 'Can't fly, Won't fly'. However, the Justice refused to allow their identities to be revealed. He said that there was no evidence of bullying by the defendants to the action and the only evidence of bullying in the case was by the plaintiff, Ruinair. Mick doesn't agree that his pilots are under pressure. *'I don't even know how I would put a pilot under pressure. What do you do? Call him up as he's coming in to land? They are paid €100,000 a year for flying eighteen hours a week. How could you be fatigued working nine days in every two weeks? They can afford to buy yachts. If this is such a Siberian salt mine and I am such an ogre then why are they still working for the airline?'*

All aircraft are left at their home base overnight so fault fixing is easier. There is no slack in the operating system. Turnarounds are scheduled to take only 25 minutes, and any delays are subject to immediate scrutiny. Timing is so tight that the only chance the pilots get to have a break is when they are safely up in the air. If the cabin is absolutely full, 25 minutes is simply impossible, so pilots rely on arriving early at the gate to achieve an on-time departure. If any aircraft become unserviceable, Ruinair has four standby aircraft at the ready: at the time of writing one is based at Dublin, one at Rome Ciampino and two at Stansted. Daily at 8am after the first wave of departures, all the base operations chiefs in Europe join a conference phone call. Each centre sends an email to the Dublin headquarters detailing performance. If there is a reason even for a one-minute delay it is discussed to see if a recurrence can be prevented. At 8.30am every Monday at the Dublin headquarters, all the department heads meet Mick and they review the week's operational performance. That must be fun. *'Late? What do you mean f****** late?'*

So it's not surprising that our aircraft is on time. I watch the disembarking passengers trudge past us. There's also an incoming flight from Liverpool so every second passenger who alights wears full Liverpool FC replica kit. Mick likes Liverpool. *'Liverpool is the low fares regional airport for the north-west of England. Liverpool doesn't have all the glass, bells and whistles that Manchester has, but passengers don't want glass, bells and whistles. It's always good to see Liverpool give Manchester a good kicking.'* All of the passengers are bleary-eyed and fatigued. I woke up at 6am to catch my flight. I dread to think at what time these fellow travellers awoke. It was hardly worth even going to bed. Often low fares comes at a high price. Having aircraft lying around doing nothing at night-time must ruin this airline. Soon there'll be 3am flights.

On the plane I read *Ruinair*, the first edition of their in-flight magazine, which I keep because it will surely be worth a lot of money in years to come. There is an advertisement from the printers of the magazine based in Warsaw. I bet they're low-cost printers. The magazine includes a model Boeing to buy; a push-fit plastic model requiring no glue or paint, with realistic take-off sounds and flashing lights, like what we fly in today. I read Mick's message on the first page. I can't believe he writes this piece himself because of the absence of swear words. He describes the amazing in-flight *Movie-Star* system. There's a sample on-screen picture, showing Mick getting on board an aircraft, hands on hips, open-neck shirt and jeans. I think that's the same shirt. I hope we don't have to pay €7 to listen to him. Six months of trials later they can the movie system because no one wants to pay to use it. There is an editorial with a quote from Saint Augustine who is the patron saint of low fares air travel. *'The world is a book and those who do not travel, read only a page.'* I keep my copy of the magazine for research purposes but the crew come through the cabin to retrieve all copies. So I sit on my magazine. They pass by. I triumph but there will be a downside. They print 70,000 copies of every issue, and 50 per cent of passengers spend thirty minutes reading it. Tonight the employee who counts the magazines in the warehouse in Dublin airport will shout over to his foreman: '*Hey, Seamus, it's happened again. We're down to 69,999 copies. Some fecker has nicked a copy.*'

The magazine has a tacky insert called *Buy As You Fly*, which features mail order products that no one would ever need or use or want as a gift. There's a wooden rocking chair. I mean who ever uses a rocking chair except Val Doonican or the elderly gentleman in the TV advertisements for Werthers Original sweets? There's a Hercules Winch which will uproot an unwanted tree, pull a vehicle out of a ditch or winch in a boat but I don't have any unwanted trees, I don't often drive my car into ditches (of which there are few where I live and in any event I would be calling the AA) and, like most of the population, I don't own a boat. There's a Snail and Slug Trap which is filled with beer to entice the slimy rascals inside where they drown but go with a big smile on their faces. What a waste of good beer. There's the Garden Kneeler Bench, a real life-saver for the avid but badly crippled gardener. There's the dog bark control collar, the sonic mole repeller and the ultrasonic cat repeller; all repelling. There's the appropriately named *Sudoku for Dummies*. There are Exclusive Football Stadium Framed Prints. How exclusive can they be if I can buy one by mail order? There's an anti-frost mat to prevent icy build-up in my freezer. What a load of rubbish.

In 1942 the US Air Force established an airfield at Stansted for its Marauder bomber squadron. In the early days of this low fares Mecca everyone flew from here for free courtesy of the US government, but mostly it was on daytime bombing runs to Berlin. Later the Air Force's Strategic Air Command abandoned the airfield, leaving a civil airport with one of the longest runways in Europe, but with zero passengers. The airport was designated as London's third and re-opened in 1991 as the greatest white elephant of its time. There was no train link from London to the airport. Air UK flew there and Cubana Airlines operated a weekly flight to Havana via Gander on a Russian-made Ilyushin jet. The BAA, with noted *starchitect* Norman Foster on board, spent £300 million on a terminal building with a floating roof supported by a frame of inverted-pyramid roof trusses, a glass and steel masterpiece in the middle of nowhere. Ideal for Ruinair.

Why do we need architects to design airports? Let's build a building and have glass walls so it's bright inside. Let's put a flat roof on it. Let's have a train station underneath and how about some bus stops outside? And then let's build a Toytown train to take people to the piers — we'll have two of those. Let's call them A & B. And hey, how about we make one half for Departures and the other for Arrivals? But Stansted is revolutionary for one genuine reason. Before Stansted, airports used to have roofs full of cabling, air conditioning and insulation. Foster put them all under the floor and opened the roof to the sky, safe in the knowledge that sunlight is considerably cheaper than paying a monthly London Electricity bill. This is the airport of choice for the authorities when a hijacked aircraft wants to land in the South-East. I rest my case. When a Sudanese airliner was hijacked and landed here, Ruinair responded with an advertisement headlined: '*It's amazing what lengths people will go to to fly cheaper than Ruinair.*' As Mick says, '*Usually someone gets offended by our ads, which is fantastic. You get a whole lot more bang for your buck if somebody is upset.*'

The BAA plan to build a new runway at Stansted. The analysis of the £4 billion spend includes £90 million for a runway, £1 billion plus for a terminal building and an amazing £350 million for earthmoving and landscaping, the latter representing a gardening event of truly Alan Titchmarsh proportions. Mick as usual offers his modest opinion. '*The BAA are on a cocaine-induced spending spree. They are an overcharging, gold-plating monopoly which should be broken up. BAA have no particular skills in building airports and are the worst airport builders in the western world. A break-up of BAA would be the greatest thing that has happened to British aviation since the founding of Ruinair. Then airline customers would not be forced to endure the black hole of Calcutta that is Heathrow, or the unnecessary, overpriced palace being planned at Stansted. The BAA*

*want to spend £4 billion on an airport which should cost £100
million. £3.9 billion is for tree planting, new roadways and Norman
Foster's Noddy railway so they can mortgage away the future of low-
cost airlines. This plan is for the birds. People can drive up the M11,
they will walk barefoot over the fields for a cheap fare. What they are
not going to do is pay for some bloody marble Taj Mahal.'*

Mick is even considering ways to avoid incurring the charges at
the check-in desks at BAA's Stansted airport: *'I could check in people
in the car park, which would be cheaper than BAA. If they don't let
me use their car parks we might let them check in at the truckers' car
park on the M11.'* Equally the BAA CEO enjoys a public spat with his
biggest customer at Stansted and rebuts Mick. *'You could probably
build the runway for £100 million if you had a flat piece of ground,
were not worried about where you parked the aircraft and were not
worried about how to get the passengers on and off the planes. The
runway would only cost £100m if all we had to do was fly some Irish
labourers over to lay some tarmac down the drive.'*

It's a rough landing at Stansted in gale force winds but it's not a
bad landing. A good landing is one where the pilot plants the
wheels onto the asphalt and comes to a stop. A bad landing is any
other sort of landing. I don't know how much these aircraft can
take, but if it had been my motor car, it would now be scrap. I turn
to a guy in the aisle seat. 'Not a great landing?' I suggest. All he can
do is mumble and then show me the open palm of his hand, slam
it down hard on his thigh and utter the single word 'Splat.' I am
reminded of the note written by a girl to the captain on a Qantas
flight. *'Dear captain. My name is Nicola. I am 8 years old. This is my
first flight but I'm not scared. I like to watch the clouds go by. My
mum says the crew is nice. I think your plane is good. Thanks for a
nice flight. Don't fuck up the landing. Luv Nicola.'*

Shortly after we land, a loud trumpet fanfare is broadcast
through the cabin, followed by *'Congratulations, you've arrived at
your destination ahead of schedule.'* I look at the crew members in
disbelief and they are evidently mortified at having to play such a
tacky announcement but it's company policy. It's also odd because
they are congratulating us for an early arrival but we didn't make

the aircraft go faster. As soon as we stop we all feel the need to instantly power up our mobile telephones. The cabin interior is suddenly a cacophony of harmonised Nokia tunes. One rough-looking older gentleman close to me immediately has to take an incoming telephone call. He swears loudly. 'Jaysus, who the hell is this? This call will cost me a fucking fortune, what with their roaming charges when I'm away from me home.'

There is an air-bridge when we arrive at the pier but we don't use it, in line with this airline's stated policy. *'When we used Jet-Way airbridges, we found that they were the fourth largest cause of delays. Either the Jet-Way wasn't there when we arrived, or the buffoon who was driving it was out by a few inches, and had to take the whole thing back and forth again before landing up at our doors. If it's raining, people will just walk a little faster.'* It is sometimes necessary to take the *Skytrain* from the arrival gate to the Arrivals hall. This can be confusing for some travellers. I once arrived here on a flight, got on the *Skytrain* and sat beside an elderly Irish lady. She turned to me in the tiny train without a driver and asked, *'Is this the Piccadilly line?'* Needless to say, I told her it was and if she stayed on board for the next fifty minutes, she would be in the West End.

Today I join the long march from the gate to the Arrivals hall, largely reminiscent of Napoleon's retreat from Moscow in the winter of 1812, although fewer of us die from hypothermia, but some are picked off by snipers or succumb to the changing seasons, dysentery or the dreaded tetsi fly. My taxes and charges today include the arbitrary *Wheelchair Levy*, so next time I'm asking for one to take me to Arrivals.

If Ruinair didn't exist, would Stansted airport shut down simply for lack of use? One in six flights out of Stansted is taken by some of the one million British people visiting second homes abroad, which they do on average six times a year. Ruinair flights here are like hailing a taxi. If you wait long enough, one will soon come along. Their aircraft are everywhere, like some bubonic plague. In the future, Boeing will manufacture all 737 aircraft with the Ruinair logo as the default livery. Boeing does not disclose production rates, but it is believed to build about twenty-eight 737s a month, or one every day. I read in the newspaper that a delay in the delivery of four new Boeing aircraft to Ruinair meant the airline was forced to cancel 1,200 flights, affecting an estimated 300,000 passengers. It is not untrue to conclude that the growth of this airline is only being impeded by Boeing's failure to build new aircraft fast enough.

The UK aerospace industry's trade surplus with the rest of the world shrank by a third one year, because of the huge volume of Boeing aircraft being brought into the UK by this single airline. Ruinair now have so many Boeing aircraft that they could easily lose one and then accidentally locate it again at some lesser-known airport.

Ruinair gave its flying angel logo bigger breasts. Mick ordered the change on all new Boeing 737-800 aircraft. The image boost was first spotted by Ruinair workers at Stansted airport. A spokesman said: 'We decided to give our customers a more uplifting experience. We think she is rather aerodynamic.' Ruinair's spokeswoman for the Nordic region said: 'We do not wish to milk the situation.'

Mick adores Boeing and he sometimes visits Seattle to collect new aircraft in person. 'Boeing made a lot of bullshit promises in 1999 but uniquely in the history of aviation they have beaten them. This is the best bloody aircraft in the world for short-haul operations. You people build the best god-damn aircraft in the world. My three favourite words are 'Made in Seattle'. I promise I won't say anything like 'Screw Airbus'. Bravo Boeing! Adios Airbus! Fuck the French. We are an oasis of Boeings in a sea of Airbuses in Europe. And I can't fly the bloody things. I can't even turn them on.' Once he bought 9 billion US dollars worth of aircraft from Boeing at a significant discount, believed to be at $28 million each rather than the list price of $60 million: 'We raped them. I wouldn't even tell my priest what discount I got.' Mick doesn't like the wider Airbus A320. 'I've heard a lot of horseshit about a wider fuselage. I've yet in fifteen years in this industry to meet one passenger who booked his ticket based on a wider fuselage.'

The terminal walls are plastered with advertisements for this airline. 'This is the home of low fares.' Here we live and breathe their Eurobrand. There is a route map but Western Europe has disappeared under a swathe of yellow arrows emanating from Stansted. This airline adds new routes at a rate only exceeded by the inflation rate in Zimbabwe. Along the way there's a Ruinair aircraft outside with the words *Arrividerci Alitalia*. Stuff it to the Eyeties, but don't get too xenophobic. Other aircraft announce *Auf Wiedersehen Lufthansa*. It must be great for a Lufthansa pilot to park at an airport stand and look at that jingoism out your cockpit window for 25 minutes (usual turnaround time). Other aircraft in the fleet have the slogans *Say No to Lufthansa's Fuel Tax, Say No to* BA *Fuel Levy, Bye Bye SkyEurope, Bye Bye EasyJet* and *Bye Bye Baby*, the latter a reference to competitor BMI Baby rather than to a 1970s pop song. They might as well put on the side of every aircraft, *To All Other European Airlines — Go Fuck Yourselves.*

I walk the concourse. The newspaper headlines in W. H. Smith catch my eye. *The Evening Standard* has 'Children Must Not Use Mobile Phones'. Unlikely. *The Daily Sport* has 'TV Star's Sex with Poodle Next Door'. Equally unlikely, I fear. *The Sun* has 'One Hundred Thousand Holidays for a Fiver'. Is this news? Another Daily is asking its readers 'What does it mean to be British?' The best reply to date is from a man in Switzerland: '*Being British is about driving in a German car to an Irish pub for a Belgian beer, then travelling home, grabbing an Indian curry or a Chinese on the way, to sit on Swedish furniture and watch American soap shows on a Japanese TV. And the most British thing of all? Suspicion of anything foreign.*'

The Stansted Express to Liverpool Street is punctual, not cheap. It's worth taking the train because the BAA tell us that last year there were 178 days of roadworks on the motorway to London and there are 571 sets of traffic lights between here and Central London. I gaze around. Airports, there's nothing like them. The variety of people and cultures, excitement and expectation, arrival and escape, the last-minute crises, the personal dramas, the tearful partings and joyful reunions. I could live in an airport. Jesus, maybe I do.

I have always loved airlines and travel; eschewing a structured social order and a daily routine of life for a flight of fancy to a new world less familiar; cheating the four seasons. Mick is not such a fan.

'*The problem with the airline industry is it is so populated with people who grew up in the 1940s or 1950s who got their excitement looking at airplanes flying overhead. They wanted to be close to airplanes. Mercifully I was a child of the 1960s and a trained accountant, so aircraft don't do anything for me. There's a lot of big egos in this industry. That might be a better title for them, including myself, rather than entrepreneurs. It's a stupid business, which generally loses a lot of money. With the exception of Southwest and ourselves, and EzJet to a lesser extent, nobody makes a lot of money at it.*'

But why go to Central London when I have shops, restaurants, cafés, a viewing gallery, ample seating and more tourists than I could ever encounter on Oxford Street or at Madame Tussauds? I decide to spend the remaining five hours of my allotted time in the UK here, and I engage in my continuing observation of my fellow users of this airport.

1. *Italian Students.* They reside permanently in Departures, sorted into large groups, surrounded by backpacks piled high on luggage trolleys. They are dressed by FCUK, Diesel and Quicksilver. They survive on communal bottles of mineral water and occasional trips to *Prêt a Manger.* They rarely venture into Central London. They keep in touch with the world via Dell laptops and Wifi G-mail. They grow goatee beards or shave only weekly. They fly home for significant events such as births, marriages or funerals but promptly return to their place of permanent residence, irresistibly drawn by fares of one euro and the absence of rent at Stansted. I don't engage in voluntary conversation because the guys wear T-shirts which advise '*Practice Safe Sex, Go Fuck Yourself*' or else '*If You Don't Like Oral Sex, Then Shut Your Mouth.*' Their spiky bohemian girlfriends wear T-shirts which advise '*Your Son is in Good Hands*'. These passengers are the key to success in the low fares airline business since they will happily take 6am flights to nowhere and catch two-hour-long bus excursions, whilst business-men love Heathrow and BA. The difference is time. Businessmen are time poor. No one has more time to spare than an Italian student.

2. *Old Dears.* They sometimes gather around in a huddle, take out a sliced white loaf, add some *Utterly Butterly* spread, select ham

and cheese from assorted baskets and self-assemble their own sandwiches in a manufacturing operation of such operational efficiency as to impress even Henry Ford.

3. *Old Blokes.* They cluster together in teams and are identifiable in sporting matching blazers and grey slacks, possibly either rightly proud veterans or members of a lawn bowling club. Often they break out into Welsh accents and talk about getting up at 4am to catch a mini-bus up the motorway to Stansted.

4. *Foursomes.* Two pairs of Old Dears and Old Blokes off on holidays. One Old Bloke is hyper-active and so refuses to sit, preferring to go for newspapers for all tastes and to search airport desks for luggage tags. His Old Dear recalls she left a cucumber in the fridge at home so she telephones her daughter to use it. The second Old Bloke is not budging and wonders aloud why anyone needs luggage tags since they advertise to all that your home is empty for two weeks. His Old Dear decides to re-lace her gleaming new sneakers. Eventually she gives up. '*Good job I don't work in a shoe shop. I'd be there for hours doing up laces.*'

5. *Check-in Ladies.* These females of a certain age wear blue uniforms which are two sizes too small. The ladies are wide, rather than tall, and teeter about on precarious six-inch heels. They wander amidst the ever-lengthening queues of the Great Unwashed disappearing over the horizon, occasionally looking at impressive clipboards and lists of flight timings, scribbling notes with Bic biros. Their job is to never make eye contact or engage any passengers, and particularly not to intervene when any check-in delays arise. But beware. Cross these ladies once and you will never fly anywhere anytime ever again.

6. *Check-in Gents.* These thirty-ish males stand in the raised areas overlooking each check-in area. They are only visible from the waist upwards, unfortunately often much like Fiona Bruce on the BBC. They wear excessive assorted BAA security ID dog tags hung around their necks like Vietnam GIs and sport tight officialdom haircuts. The Check-in Gent's job is to closely examine all the female talent below and to nod approvingly in small groups when

a fit Italian brunette or a Nordic blonde with big tits leans over the desk below.

7. *Trolley Dollies.* Not flight attendants but guys in luminous jackets who gather the baggage trolleys from the concourse. Their job is to steal back the trolleys from sleeping Italian students, make the world's longest snake of inter-connected trolleys, apply for an entry in the *Guinness World Records* and drive their trolley snake through the heart of the dormant student population, forcing them to rise from their slumber and scatter like the parting of the Red Sea by Moses. '*Sorry mate, I didn't see you down there.*'

8. *Dixon's Homing Businessman.* Guys in suits with an overnight bag, laptop PC, briefcase and duty free bag. They stand carrying all four items whilst on a mobile telephone, broadcast to the Departures lounge about sales forecasts and cash budgets, refuse to sit and lessen the load, instead irresistibly drawn to the threshold of Dixon's electrical store, worried that the latest digital nano-gadget might pass them by.

9. *The Well-Heeled Couple.* He is tall with proud features and silver hair and wears chinos with a crease, open-neck Ralph Lauren Polo shirt and blue blazer with gold buttons. She wears make-up, a tan, jewels, and heels. Both are fifty-something. Their luggage matches, mostly it's Louis Vuitton, and they lug golf bags or skis over to the oversize baggage. They ask for directions around Stansted since they are only used to the confines of Heathrow Terminal 1 or 5. 'We usually fly BA Club Europe but this cheap little Irish airline flies to somewhere near our summer holiday home / winter ski chalet / golf course / friend's yacht.'

10. *Lost Elderly Irishman.* He is alone and is bewildered by Stansted, having left his Cricklewood or Kilburn digs on a rarely taken journey back to his roots, usually to Knock Ireland West, maybe sadly to a funeral. Or I suspect some well-meaning relative bought him a ticket home for two pence so he feels obliged to use it. I doubt he is sitting at home Googling away all day looking for free seat sales. Personally I blame low fares airlines for upsetting his ordered life. He wears his Sunday best, an old navy suit, perhaps

his only suit, and his passport shakes in his rough hands. I always offer him as much assistance as possible.

I am early for check-in. It's two hours to departure. I sit opposite a screen showing my flight. The desk opens soon after and I amble over. I am overtaken by a woman with a walking stick who runs to the same check-in desk. She is using the established *Old Woman with Fake Walking Stick* ploy to get ahead in the queue.

In the security area we watch a statuesque six-foot-plus lady passenger. She sets off the X-ray machine so she stops by the BAA staff, holds her arms out and waits to be frisked. It's a male staff member, about five foot five and his eyes are at the level of her breasts.

He smiles. 'Darling, I'd love to search you but I'd lose my job.' A female staff member rescues him.

The Metro Café in Departures is crammed with Ruinair staff; less passenger fare and more works canteen. It's terrifying to sit near the departure gates at Stansted, with the constant stream of threats they unleash at us poor passengers over the tannoy. '*Pre-boarding call. Come immediately to Gate 42. Last few remaining passengers. The gate is now closing. Your luggage will be offloaded. You will be denied boarding. Last and final boarding call.*' And there's the public shaming of passengers by name.

If you wish to break a terrorist suspect, don't play white noise. Make them spend a day at Stansted.

The Low Fares
Airline (2)

THE LOO FARES AIRLINE

Picture the scene. The plane lifts off. Then only minutes into the flight the fasten-seat-belts signs throughout the cabin start to flash. You return to your seat, anxiously awaiting turbulence, perhaps worse. The next thing you see is your captain striding purposefully up the aisle to the cupboard-sized water closet. Pinned to your seat in terror, you wonder who is flying the plane in his absence. But a few minutes later the pilot saunters back down the gangway and the emergency lights are extinguished. Only then do you discover that the whole performance was just to ensure the pilot can visit the facilities without having to join a queue. And the airline where this is standard procedure? Well, it's Ruinair. Mick O'Leery explains: 'Look, even the captain has to take a leak occasionally. When such times arise, it is normal procedure to switch the seat-belt sign on to ensure all passengers are seated.' *One of our readers, who was interrupted while ensconced in the lavatory, isn't reassured.* 'It was very alarming,' says *the flyer, who was 20 minutes into a two-hour journey to the south of France when the seatbelt lights lit up and the stewardess announced that the plane was beginning to land.* 'The passengers were confused, we were all looking at our watches. Then the stewardess came on again to say we weren't landing and that the captain had just needed to relieve himself.' *But O'Leery remains unrepentant.* 'I agree it's not ideal interrupting customers mid-pee for the captain, but it's all part of ensuring a fast turnaround at the other end.'

DAILY TELEGRAPH

THE LOW IQ AIRLINE

Three Norwegian tourists who planned a holiday on the Greek island of Rhodes landed in the south-western French town of Rodez after misunderstanding their destination on a Ruinair internet booking, officials said. The three, identified as Bente, Marit and Knut, appear to have been surprised when their Ruinair flight landed in Rodez, which boasts a medieval town centre with a 13th century cathedral but none of the Greek island's beach resorts. 'We were told of the mistake when the three tourists arrived at the airport and we tried to make their stay as agreeable as possible before they decided to return to Norway,' said Florence Taillefer, the head of the Rodez tourism office.

REUTERS

THE LOW FEES AIRLINE

Aware of the need to step up its promotional efforts in an increasingly uncertain market, Truro School in Cornwall has mounted a publicity campaign in Essex to capitalise on cheap Ruinair flights from Stansted to Newquay. Simon Price, the boarding school's deputy head, said: 'It would make perfect sense for someone from the Stansted area to board here. The flights are normally £10 if you book in advance, although we've got someone coming to visit this week who paid 79p.' Bill Levene, 17, who is studying chemistry, physics and maths at A level, said: 'The boys learn about co-operation and teamwork living in a boarding house. And I've learnt how to use the washing machine,' he added.

TIMES ONLINE

THE LOW ESTEEM AIRLINE

A man who made bizarre attempts to kidnap female Ruinair staff had a toy gun and pieces of rope in his pocket when he was arrested.

Gavin Plumb, 20, targeted women wearing the low-cost airline's distinctive blue uniform as they travelled by train from Bishop's Stortford to Stansted Airport. He sat in front of Ruinair employee Katazyna Pasek and handed her a note which read, 'I will do anything'. She moved to another seat, but Plumb followed and showed her a piece of paper which read, 'I will do anything, so keep quiet and get off with me at the next station. Otherwise I will shoot you and everyone on this train.' He put his finger to his lip, indicating she should keep quiet, a prosecutor told Chelmsford Crown Court. Fearing she was going to be killed, Miss Pasek became upset and other passengers intervened. Plumb moved down the carriage and got off. Two days later, air stewardess Marlene Gaborit, also wearing her uniform, was in an almost empty carriage when Plumb sat beside her. He showed her a note which read, 'I'm a police officer. You have to get off at the next station for a quick chat.' He asked her if she wanted to see his ID and he produced a card. As Plumb got off he touched her leg and said: 'No worries.' He was still on the platform when transport police saw him later. He was asked if he had claimed to be a police officer, which he denied, but seemed agitated, said the prosecution. When asked if he had any police ID, he said: 'My little brother uses my coat. He pretends to be a police officer. I've just remembered, there's a gun in my pocket.' He had a black toy handgun and three pieces of rope on him. When arrested, he said that he wanted to be a police community support officer. During questioning, he said that it had all been a silly prank because he was bored at home. Plumb, of Upper Stonyfields, Harlow, pleaded guilty to two charges of attempted kidnap. Defence counsel described the offences as very unusual with disturbing undertones and said Plumb, who was of previous good character, was a vulnerable young man who suffered from low self-esteem.

THE GUARDIAN

THE LOW AIRLINE

A Ruinair pilot was demoted following a serious incident on a flight carrying 128 passengers from Stansted to Cork, it has emerged. Poor communications between the pilot and co-pilot led to the incident, where the Boeing 737-800 aircraft flew too low over Bishopstown. The Air Accident Investigation Unit of the Department of Transport (AAIU) has published its investigation into the incident, which took place with 134 people on board. The AAIU report says the flight over Bishopstown was reported to the Cork Airport Authority by 'at least 16 upset residents, whose independent and consistent complaints, submitted by telephone and in writing, referred to noise and how low the aircraft was being flown'.

THE IRISH TIMES

THE LOW VISIBILITY AIRLINE

A passenger jet which was destined for City of Derry Airport has landed at an Army base six miles away by mistake. The Liverpool to Derry service, operated by Eirjet on behalf of Ruinair, landed at Ballykelly airstrip. Ruinair said in a statement it was due to an 'error by the pilot who mistakenly believed he was on a visual approach to City of Derry airport'. Ballykelly airfield, formerly RAF *Ballykelly, has 2,000m of partially-paved strip, of which only around half is understood to be usable, not least since it is now intersected by a railway line. It has not been used for fixed wing aircraft since 1971. One of the passengers said 'The pilot apologised and said, "We have arrived at the wrong airport. I ask you to be patient."' Another passenger said he knew the flight was landing at the wrong airport. 'I tried to tell the crew that we were landing in the wrong place, but it was too late to do anything because the descent was almost over. It was hilarious.' Brian Mather, a passenger, said the soldiers treated the passengers well. 'They could see the funny side of it. Some of the soldiers came on board and laughingly welcomed us to their international airport.' Captain Mervyn Granshaw, chairman of the British Airline Pilots' Association, said there were several reasons why such an incident could occur. 'Human beings are fallible — from simple things like putting teabags in a milk jug to the other end of the spectrum of landing at the wrong runway.' Ruinair chief executive Mick O'Leery said, 'The pilot seems to have made a stupid mistake.'*

BBC NEWS

RUINAIR ANNOUNCES 16th EUROPEAN BASE
IN DERRY BALLYKELLY

Ruinair, Europe's largest low fares airline, today announced its 16th European base, in Derry Ballykelly airport. On Wednesday last, the independent surveyors, Eirjet, working on behalf of Ruinair held an impromptu meeting with representatives from Ballykelly Airport Loading and Logistics Services (BALLS). The military precision of the operation, un-congested, low cost facilities, impeccable turn out and well-drilled staff led Eirjet to advise Ruinair that these were clearly people it could do business with. Announcing the new base today, Leo Hairy Camel, Ruinair's CEO designate, said: 'This is not a load of Barracks. Since its inception, Ruinair has been waging war on high cost airports, and our announcement today of a new base at Costa Del Ballykelly is just another of our military manoeuvres to continue to lower fares for European consumers. Ballykelly Airport is a breath of fresh air and this development marks the demise of Taj-Mahal airports run by fat cats. Ballykelly secured this base by fluke despite intense competition from over 50 airports throughout Europe. Airport operators the length and breadth of Europe are today taking note that the future of airports lies in simple, functional, low cost facilities. Ruinair's new route from Ballykelly to Nocincz (pronounced Nochance) go on sale today on www.ruinair.com/aprilfooledyou.

Belgium

Ruinair Flight FR44 – Tuesday @ 11.50am – DUB-CRL-DUB

Fare €1 plus taxes, fees and charges €33

I must drive rather than take public transport because Dublin is the only large European capital without a rail link to its airport. I pass the Port Tunnel into which the government has poured €750 million of taxpayers' money yet the builders want €350 million more to finish it and the tunnel roof leaks water on occasion, making it the most expensive car wash in Dublin. It's a black hole. I stay out of the bus lanes since these are exclusively reserved for Polish motor cars. On the way to the airport there are *Irish* roadworks. A sign confirms the M1 is closed and there is a diversion along Griffith Avenue. However, in the best traditions of Irish motoring, all the cars ahead of me carry on along the M1. I follow. As expected, the M1 is open to traffic all the way to the short-term car park opposite the terminal. Sure we only put these sort of alarmist road signs up to present a challenge to our overseas visitors when travelling to the airport.

In a move reminiscent of Al Capone's hey-day, the Dublin Airport Authority has increased the cost of short-term car parking by 50 per cent, so I drive the fifty miles to the barren wasteland of long-term. To park in short-term, one must now deposit several close family members in a bank vault as a security deposit. The *Beautiful People* of Dublin used to frequent Brown Thomas, the Ice Bar and Lillie's Bordello but now they can ostentatiously display

their personal wealth in the Lower Level of short-term car park A.
In long-term the DAA has kindly provided visual reminder signage
of the parking zones to aid those who return from two weeks in
Majorca only to utter '*Jaysus, where did I leave me feckin' wheels?*'
So there's a Zone G for Guitar, Zone H for Helicopter and more
recently Zone C for Criminal, Zone M for Monopoly and Zone R
for Rip-off. There's also a Zone Y as in Y is this car park so fecking
far away from the terminal building? It's only called long-term
because of the average time it takes to get from your car by bus to
the Departures terminal. I park in Zone F, so-called because today
there's no *F'in* spaces left anywhere. My parents have given up
parking in the long-term because they find it's too complicated
and too difficult to find their car on their return. They claim to
have lost several rather desirable and sensible Peugeot 406s here in
the past.

It's freezing in Dublin so on the apron they are de-icing our
aircraft. I don't know why they bother with the expense of de-
icing. Why not get Mick to stand near the wings and tail and speak
for ten minutes? There is much chaos at the gates, almost a
bloodbath. '*Flights FR206 and FR112 to London are cancelled due to
the weather conditions. Would passengers make their way to the
baggage carousel to collect their luggage and go to the Ruinair ticket
desk in the Departures hall.*' A day ruined. We are the lucky ones.
The ramp guy who boards us is professionally attired in a woolly
Manchester United bobble hat. 'Will yez all stop pushing. If yez
don't stop pushing, then none of yez will be gettin' on de plane.'
They don't hang about even in freezing weather so some of the
passengers who board by the rear steps receive a fine coating of de-
icer from the man on the gantry who knows there is always a
25-minute turnaround, hail rain or shine.

A University of Miami professor addressing the Airline Pilots
Association claimed that in the future the crew in an aircraft will
consist of a pilot and a dog. The pilot is in the aircraft to feed and
take care of the dog. The dog is in the aircraft to bite the pilot if the
pilot tries to touch any of the buttons or switches. The primary
requirement to becoming a pilot continues to be the ability to
speak with a posh accent, and being a pilot means starting your

career with a bag full of luck and a bag devoid of experience, the trick being to fill the latter before the former empties. As BBC's Frank Spencer once said, 'There are old pilots, there are bold pilots, but there are no old, bold pilots.' I wonder do Ruinair pilots place wagers on whether they will be able to find these remote airfields? Our pilot locates Charleroi amongst arable fields. We land. It's Brussels but not as we know it, Captain. It's quiet, and I wonder: are they expecting us? The airport is deserted. There have been no air traffic control delays here since Sopwith Camels took part in the Allied offensives in the Great War. Immigration hardly requires a passport; it's more like a nod and a wink.

There is a tourist desk in the airport and I'm suddenly hopeful that there may be a tourist industry in Charleroi. Five years ago 200,000 passengers passed through here annually. Now it's two million plus of us annually. Back in the nineteenth century a place on Europe's rail network could make a city's fortune. Now it's a listing in the schedules of a growing list of *low fares, low cost, budget, low frills, no frills, etc* airlines. Charleroi's tourist office is in town on *Quai des Martyrs de 8 Aout* and so I am sure something very grisly happened on that date. But I remain pessimistic. A colleague told me that some years ago when he worked in Brussels, he and some friends went to visit Charleroi one day. They entered the tourist office and asked the charming girl behind the counter what they should go and see. She replied rather sheepishly, '*Well, there isn't anything to see.*'

Mick has never been a fan of Brussels. '*Consumers have been ripped off for the past fifty years because governments got together with the airlines after 1945. British Airways got the monopoly in the UK, Air France the monopoly in France and Lufthansa the monopoly in Germany. The airline industry is the only industry where the producers are allowed by the idiots in Brussels to get together once or twice a year to fix the fares and route capacities and they get anti-trust immunity to do it. It's a joke.*' Today's nearby destination is in the newspapers. The European Commission rules that four million euros of financial incentives received by Ruinair from the Walloon government amounts to illegal state aid.

Mick's reaction is choice. '*It would be easier for a camel to pass through the eye of a needle than for Ruinair to get a fair hearing in Brussels. It's a complete fuck-up which is going to overturn twenty years of competition in air travel, but it wouldn't be the first time the EU has made a balls of an investigation. Any time politicians get involved in an industry or regulating an industry, they fuck it up. It's what they do best. I think we should blow the place up and shoot all the regulators and the airline business might actually prosper. Bureaucrats in Brussels have been blathering on about European unity for ages but the low cost airlines are at the forefront of delivering it. We are the means by which hundreds of thousands can now travel back and forth; they are almost commuting. It looks like the EU are trying to come up with some communist rules. The judgment is just blindingly wrong. There will be a repayment over my dead body. We have written back to say fuck off.'*

The chief executive of the almost-Brussels airport replies: *'A letter is going to be sent shortly to ask the airline to repay the amount.'* Mick retorts: *'We haven't received a letter, but if we do I think it would get a pretty short reply. I think it would consist of two words: Foxtrot Oscar. We have spent much more than we have ever received from the Walloon region. We spent over a hundred million euros building the bloody base. We created their airport from nothing. So our reply will say we're paying nothing, love Mick.'*

Mick was not best pleased either when the EU Competition Commissioner Neelie Kroes blocked his bid to take over Aer Lingus when she had previously permitted an Alitalia and Air One merger: *'She'll be rolling over like a poodle having her tummy tickled and rubber stamping the thing. We think the EU Commission is biased against us, but then we would say that, wouldn't we.'* Mick is appealing. Now that doesn't happen too often. *'Given our outstanding record with legal actions we're very confident we'll be successful. So far the tally's running at 99 losses and 2 wins.'*

Mick is left holding a 29 per cent stake in Aer Lingus which some investors want him to sell: *'It has been mentioned by our shareholders; the response was two words, and the second word was "off". It is in the national interest for us to help out our national airline. The €300 million invested by Ruinair in Aer Lingus is just a drop in the ocean, this isn't a lot of money. I sit in front of* our shareholders and say, "I own more shares in the company than you do".'

At the time of writing Mick is down sixty million euros on the stake in Aer Lingus. 'I'm celebrating the fall in value in our investment in Aer Lingus. It's an accurate response to the management's current performance. Aer Lingus is likely to be taken over and the most likely candidate to take over Aer Lingus is Ruinair, because frankly nobody else has any interest in taking over Aer Lingus. It's too small and too high-cost to survive as an independent airline.'

Charleroi is not the same as Brussels, and even the Advertising Standards Authority spotted this when it banned Ruinair from claiming its London to Brussels flights were faster and cheaper than the *Eurostar* train service. The airline's advertisement compared its one-hour, 10-minute flight to the two-hour, 11-minute train trip. The ASA found that because London's Stansted airport is around 25 miles (40 km) out of London and Charleroi is around 28 miles (46 km) out of Brussels, travelling from London and Brussels city centres to the two airports adds 1 hour and 45 minutes to the total journey time. A Ruinair spokesman retorted by saying: 'Only in the parallel universe of the ASA can a one-hour, 10-minute flight be declared to be longer than a two-hour, 11-minute train journey. Even a four-year-old with basic maths could tell you the flight is shorter. Ruinair has today sent a *Dummies Guide to Mathematics* to the ASA who clearly can't add and they can't subtract either. This false ruling should be reversed.' Not so fast, Ruinair.

But Ruinair did not let the matter lie and shortly after ran the following job search on their website:

Maths Test for Morons: Are you slow enough to work for the UK Advertising Standards Authority?

The UK Advertising Standards Authority is looking for an 'investigations executive' but if you want to work for them you'll have to show that you're a dummy. Take our test to find out if you are a big enough moron to join the ASA's crack team.

A Ruinair flight from London to Brussels lasts 1 hour and 10 minutes. The Eurostar train takes 2 hours 11 minutes.

Which is shorter?   *A) Ruinair*   *B) Eurostar*

A Ruinair flight from London to Brussels costs £15. A Eurostar train from London to Brussels costs £27.

Which is cheaper?   A) Ruinair   B) Eurostar

If you answered B you're just the kind of mathematically challenged 'Investigations Executive' the ASA is looking for.

I look around the airport and try to decide where to spend the night. I could follow the herd and board the bus north to Brussels; the 46 kilometre trip. But I've been to Brussels before. On the first occasion I went to the Grand Place and the famous *Manneken Pis*, a pitifully small urinating national icon. I didn't fondle its well-rubbed private parts. It's the sort of tiny national statue you could stick in your backpack and make off with and no one would miss it much. It's the same statue that today's airline used for its aggressive press adverts along the lines of '*Pissed off with Sabena's high fares?*' There's a deal on offer I cannot refuse: a bus ticket and a train ticket to anywhere in Belgium for ten euros. I approach the ticket office in the airport terminal and ask the bored guy inside for a return ticket.

He stares back at me. 'To where?'

I too stare. 'Why, back here of course.'

There are three buses outside. One goes to Brussels, one to Charleroi and one to the car park. There is much confusion. Folks who really want to go to *Gare du Midi* will be deposited in the long-term. Irrespective of my primary issue with going to Brussels (it's full of Belgians), I am not taking the Brussels bus because I have flown here. I will go to cosmopolitan Charleroi, first metropolis of Wallonia, third city of Belgium, located in the province of Hainaut. Population seventeen, including one dog, in peak season. The glamorous Line A bus takes me to Charleroi in ten minutes. The landscape looks like one of those roadside signs you see for industrial estates, the ones with rows of warehouses and plumes. Chimney stacks here belch smoke into the grey sky. There are many small hills, each perfectly formed with neat peaks, unnaturally so. They are covered with trees, hiding something dirty. Slag heaps.

I am aware Charleroi has suffered from depression and it's

starting to have the same effect on me. This is the Black Country, with important steel, glass and coal mining industries in the nineteenth century. You know the sort of place from Monty Python and the *Hovis* adverts. Folks here had to get up before they went to bed, walk twenty miles to work barefoot, and eat rough gravel rather than muesli for breakfast. Times here are still hard. Unemployment here is 20 per cent, twice the Belgian national average. I alight at the train station and receive funny looks from the puzzled locals. Yes, we are the people who choose to come here for our annual holidays rather than risk a sunny sandy beach with talented top tottie in southern Spain.

Charleroi was founded in 1666, built as a fort by the Spanish King Charles II and later abbreviated to Charle-Roy. Charles II was a four-year-old child placed on the throne after the death of his father Philip IV. I bet he made some inspired decisions in the first few years of his reign. *Free Farley's rusks and late bedtime for all.* It takes some time to get my bearings and orientation in the city. Okay, so I get lost. It reminds me of the time a friend went on a motoring holiday in the UK's South-East and he and his wife got lost on the roundabouts of Poole. He eventually pulled over and asked a local how to get out of Poole. To which the bemused local paused for thought and replied that first he would have to be *in* Poole. And don't ever ask anyone in Ireland for directions. Their response will be, '*Well, I wouldn't start from here if I was you.*' This is a derivation of what is known as *Irish Logic*, another example being the guy who drinks in one Dublin pub because the pints are so cheap and tells his mates, '*Sure the more I drink, the more I save.*'

The population of Charleroi is 200,000 and all of them drive their lead-spewing cars around the city's ring roundabouts in a 5pm rush-hour frenzy. I am not sure where they all come from since there is nowhere to leave. There is one office tower block in the city and it's an incomplete eyesore with scaffolding. The refurbishment is half-finished and it's so ugly I'm not sure which is the new half and which is the old half. I don't know what people do around here, apart from engaging in an ongoing competition for the worst parked car in the city centre. I attempt to cross the teeming *Boulevard Tirou* at the zebra crossing. This is an important test in a new city. Either they will allow pedestrians to cross or run us over. I step onto the first white marks and a local almost takes off my lower leg. Drivers take aim for pedestrians in these parts.

Place Charles II is the heart of the old city and is quite a climb. I recognise the square immediately. The last time I saw it chairs were being thrown through bar windows and the police were spraying water cannon jets over the tourists. It was Euro 2000, when soccer supporters came to play hardball. I sit and wait until an enterprising beggar speaks to me and asks for a few euros. I decline his request but admire his excellent French. *Rue de la Montagne* is a cobbled pedestrian thoroughfare which links the upper city to the lower city, otherwise known as a sheer vertical drop disguised as a shopping street. I come to rest at *Le Pieton* café at *Rue de Dampremy*, the oldest street in the city. The café name is appropriate because I have been walking for miles. I wonder perhaps if there is a sister café a few streets away called *Le Pieton Mort*, near a zebra crossing. I have a coffee and a big crêpe. A bloke always feels better after a decent crêpe.

Along the way back to my hotel, important sites are marked with monoliths in the shape of upturned oars with text. Near the back of the train station I see a few more local oars, plying their trade. Please do not go to Charleroi solely for the nightlife. It's Tuesday and 8pm but everywhere is closed or empty. I think the government organised a civil defence exercise for a simulated germ warfare attack and perhaps asked the population to stay indoors for the duration of my stay. *Chez Walters* bar only has one drinker inside and it looks like Walter himself. A trendy Italian bar I saw open at 4pm is closed as darkness settles. The one and only cinema is doing a roaring business so this is conclusive proof. The highlight of my evening is watching a driver parking his car illegally on a curb. A crowd gathers wherever I stop in the street. I have a paranoid fear of dining in empty restaurants. Either I get poisoned or ripped off. In absolute desperation I dropped into *the* McDonalds. They do a good Big Mac but they made me wait ten minutes for fries. I suggest if you go there you telephone in advance so they have the fries ready when you arrive.

In a few hours I have done Charleroi. Or rather it's done me. Next morning I check out and cross the *Sambre* to the train station. I have a train ticket and I'm not afraid to use it. The next inter-city train to Brussels is due to leave at 10.07am. At 09.52 an IC train arrives at the correct platform. It looks like my train but it cannot be because it's so early. This is not Germany. I ask the guard, who confirms it is my train. I tell her it's fifteen minutes early. She shrugs, *'C'est normale.'* Not where I live, dear. When we depart in the opposite direction, I am the only passenger facing the wrong way. Charleroi is the end of the line.

In Brussels in the mid-afternoon I go to *Gare du Midi* to catch the bus back to Charleroi airport. The timetable advises this bus serves two flights, one to Dublin and one to Rome Ciampino. I am anxious since this bus can hold a maximum of a hundred people and a Boeing 737 holds 189 people. There seems to be some imbalance here. I make sure to get to the bus on time, to get a seat, to just be on it. I am very early. Low fares airlines love anxious passengers. They are on time. The bus journey takes an hour. It takes an hour to get from Heathrow to Central London by tube, reinforcing the fact that the only airport actually in London is the City Airport in London's Docklands, used exclusively by suited City Blackberry users. I'm not sure what all the fuss is about the location of this airport. Within a minute I exit the bus and check in.

At the departure gate a couple of Belgian teenage girls study an *Irland* guidebook excitedly. They are the frequent-flyer Generation Y'ers who fly, not because they want to, but because they can. They are young, young enough never to have lived without Vodafone and DVDs, email and IMS, Playstation and Gameboy, Yahoo! and Google, and pan-European low fares air travel courtesy of Ruinair. But I am from a different generation, where only wealthy adults had mobile telephones and nobody outside of academic and research laboratories possessed an email address. A URL was a really exotic address. Amazon was a river in South America. Orange was a bright colour. A googol was the technical term for an enormous number, a 1 followed by one hundred zeros. XBox, eBay and iPod were typographical errors. An instant message was something you sent via a bloke on a motorbike. No one wanted to drive a Mini. There were little shops on the High Street called travel agents and Ruinair was a small Irish airline which lost money annually and which most Irish people were sure would never amount to much more than an embarrassment.

17.17. A Ruinair Boeing 737 lands and flashes by the huge plate glass window at speed. Such relief.

17.19. The aircraft pulls up outside the gate, only twenty feet away, filling the glass window with its logo. The sun shines suddenly and bounces off the white paint in an almost ecclesiastical experience.

17.21. The first passengers disembark. The ground crew work at speed, actually running around the aircraft. The last time I saw a team work this fast they were refuelling a Ferrari at the Monaco Grand Prix.

17.23. The aircraft is empty. Thumbs up signals are given and reciprocated between ground and cabin crew, the latter immediately coming down the steps to the gate to board us.

17.45. We take off five minutes ahead of the scheduled departure time. I have been flying for twenty years and I have taken hundreds of flights. I can't ever remember taking off before the scheduled time.

The flight is uneventful except for one announcement from the crew supervisor: '*If anyone has change of a fifty euro note would they make themselves known to one of the cabin crew.*' They are tight. I sit next to someone I vaguely recognise from Irish politics. I take a second look at the only guy in a suit and risk all.

'Are you a TD?' I ask.

'MEP.'

Myself and an Irish MEP discuss low fares airlines. He seems to be a fan of the concept.

'I receive a fixed EU allowance to travel to Brussels. I only paid forty euro today. I keep the rest.'

I tell him I'm writing a book about this airline and others and he likes the idea. I agree to send him a copy if it sees the light of day. He offers to attend the book launch and say a few words. I wonder will he? We exchange business cards. A few months later I get a personal invite to his Golf Day. I don't play golf.

After one hour the eastern coastline of Ireland is in view, with the undulating hills and pastures of Wicklow sweeping seamlessly towards the finest coastal residences of Killiney and Dalkey, home to Bono, The Edge, Enya, Eddie Irvine and Neil Jordan, and of course little old me. We cruise over Dublin Bay, past lush golf courses and white sands to touch down on cue. Ireland never looked so good.

We land in Dublin at 18.10, twenty minutes ahead of our scheduled arrival time. What with the one-hour time difference, I think we landed before we took off, which is surely impossible. I'm amazed, since this is an Irish airline. Sure, we're always late for everything. Stephen Hawking's weighty tome called *A Brief History of Time* was not a great seller in Ireland. Oscar Wilde once remarked there's no point in being on time for anything in Ireland since there will be no one else there to appreciate it. The poet Patrick Kavanagh advised there were thirty words in the Irish language equivalent to the Spanish *mañana* but none conveys the same sense of urgency. When God made time here, sure didn't he make plenty of it.

Inside the terminal building at passport control, our queue is stopped by the officer sitting in the box.

'Where are you travelling from today, madam?' he asks the elderly lady ahead of me.

'From Murcia. In Spain,' she replies.

That should be sufficient information but it's not. 'Did you have a pleasant time?'

What? She nods. 'Yes, it was good enough. Weather was a bit mixed. Cloudy for a few days.'

'But you enjoyed the break?' he perseveres.

Jesus Christ. The rest of us need to get home sometime today. 'Yes, it was nice.'

That must be it. But not so. 'Would you go back there?'

'Ah, I think I would. But not this year. Maybe next year.'

They don't know each other. I am sure of that. 'Right then, all the best.'

'Thanks again.'

He bids her fond farewell. 'Safe home.'

Next it's my turn. I am dreading another Spanish inquisition.

He gives my passport a quick glance. 'Fine, Paul.' I mean, I don't know him or anything either. I don't travel *that* much. It's only an Irish welcome.

I am beginning to understand the real challenge I have set myself. It's not the getting there and back that's the difficult part. It's having to spend time in these continental places much beloved by Ruinair.

The Low Fares
Airline (3)

THE LOW FARES TAXI

A row over security at Stansted Airport has broken out after it was alleged an aircraft was flagged down 'like a London taxi' as it moved towards the runway for takeoff. The GMB union says a Ruinair plane was stopped by one of the airline's employees, breaching safety and security rules. Ruinair has confirmed the incident took place, but says safety was not compromised. A GMB spokesman said the plane, with approximately 100 passengers on board, was flagged down as it taxied towards the runway. Ruinair denies the plane was taxiing but admits it had moved off its stand. In a statement the airline said one of its co-pilots had asked to travel home to Esbjerg as a supernumerary crew member. The airline's statement confirmed that the co-pilot, who had a fully authorised air-side access pass and was wearing full reflective clothing, did board the plane. 'He boarded after the aircraft had pushed back early from the stand, and before the engines had been started up. While it was unorthodox and the co-pilot was disciplined, there was no breach of safety procedures and no delay to the aircraft. The flight continued onwards on its journey and arrived 22 minutes ahead of schedule in Esbjerg.'

BBC NEWS

THE NO FARES TAXI

The head of Ruinair has come up with a novel way to beat Dublin's notorious traffic jams – his own taxi licence. Tired of crawling through the capital's frequent gridlocks, multi-millionaire O'Leery has bought a taxi licence, number MG99, which allows him to drive his luxury Mercedes s500 saloon in restricted bus lanes. Since the deregulation of the taxi industry three years ago, the number of licences in circulation in the city has tripled to around 10,000. A spokesperson for Ruinair confirmed the move by O'Leery. 'To the best of my knowledge it's true and what is reported in the papers is correct,' the spokesperson said. While it is not illegal to use the licence, O'Leery would be obliged to pick up customers if hailed while driving without a passenger in his car, the papers said. O'Leery was quoted as follows: 'Last time I checked this was a democratic republic. As long as I pay my taxes I'm free to do with my money what I like. It's a black taxi registered in Mullingar. I have a driver who drives it for me. It appears to be alright if I rent a taxi but if I own a taxi there's a problem. If you're in Mullingar then give me a call. I'd be happy to look after you. If they want to amend the taxi regulations which says I'm allowed to pick up people in Dublin, I'll be happy to pick up people in Dublin. And I'll do it a lot cheaper.' There is a meter in his taxi and it produces receipts. The fare from Mullingar to Dublin Airport is eighty euros. 'We are a low-cost airline so we wouldn't entertain mileage allowances like that,' he added.

INDEPENDENT ONLINE

Mercedes Bends the Rules

THE LOW FINES AIRLINE

Ruinair boss Mick O'Leery had his wings clipped for dangerous driving yesterday. The multi-millionaire was fined €1,269 and had his licence endorsed at Trim District Court in Co. Meath. Impeccably dressed in a navy suit, white shirt and tie, a grim-faced Mr O'Leery faced three charges of dangerous driving, careless driving and dangerous overtaking. Witness Catriona Cunningham said she was driving along the main Dublin - Trim road and a BMW overtook her, quickly followed by a 97D registered Mercedes, which also passed her in the face of oncoming traffic forcing her to brake and allow Mr O'Leery's Mercedes to pull in, in front of her. She witnessed the Mercedes overtaking between 10 and 15 cars on a straight stretch of road. She dialled 999 and got through to Trim garda station. Garda Fergal Quinn said he followed Mr O'Leery as far as Athboy Gate in Trim, where he pulled him over and informed him there had been two complaints against him. Mr O'Leery said he felt he had done nothing dangerous. Speaking outside court to reporters, Mr O'Leery said: 'I'm very sorry, I will try and learn from the experience. I clearly made a mistake. I'm sorry to have wasted the Garda and court time.'

INDEPENDENT ONLINE

The Rough Guide
— An official handbook for Crewlink staff working on Ruinair aircraft

www.crewlink.ie/Handbook.doc

Are you bored of nine-to-five? Want something different? Want a career that will get you places? How about a job that gives you wings! We are recruiting for exciting Cabin Crew positions at Ruinair's bases throughout Europe. What is this Rough Guide? Well you need it because anything else that claimed to give you all the answers would either put you to sleep or be out of date before you finished reading it. This guide is not intended to give you all the answers but give you a flavour of what it's like to work for CREWLINK *operating on Ruinair aircraft, what's expected, what are the definite no no's and what you have to do to excel. As a* CREWLINK *employee you will interact with various Ruinair departments on a regular basis:*

In-flight *are the part of the airline that spend the most time with passengers. They are the front line troops of Ruinair, they are capable well-trained individuals who can handle pressure and deal with all types of people. Apart from delivering a first class service, they are also famous for wild nights out and asking complete strangers how well they look in their uniforms.*

Engineering *are the heroes, from sun up to sun down. These technical wizards ensure the planes are the best maintained in the business. They are a proud and hardworking bunch that pursues an uncompromising approach to safety and the highest engineering* *standards. While the majority call the hangar in Dublin airport home, a growing number are located in other bases. Not all of engineering are required to wear overalls, high visibility vests and smear themselves with oil.*

Flight Operations *are the very core of the operation, the men and women whose vast experience and know-how ensure that the planes fly, without them Ruinair would be a bus company! Well that's what they claim. As a group they are famous for their modesty, humility, meekness and unassuming nature.*

Commercial/Head Office *functions provide support to the operational sections of the airline. Included among their ranks are the Finance team, 'show me the Money' is their mantra.* MIS *are the tech people; if it's plugged in you can bet these bright sparks are taking care of it. The Marketing team attract passengers whether it's in Stockholm, Glasgow or Pisa. The Yield team decide how low ticket prices can go; also called the limbo department. The New Route Development team trawl Europe in search of new and exciting routes and finally Personnel, the hidden treasures of the company, good looking and hard working, the people who ensure they get the best that Europe has to offer. As Ruinair tries to minimize the number of people who are not involved in the front operation of the airline, these teams are small and happy — they also get to go home at weekends — sometimes.*

Ground Operations *which includes Check-in and Ground Handling, are one of the most important parts of the airline. The Ground Handling Agents (Rampers) have a flight turnaround time which is an unbelievable 25 minutes. This turnaround allows Ruinair to utilize their planes more efficiently than anyone else; it also ensures Ruinair maintains its position as the most punctual airline in Europe. As the uniformed front line, check-in/Customer Service are people who must have a good sense of humour, and the ability to work in a demanding environment. Renowned for their exceptional speed, whether checking passengers in or working their way through a free bar.*

Ruinair.com — *The jewel in the crown. Powered by a computer server who works 24 hours a day/seven days a week, no pay, sick days,* or cigarette breaks. On a good day their web site can account for over 94% of all bookings. This outstanding employee is supported by a small but dedicated team of web masters, or whatever they call themselves this week.

Duty Station Manager. *Responsible for ground operations at a particular airport. These unfortunates sometimes have to tell a departure lounge full of passengers the flight's delayed or snow has set in for the weekend. Sense of humour, athletic build and sub 10 second 100 meters ability are all helpful.*

Z Level Managers. *The clowns with the pea sized brains that make most of the decisions at Ruinair. They meet every Monday morning to wreak even more havoc.*

Netherlands

Ruinair Flight FR1964 – Monday @ 4.10pm – DUB-EIN-DUB

Fare €2 plus taxes, fees and charges €46

I vaguely remember how I booked a European city break ten years ago with a travel agent. *'Screw the travel agents. Take the fuckers out and shoot them. They are a waste of bloody time. What have they done for passengers over the years?'* Mick even declined an invitation to attend the Association of British Travel Agents' annual convention in Cairo: *'I certainly won't be going to the ABTA convention. I can think of no more useless a convention. It's a bit like holding a meeting of Alcoholics Anonymous in a big pub.'*

I read that travel agents hit back after Ruinair referred to them as the 'greatest deadwood' and 'the costliest parasites in the travel industry'. Boston-based Spa Travel partner Paul Dayson said Ruinair needed to look closely at how many agents book its flights. He said: 'Ruinair thinks it can do without us. It is getting a lot more from us than it realises. It should look at how much product is booked through the trade.' Karen Forrester, owner of Cumbria-based agency Travel On, said: 'We have to use the airline so to call a travel agent a parasite is totally disgusting. We are all people and we all have to work and earn a crust.'

I used the same local travel agent as my parents used, where the husband and wife owners knew the travel patterns of my entire family tree over prior generations. I would express interest in a weekend in some glamorous *Eurocity*. They'd look at each other in a Harry Enfield sort of way and say, 'Oh, you don't want to go there, now do you?' But I did. Eventually we would agree on a suitable destination, one they liked, one they had been to many times and one they insisted I try. It was a sad fact of life that travel agents, remember them, had been to everywhere on earth on freebie press trips. I'd mention the weekend I wished to travel and they'd look at each other and say 'Hmmmnnnn .... Now that could be expensive.'

This all happened so long ago that people used to dress up in their Sunday best before flying anywhere in public. There was never a range of air fares since two national airlines only flew between the two cities and their fares were identical. What a coincidence. The travel agent made the reservations by telephone to some unseen voice. In the week of departure I'd return to get a little plastic wallet with flight tickets, hotel vouchers, an itinerary and best of all two natty little paper luggage tags for my bags. These were essential since if my luggage went missing I could be sure the paper baggage tags would endure.

In the final week I would go to the bank at lunchtime to get my foreign currency. I'd queue for half an hour but because I was in the elite *Bureau de Change* queue I felt hyper-important. It was a two-stage process whereby you ordered the currency one day and then returned to collect it the next day. The teller would count it out at such speed that I had no idea how much I ever got. All change now. Travel in the old days meant that planning was often the most time-consuming yet enjoyable part of a holiday, such that couples would plan several holidays a year, but go nowhere, and so enjoy all the fun yet save a fortune.

Travel has gravitated to the internet. We book our flights online. We book our car hire online. We book our hotels online once we see the map of the hotel location and the photographs of the hotel rooms, including the colour of the duvets and the size of the bathroom. We check train and bus times online. We download free pdfs of attractions and events from the tourist office websites. On some tourist websites they offer a free movie of the city which, once viewed, completely obviates the need to actually travel at all. And of course we can check the five-day weather forecast at our destination before we travel so if there is even a chance of a speck of rain we cancel the trip entirely because we only ever paid one cent for the flight.

The Sunday Independent reports that Irish people on average now take two trips abroad per annum. Baloney. Dublin airport is the 17th busiest airport in the world and sometimes it feels like Heathrow because it is bursting at the seams and I blame certain low fares airlines for enticing us away so often. Twenty years ago we only went to the airport once a year and that was to emigrate to New York or London. Ten years ago we only got two weeks away in Lanzagrotty or Playa del English courtesy of Gillian's *Budget Travel*, plus if we were lucky we got a dirty weekend in London via Sealink and Holyhead. Now we hop off for city breaks as if there is some sort of social stigma to being marooned in Dublin. Friends of mine are going to Johannesburg and Buenos Aires like they are off to Cork or Belfast. For the first time ever Irish people now make more visits annually overseas than tourists make coming to Ireland. Some weekends I am the only local person left in Dublin and I have to mind the city on behalf of those who travel to stags, weddings, festivals, matches, races and tours in Europe. Plus I welcome the Boeings of tourists arriving to see the Guinness Storehouse, Temple Bar, Windmill Lane and all other authentic Irish things.

Heathrow spent £4.2 billion on Terminal 5 and Hong Kong spent $20 billion on an airport on a man-made island, but we had a temporary solution to expand Departures at Dublin airport: *Portakabins*. Dublin airport built a new check-in area for Ruinair in the basement but Mick is not keen. '*Unless there's some incentive for us to move to the basement of the black hole of Calcutta, we'll stay where we are.*' There are signs advising that I should allow ten minutes to reach the furthest gates in Pier A, which is true enough if you have recently participated in an Olympic athletics final. Mick hates the way this airport is run. '*Dublin airport has descended into a farce. The Dublin Airport Authority, which is responsible for this third-world facility, is to be rewarded for its incompetence.*' He traces the problems back to a former transport minister called Mary and her boss called Bertie. '*She's an idiot. I'm very supportive of people who come from the Midlands but I'm not supportive of an idiot no matter where they come from. Most politicians are idiots, but if you look on the scale of idiocy she'd be right up there at the top. I would have to ask why you would let a schoolteacher run such an important ministerial portfolio? I am disrespectful towards authority. Like I think the Prime Minister of Ireland is a gobshite.'*

The queues at security are lengthy, so much so that one woman says: *'It's worse than bleedin' Disneyland.'* The diligent staff always ask me if I have a laptop computer inside my baggage, so now to save time I display a prominent sticker on my baggage which proclaims, 'I don't own a fucking laptop.' We are asked to take off our jackets, hats, belts and shoes. If I go through any more airport X-ray machines, I will become a shadow of my former self. The way things are going I won't be surprised to be seen in a few years' time walking through an X-ray machine in public wearing only my boxer shorts. A man sits down next to me to replace his belt. *'Jaysus, I almost lost me bleedin' trousers there.'*

Security is even tighter today following a terrorism scare in which a Ruinair plane was diverted to a remote spot in Prestwick airport. Mick was not so impressed. *'The police force were outstanding in their field. But all they did was stand in their field. They kept passengers on board while they played with a suspect package for two and three-quarter hours. Extraordinary.'* Or it could be because of a foiled terrorist plot which led to extra security measures. *'These are farcical Keystone Cops security measures that don't add anything except to block up airports. We are not going to die at the hands of toiletries. Ladies' padded bras with gel inside are not weapons of mass destruction. Searching five- or six-year-old children and elderly people in wheelchairs going to Spain on holidays will have the terrorists laughing in the caves in Pakistan. It feels like Laurel and bloody Hardy are working at the Department of Transport coming up with these security measures.'* Mick is not so bothered by terrorism. *'Generally, the best time to visit anywhere is after a terrorist attack because the hotels are discounting like mad and the place is crawling with security. You might be scared of flying at £200 return, but you'll be a lot less scared flying at £20 return. We need visitors to fly to Britain or the economy will be in the toilet.'*

I travel light so only occasionally is my backpack opened and inspected, and usually this check is performed in German airports by an elderly matron in a security uniform, with the sole purpose of causing me the maximum amount of public embarrassment. Inside she will only find socks and smalls, shirts and executive *jim-jams*, a small supply of notes and coins from those nations which refuse to join the Eurozone (e.g. the UK), and emergency rations such as chocolate, bananas and lightly buttered salad rolls because you never know when a cheap Irish airline might abandon you in a foreign field. Of course I must display my intimate toiletries in a little plastic bag for fear I combine my shampoo, toothpaste and shaving gel into an explosive device. There is a real need to manufacture miniature toiletries of no more than 100 ml each in size and in due course no doubt the Japanese will too come to dominate this miniature industry.

On the way to the departure gate I read an advertisement from Budget car hire. '*Last year Ruinair made €27 million on car rental. Don't pay more than you should. Cut out the middleman. Book direct with Budget.*' Near the gates I pass the luggage shop with suitcases stacked up. This always puzzles me. This shop is airside, on the far side of security. Why would anyone want to buy a suitcase in an airport? Do people in a hurry say '*Oh, just grab a few things and sure we'll get a suitcase in the airport.*'

Walking through the confusing airport is a journey in itself, despite the fact that Dublin airport is small in passenger volumes; small in the sense that you can sit next to a loony on the bus from the long-term car park safe in the knowledge that an hour later when you board your B-737 the same loony will be sitting in the next seat. It's easy to spot the seasoned Ruinair passengers. They're the ones having bananas and chocolate, Red Bull and Lucozade, multi-vitamins and health supplements, ready for the endurance test that lies ahead. Our experience and fortitude binds us together so that whenever two or three of us are gathered together in Mick's name, we surreptitiously share our collective tales; the earliest departure, the longest delay, the smallest airport, the remotest airport, the longest bus trip, the last flight we took, the next trip we plan, how to beat the ever-changing rules for carry-on and hold baggage, but most of all pride in the lowest fare we ever paid. We have all been there, done that, bought the cheap ticket and lived to tell the tale.

Refreshingly, there are few Suits, minor-Celebs and pseudo ABC1 airline snobs amongst our egalitarian bunch. Ruinair's market research says 57% of their passengers are between the ages of 25 and 44. A third regard themselves as 'Innovators' or 'Early Adopters'; 82% rate Ruinair's service as 'good' or 'excellent' but I am not sure why; 21% are travelling on business; 40% travel five times or more each year with Ruinair (I am one); 90% would 'probably' or 'definitely' recommend a friend. Their average total spend per trip is €510; 64% have an income in excess of €40,000 so they could easily afford to travel on another airline; 21% own a second property in another country; 46% originate from the UK, 12% from Germany, 12% from Ireland, 12% from Italy, 6% from Spain and 5% from France. That's enough numbers for now. *'Most of our frequent flyers would be what you'd call upper class: the very rich. Our most frequent flyers during the summer are people who have large holiday homes in Malaga, Marbella, south of France, Italy, sending their kids, nannies, gardeners, wives, girlfriends, mistresses up and down on our flights.'*

As we wait, a plume of black smoke rises from dense trees adjacent to the runway. It's the sort of sight you don't wish to observe at any airport. However, I take some comfort from the fact that the crew at the airport fire station, some one hundred yards away, have not budged from their morning slumber. But two Ruinair ground staff have seen the same dirty big plume and they wander over to the window.

'What's that?' one of them asks.

'Smoke,' the other replies.

We're running slightly late but an elderly gent alongside is confused. 'We're already an hour late.'

'We're not,' I reply. 'We're about fifteen minutes late. Relax, we'll be there on time.'

'Are you sure?' he asks.

Do I look like I work for this airline, yet? 'They're the most punctual airline in Europe.'

He remains unconvinced. 'Says who?'

'Says Mick.'

He nods. 'It must be true then.'

We wait as faltering Ruinair staff make Tannoy announcements. *'Would the last three passengers, Reilly, Murphy and Byrne, on Ruinair flight 123 to London Gatwick please make their way immediately to gate 11 since their flight is fully boarded and awaits an on time departure.'* But of course if there are three eejits who are late, then their flight is not *fully boarded* and the announcement is completely erroneous.

Today's crew again display disinterest, almost disdain, towards their passengers. They cannot muster even a false smile, as other airlines can, and it's due to their flight attendant training course. If they exhibit any sense of humour or a glimmer of a personality, they are taken aside midway through the course. *'Look, we're sorry, but we saw that smile, you're not the sort of person we look for at this airline.'* The vitamin-starved girl who boards us at the gate looks at us. 'This way. Stand here.' Soon she is shouting at us. 'Come over here. Wait. You first. 1 to 90 only. I said ... 1 to 90 only.' I don't much like being shouted at. They tell us to take our seats quickly because the flight is 'full', but when they close the doors there's a free seat beside me and one in front and one behind so either they cannot count or I cannot count. This airline does not overbook flights (they don't sell more than 189 seats per Boeing) so the only flights that are ever 'full' are their three hundred euro flights to see Liverpool FC play their Champions League Final annually.

We have Loud Americans on board. He stands in the aisle in the middle of the aircraft and booms to his wife some rows back, 'Honey, I got three seats in a row. Over here. They're free. Get here, quick. Run. Lots of room on top.' She replies. 'I got three here. I got 'em saved for you. Come here, Jim.' Back and forth they go. 'You come here.' 'No, you come here.' Tempers fray. 'Jeez, come up here.' Soon they are the only two left standing in the aisle and all the free rows are taken. 'Jeez, can you see two seats together?' I can't help but overhear their audible conversation to nearby passengers. 'We're using this airline to see all of Europe. It's a bit daunting, like we often have to figure out where the hell we are. We've been to

Paris, Berlin, Barcelona, Rome.' And rather belatedly they add, 'And to here, of course.' Only 20 per cent of Americans possess passports so we must be grateful for small mercies but some of them are well travelled, except for those who arrive in regional French towns and make straight for the *Hotel de Ville* as the best place for board and lodging, only to discover it is where elected council officials direct municipal policy.

Our cabin crew supervisor, amazingly enough, is once again Gavin. I fly on this airline too often. He excels in dealing with twelve Culchies from Mohill GAA club who sit close by. It's their first time out of Ireland, perhaps even their first time out of Mohill. When Gavin hands out copies of the Ruinair magazine, one of the langers asks him for crayons. When one buys a chicken salad sandwich they play a vocal game of '*Find the Chicken*'. When we hit turbulence one of the Culchies asks the fattest bloke to move seats to the other side of the plane so as to balance the load. Gavin enjoys some revenge when he stops by the Culchies with the gifts and fragrances trolley to ask, 'Anyone here for a Teddy bear?' After we land Gavin welcomes us to the Netherlands whether our trip is '*for business or*' ... a long pause and an evil grin ... '*pleasure.*'

It's good to avoid nearby Amsterdam Schiphol. Last time I arrived at Schiphol a few hundred of us passengers set off on a forced route march through inhospitable terrain and arrived at immigration some hours later. We lost a few on the way, picked off by snipers in duty-free and at the shoe-shine. Schiphol is too big to be an airport. It's more of a giant shopping mall which happens to have a runway attached. Immigration today is a thirty-minute nightmare as we queue outside the terminal onto the apron. Two quizmasters in uniforms ask excessive questions: '*Where have you come from today? What is the purpose of your visit? Where are you staying? What is your date of birth? What did you have for breakfast? Any terrorism plans for the weekend? What's the fastest land animal?*' I feel like a contestant on *Mastermind* who has taken as his specialist subject *Useless Questions asked by Bored Policemen*.

The 401 bus trundles from the airport to the city centre *Centraal* station via industrial suburbs. The landscape is so awfully flat. They must kill for a hill around here. Remember that movie with

Hugh Grant called *The Man Who Went Up A Hill and Came Down A Mountain*, where locals added twenty foot of soil to a hill so they had a mountain for visitors? Well, that movie wasn't made around these parts.

Sitting opposite is a thirty-something girl in faded jeans and scuffed boots who chews her nails avidly for afternoon tea. Worst of all she uses her Nokia mobile with its trailing earpiece incessantly, seemingly working her way through her entire address book. She will only be parted from this telephone if she has it surgically removed. I listen to her. I worry she's trying to rip out her vocal cords, or perhaps has acute pneumonia. She has at least acute something as she stands and stretches to retrieve her luggage. Maybe she has a throat ailment, or advanced bronchitis. No, I eventually decide. She's speaking Dutch. Dutch people speak as if they are trying to bring up something, and it's not only a conversation. Retched. When first learning to speak Dutch it's best instead to cough violently and produce as much phlegm as possible.

All I know about Eindhoven is that it has a decent football team in the Champions League and a substantial factory manufacturing a lot of exciting light bulbs. I gleaned the latter from my secondary school geography class, because we enjoyed Miss Glynn every Tuesday at 10.30am, so to speak. She was young and slim with long dark hair and bright eyes and a penchant for leaving a few top buttons open. Sadly, everything else we covered in six years of global geographical discovery largely remains a blur due to her appearance, apart from the time I read aloud to the class from the chapter about Cornwall. Every one of us knew one particular town was coming up and the room went deadly quiet as I drew near, but sadly pubescent boys all around the British Isles always get a snigger when hearing of the town of Newquay.

The first connection I make is at the city's rail station, a building from the 1920s. It is rectangular and long, with recessed windows on the front, a flat squat roof and a side clock tower built like an aerial. The building was purposefully designed to look like a wireless set and I have to admit it offers me a good reception. Nearby lies an industrial tower called *Lichtorren,* and close by lies

Lichtplein and *Lichtstrasse*. Already my Dutch is improving and Eindhoven is proving to be an illuminating experience. Around the corner on *Emmasingel* is their first factory, founded in 1891. A bright spark named Mr Gerard Philips brought his idea to Eindhoven because land and staff were cheap and the south of Holland was as depressed as I am when I sign up for the one-hour light bulb factory tour offered only in Dutch.

Gerard was not as good a salesman as his brother Anton. To date they have manufactured two and a half billion light bulbs. Here's how to make a light bulb if you ever need to knock one together. Tease out a piece of purified cotton and soak in some stinky chemicals. Add some carbon and graphite and bake in a moderate oven for twenty minutes, turning once. Twist the cotton wire into loops and connect to two electrodes. Insert into a hand-blown glass bulb, suck out all the air and vacuum seal. Insert into light fitting. Pray. The early days were dark. Electricity wasn't freely available, so they had to build their own generator to make electricity to test the light bulbs. Few citizens could afford expensive light bulbs so they were used in shops, restaurants and theatres. They didn't last long either. Oops, there goes another bloody bulb.

Sepia photographs on the wall depict early staff. The men sport dodgy handlebar moustaches last seen in a *Village People* video, and some were called Hans because it's a proven scientific fact that many Hans make light work. The factory girls were as young as twelve years old because young girls were good at handling the fiddly little bits of bulbs. Some of the girls making the light bulbs used to work previously in a matchstick factory. If you were a guy on the pull in Eindhoven's hottest nightspot in the early 1900s you could tell much from afar. If a girl had pink fingers she worked with sulphur making matchsticks but if she had black fingers she worked with graphite making bulbs at Philips. If her fingers were clean, chances were she was, unfortunately, unemployed. I find myself soon listening attentively to the guide speaking double Dutch about the riveting manufacture of the carbon filament inside the inert vacuum of an incandescent light bulb. This is particularly sad. Listening to the guide conduct the world's most serious tour all in Dutch is hard work. At various stages in the tour I wish to offer him a handkerchief so that he can clear his throat and continue.

The Philips brothers made Eindhoven. A city map shows that the Philips complex occupies one tenth of the city centre. If you want to watch PSV Eindhoven, you can walk ten minutes to the *Philips Stadion*. Eindhoven is the fifth largest city in the Netherlands, embracing electronics, invention and the digital age. It's a switched-on, high-tech, illuminating sort of place. Philips did for this city what Bill Gates and Microsoft did for Seattle, what Boeing did for Seattle, what Starbucks did for Seattle. Seattle's done well, hasn't it? In Piazza Square a flea market offers bootleg CDs of a U2 concert. It's appropriate because the CD was invented in Eindhoven. Yes, by Philips. Some think the CD was invented to deliver improved audio quality but not so. It was invented so that forty-year-old men would repurchase their entire record collection. For those who like trivia, the 15 mm hole in every CD is the size of the smallest Dutch coin of twenty-five years ago.

Next morning after a quick shave, that's with a *Philishave*, and a catch up on the news on TV in my hotel room, and that's not on a Sony or Sharp, and wearing a well-ironed shirt courtesy of a Philips *Mistral* steam iron from back home, I take in the sparkling new Van Abbemuseum. Every low fares destination in Europe has such a venue, but sadly modern art now passes me by. It's an edgy building with metal cladding on the walls designed by a celebrity architect. There are rooms of black and white block paintings in empty minimalist space, chairs hanging from walls and a shelf of cellophane-wrapped Lever Arch files, a pile of rusty nails or whatever on a wooden floor in the shape of a crescent, rotating slide projections and repetitive videos of two men inside a car in a storm where not much happens. Abstraction, modernism, cubism, confusion, refraction and reflection lead me towards the *Uitgang* at the speed of light.

What is with the Dutch and their bicycles? There are bicycles everywhere, mazes of red bicycle lanes and chained rows of bicycles at every tram and bus stop. Walking back to the rail station means being *tringed* along the way by trigger-happy cyclists and at the rail station all the bikes ever manufactured have been abandoned in front of the giant wireless set. I saw a perfectly good set of railings in an Eindhoven street without any bicycles attached so I took a photograph of the scene for posterity.

There's the relief of passing a difficult exam or a driving test, the relief after a tense job interview, the relief of a sick relative making a full recovery, and even the relief of visiting an Amsterdam strip joint, but nothing compares to the relief of being in a remote airfield and seeing your Ruinair aircraft arrive on cue. The lone female crew member who descends the steps to board us looks lost. She makes for the nearest door but cannot open it so she walks off to another door. It might be her first time at Eindhoven airport, perhaps even at any airport. Eventually she is let in, tries to operate a PA system and slowly reads from a hand-written piece of notepaper in faltering English. We are both fluent, but sadly in different languages. I wonder how she will manage if she has to tell me about some emergency on board the plane later. It is embarrassing when she invites us to board. Those with boarding sequence numbers 1 to 90 don't move since they expect families to board first. She doesn't invite the families forward. We all look at her from ten feet away in her over-sized blue coat plus pancake makeup and neat bun. I feel sorry for her. I plead with her to seize the moment. I make eye contact and nod encouragingly at her. She speaks. 'Come.' We board.

Soon we are belted in, rear doors shut with steps removed and ready to go twenty minutes before departure when I see a rather excited Ground Operations Supervisor through my port window. He bounds up the forward steps in his fluorescent jacket and engages Leena in conversation. She's the wee Scottish lassie with the perma-tan who's our cabin supervisor. She looks out the starboard windows, sees the light and makes a PA to ask us to open our seat belts since refuelling of the plane is still underway. Behind me the rear steps are returned to the plane, the rear doors are re-opened and the crew take up positions by the three sets of emergency exits. The Ground Operations Supervisor waits with a colleague on the apron, shakes his head and points to the Shell tanker on the other side with much evident frustration. Phew. We depart on the dot, destined to land in Dublin ten minutes early. As we soar above the clouds, light streams into the cabin. Below us Eindhoven recedes; the *City of Blinding Lights*, the ultimate *electri-City*.

A full 737-800 with 189 passengers on a four-hour round trip spews out about 60 tonnes of carbon dioxide, so Ruinair's fleet of aircraft belches out two to three million tonnes of greenhouse gases across Europe annually. By now my own personal carbon footprint is the size of the footprint left by the Yeti in Yellowstone National Park. Even the Bishop of London, Richard Chartres, spoke out to say that we should desist from flying, saying it was sinful to pollute the planet by jetting away so often on holiday. Mick disagrees: '*The Bishop of London has got empty churches — presumably if no one went on holiday perhaps they might turn up and listen to his sermons. God bless the bishop. The bishops have got their own crosses to bear. Goodness knows what he would know about greenhouse gases. He was obviously at some dinner party with the chatterati. It's the usual horseshit that we hear. There is a fundamental misunderstanding about aviation and environmental taxes at the moment. No one knows what they are talking about.*'

Despite the fact that airline travel accounts for a tiny 1.6% of global greenhouse gases per the authoritative Stern Report (and we don't hear so much about the 18% from road traffic and the 26% from power generation), many want environmentally based taxation charges to be levied upon the airline industry. But aviation is not the world's biggest polluter — that's the CNN TV channel. Mick likes a rant. '*I don't believe in trotting out all that politically correct claptrap just so as not to upset a couple of environmental lunatics. I say keep flying. Environmentalists are often very aggressive with their baloney, but these numb-nuts don't realise that aviation is already the most taxed form of travel. Remember all these green protestors still take flights to go on their eco-tours, and how do you think they get to their demonstrations? The Swampies of this world are climbing up trees to protest about airlines and airports. They should all get a job and get a fucking life.*

'*The Sustainable Aviation Group, God help us, is another bunch of lemmings shuffling towards a cliff edge. A lot of members of the*

*Sustainable Aviation Group won't be around in ten years' time.
That'll be their main contribution to sustainable aviation. I don't
think the advice of a bunch of UN scientists should be taken as gospel
truth. Human breathing is one of the biggest problems as far as I can
see, so why don't the environmentalists just shoot all the humans?
Let's go nuclear if you really want to do something and then let's
watch the eco-nuts go crazy.*

'*There's a lot of bullshit being peddled, mainly by environmental
nutters, that aviation is the cause of global warming, climate change
and everything else. The newspapers target airlines as the cause of
everything that's bad: pollution, greenhouse gases, emissions, floods,
war, pestilence and famine in Darfur. It's crazy that these people in
leafy suburbia in the UK think they can fix all the problems. I smile at
these environmental loons who drive their SUVs down to Sainsbury's
on a Saturday morning and buy kiwi fruit from New Zealand and
kumquats from Latin America. If you're concerned about the
environment, stop driving. Aircraft account for a Mickey Mouse 2 per
cent of emissions in Europe, motor cars account for 18 per cent. Our
planes use a lot less fuel per mile than a one-person car. These hairy
environmentalists go to the health store to buy their organic
strawberries flown in from South Africa. Why aren't they whacking a
huge tax on bananas and grapes from halfway round the world?*

'*I don't think emissions credit trading will come in, and anyway I
am far too busy doubling Ruinair over the next few years to be joining
any carbon emissions trading scheme. It would bankrupt British
Airways, Lufthansa and Alitalia. It's lots of political talk. And how
are you going to get the Italians to pay?*

'*China and India are laughing at us while they build more coal-
fired power stations. The European middle classes are having a
mid-life crisis and the sooner we wake up and say so the better.*'

Later a UK government minister's criticism of the green
credentials of his airline sparked a furious response from Mick,
who said the UK environment minister Ian Pearson was 'foolish
and ill-informed' and 'hasn't a clue what he's talking about'. Mick,
who had been described by Mr Pearson as 'just completely off the
wall', added that the minister 'talks a lot but does little'. Mick's
attack followed Mr Pearson's comments in an interview with *The*

Guardian in which he said that when it came to climate change 'Ruinair are not just the unacceptable face of capitalism, they are the irresponsible face of capitalism.' In response, Mick said Ruinair was 'Europe's greatest green airline', adding that it was time 'Minister Pearson and other equally foolish politicians actually tackled the real cause of climate change, which is road transport and power generation'. Mick recalled former Labour minister Denis Healey's famous remark about being criticised by former Tory minister Geoffrey Howe when he said that being attacked by Mr Pearson was like *'being savaged by a dead sheep'* and said that Mr Pearson was *'probably interviewed by* The Guardian *late at night in a pub.'* He added *'If you really want to do something you could penalise business class people flying around in low density seating. If you want to tax anybody, tax the rich, tax business class.'* To observations that such a move would not affect Ruinair because it had no business class, Mick retorted: *'Do we carry rich people on our flights? Yes, I flew on one this morning and I'm very rich.'*

Flying for Peanuts

Like most great ideas in life, it's been done before by someone else. Southwest Airlines has been flying passengers in the US using the 'low fares, quick turnaround, out of town airport, unassigned seating, pay for your food' business model since 1971, which is based on the revolutionary premise that if you give customers a good deal then they will find their own seats and will bring their own food on board.

Southwest Airlines was the brainchild of Rollin King, a Texan entrepreneur who owned a small commuter air service, and his banker John Parker, who both thought it was inconvenient and expensive to travel between Dallas, Houston and San Antonio, the so-called 'Texas Triangle'. They asked their lawyer Herbert D. Kelleher to do the legal paperwork to get approval for their new airline. In 1966 the three met for cocktails at San Antonio's St Anthony Club and used a cocktail napkin to draw the three-city route. That napkin still hangs in their boardroom along with the words spoken at the time. King said, 'Herb, let's start an airline.' Kelleher replied, 'You're crazy. Let's do it.' Other airlines got many court injunctions to prevent the Texas authorities giving Southwest a licence to fly. It took four years of legal battles led by Kelleher before the authorities agreed Southwest could take off. On the day before the first flight on 18 June 1971 there were fears that a Texas sheriff would show up to block the flight so Kelleher told his head of operations, 'You roll right over the son of a bitch and leave our tyre tracks on his uniform if you have to.'

Southwest are based at Love Field, a small airport outside Dallas, Texas. It's the airfield where JFK last touched down alive on Air Force One in November 1963. Love Field is named after a Lieutenant Love who crashed his aircraft in California in 1913, which is not a great reason in itself for naming an airport. In the early days Southwest played on the love theme and marketed themselves as a sexy, irreverent Love Airline, using the word 'love' in advertising slogans, putting a red heart in their logo and serving in-flight drinks called Love Potions, peanuts called Love Bites, whilst the tickets came from their Love Machines. They decided to make the airline as outrageous as possible, on the basis that the more outrageous it was, the more people talked about it. They hired attractive, extrovert, fun-loving, cheer-leading cabin crew and used the girls as a marketing image, attiring them during the less PC 1970s in hot pants, short skirts and go-go boots. One of their early advertisements for cabin crew said '*Attention, Raquel Welch: You can have a job if you measure up.*' Interviews were conducted in hot pants to show off long legs and amongst the Southwest selection team was Janice Arnold, who had trained the bunny girl hostesses for Hugh Hefner's Playboy jet.

Southwest began with four planes serving three cities and with revenues of $2 million but now fly 100 million passengers each year. They email updates to four million subscribers weekly. They fly to 64 cities in 31 states. They fly 3,200 times every single day. They are gargantuan. For example, they operate 230 flights from Las Vegas daily. Each plane in their fleet of 500 jets (four times the size of Ruinair's fleet) flies seven trips per day and is in the air twelve hours a day. They work those babies hard, much like Ruinair. Southwest is the most valuable airline in the world, valued at 12 billion dollars on the New York Stock Exchange. That's because it has been the only consistently profitable airline in the USA every year since 1973. Investors hate shocks. In 2002 the market value of Southwest was more than that of all other US airlines combined. Southwest's shares have outperformed the main US stock market by 10,000 per cent over the past twenty years. If you wish to check Southwest's current price, the code for the stock on the NYSE is, naturally, 'LUV'.

Southwest are so much admired that they hold a corporate day for other airlines twice a year, a sort of open house. They started off one day with the *Macarena*. Kelleher said that the other attendees were wondering, 'I was looking for $E=mc^2$ and I'm getting the *Macarena*?' But an attendee from Swiss Air was later asked, 'What's the most important message you're taking back to Swiss Air?' And he said 'For everybody to learn to do the *Macarena*.' Southwest always fly in the face of convention and conformity. They are a maverick.

Southwest invented low fares and challenged the assumption that permanently low air fares lead to lower revenues. Not if enough people flew. Instead of raising fares when load factors are up, they increase the number of flights and expand the market. They charge only a few bucks and have lots of flights while other airlines charge more and have fewer flights. Southwest stick to what they do best. They do not take on the major US carriers on the same routes, they do not wish to own a Boeing jumbo nor fly to Paris, France as opposed to Paris, Texas. They believe that arrogance is the quicksand of success and their number one threat is themselves. Kelleher has said, 'We must not let success breed complacency; cockiness; greediness; laziness; indifference; preoccupation with nonessentials; bureaucracy; hierarchy; quarrelsomeness; or obliviousness to threats posed by the outside world.' Southwest's business plan is to stimulate a huge amount of new travel. Their competition is not other airlines but bus and train transportation between American cities. Southwest is nimble, quick, opportunistic, responsive, egalitarian, democratic. It is lean, thinks small and keeps it simple. It still advertises itself as *The* Low Fare Airline.

Southwest invented the quick turnaround now favoured by all low fares airlines but it was accidental. In 1971 Southwest sold one of their aircraft to get some extra cash but found they could not maintain their schedules with only three aircraft. They realised they could avoid cutting back on flights if they could get the aircraft back into the air quicker, so the head of operations told staff to get an aircraft to the gate, unload and load it and get it pushed back in a mere ten minutes. No one thought it could be done. The station manager in Houston was told: 'We're going to do ten-minute turns with the airplane. If you can't do a ten-minute turn, then you're going to get fired and we'll bring someone else in. If he can't do a ten-minute turn, we'll fire him, too. And we'll just keep firing until we can find someone who can do it.' They succeeded and to this day the ten-minute turnaround is Southwest's signature and proof that their employees can think creatively. Southwest has further developed the concept of the quick turnaround into an art, so that employees and passengers alike participate in a veritable ballet of motion each time they load and unload an aircraft, because aircraft stuck on the ground don't earn much money, or zilch, for the airline.

Southwest invented flights to local airports rather than to international hubs. As far back as 1971 they transferred all their Houston flights from the giant Houston Intercontinental to Houston's appropriately named Hobby airport. As Kelleher said at the time, '*Why drive 45 minutes to take a 40 minute flight?*'

Southwest invented unassigned seating on flights but it wasn't a strategic brainwave. On the first flights their aircrafts were so empty that assigning seats to passengers was embarrassing. '*Hey, sit anywhere, folks, we don't mind.*' Southwest prefer to say they offer Open Seating. It's just that passengers don't know precisely which seat is open for them. But it was an act of genius. They created a level playing field where the passengers can fight it out. If they assign seats then there is little pressure for us passengers to ever perform. Their way, the pressure for a good seat begins the day we buy a ticket. Passengers are in a nice competitive frame of mind even before we get to the airport. By the time we get to the departure gate, we are well pumped. Like cattle moving towards water, nothing and no one will stand in our way. Some of their airport scenes will have been last seen at the annual running of the bulls in Pamplona, Spain. Even the last person who made a reservation maybe only today can battle fairly for a good seat with someone who bought a ticket six months ago. Everyone gets to play the game but no one wants to be a loser stuck with a middle seat or one of those seats next to the honking toilets. Passengers with a conscience will lose. If you see an unused wheelchair near a gate then sit in it and get to the front. If you enjoy waiting in line then join the Army. If you want an assigned seat then go commit a murder in Texas.

Southwest only offer free *cawfee*, juice and lots of peanuts on board. Last year Southwest served 52 million cans of soda (soft drinks to you and me), juices, and water; 9 million alcoholic beverages; 3 million bags of pretzels; 32 million fishie-shaped cheesy snacks and 90 million bags of *Kings Delicious Peanuts* to its passengers. And we wonder why there is so much obesity in the US? Southwest know that while most people hate rules and responsibility and accountability, everyone loves flying for peanuts, in every sense. Southwest are nationally famous in the USA for serving peanuts but scientists have proved that the more peanuts eaten by an individual, the more vulnerable he is to suggestion. When you get a drink and your peanuts on Southwest, you always receive a little paper napkin which says *Fly Southwest*. The humble nut holds the key to repeat business.

Southwest are in the customer service business but they happen to also provide airline transportation. So many passengers use Southwest to maintain long-distance relationships that the airline annually receives invitations to attend their subsequent weddings. Company policy is not to attend but to send a gift. A nice to know fact if you ever need an extra wedding gift. They share the same sense of corporate humour as Mick and Ruinair. Herb once said about low fares airlines, '*If the Wright brothers were alive today, Wilbur would have to fire Orville to reduce costs.*' The history page on their website is headed up *We Weren't Just Airborne Yesterday*. Their humour extends to painting three of their Boeing 737s like huge killer whales, like Shamu in Seaworld, San Diego. Southwest, like Ruinair, don't do Airbus. *Non.*

Southwest are a people-oriented organisation and are proof that flying can be fun both for the passenger and the airline employees. Some passengers say that flying Southwest is more fun than spending a day at Disneyland. Southwest hire people with a sense of humour. Fun is taken very seriously at the airline. Media advertisements include *Austin Auften, Phoenix Phrequently, El Paso Pronto and LA A.S.A.P.* They have a People Department which hires for attitude and trains for skills. They encourage employees to be real and authentic. Staff make safety announcements that include '*If you haven't been in an automobile since 1965, the proper way to fasten your seat-belt is to slide the flat end into the buckle*' and end with '*there is no smoking on board and if we catch you smoking you will be asked to step out onto the wing and enjoy our feature movie presentation Gone with the Wind.*' Southwest is probably the only carrier in the industry having any fun at all, not least because 2,000 of Southwest's 34,000 staff are married to each other. That's what I call a LUV airline. They must have some excellent arguments. I expect too they have a few married members of the *Mile High Club*. Staff care about their airline and made it one of *The 100 Best Companies to Work For in America*. Ramp workers and flight attendants know what the company stock price is each day. Some employees work fifteen years without a sick day. Staff swap jobs in the *Cutting Edge* programme where pilots get to spend time out of the cockpit and on the ramp to promote communication and teamwork between flight crews and ground operations teams, but they don't let the baggage handlers fly Boeing 737s. Staff morale, output and retention are high when employees have fun.

Southwest receive 250,000 CVs a year from candidates wanting to join the airline. Applications filled out in crayon or on the inside of pizza boxes are always appreciated. At interview selection they let groups of candidates speak in turn about themselves but they watch the reaction of the audience to select those who laugh and encourage but reject those who selfishly focus on reworking their own speech for when their turn comes. They hire only 1,000 of the applicants. It is statistically easier to get into Harvard than it is to work for Southwest. Staff wear polo T-shirts, khakis or Bermuda shorts. The corridors of Southwest offices are filled not with corporate art but with newspaper clippings, family memories, greeting cards, photographs of company events, classic advertise-ments and letters from competitors and customers. They have a staff tabloid spoof magazine modelled on the *National Enquirer*, called *Plane Tails*.

Every low fares airline needs a personality and Southwest has Kelleher, or Herb as everyone knows him. He's the Chairman and his former legal secretary is the President. Happy Families indeed. Ruinair idolises Southwest. Mick says Herb is '*like God*'. When Ruinair went public on the stock market it offered 5 per cent of the company to the Southwest founder for absolutely nothing. Like every great businessman Herb turned down the free offer since it would distract him from running his own company. Herb stories abound. A Wall Street analyst had lunch one day in the airline's canteen when Herb, seated at a table across the room with several female employees, suddenly jumped to his feet, kissed one of the women, and began leading the entire crowd in a series of cheers. When the analyst asked what was going on, he was told that Herb had at that moment negotiated a new labour contract with Southwest's flight attendants. Another financial analyst asked Herb why he had no strategic plan. 'We do have a plan,' he replied. 'It's called doing things.' He was further pressed if thirty years of unbroken profits was a matter of luck? Herb replied, 'I *am* Irish.' Herb once said, 'Our pilots have accused me of predicting eleven of the last three recessions.' Herb even arm-wrestled the chairman of Stevens Aviation instead of going to court over an advert slogan.

In case you now have the mistaken impression that Southwest Airlines invented the low fares model, please think again. In 1949 Pacific Southwest Airlines began flying along the west coast of the US, from San Diego, to Burbank and on to Oakland, all out-of town-airports. PSA for short, or the *Poor Sailors Airline*, what with all the naval personnel in the bay areas. The fares were cheaper than their competitors. The aircraft were in the air as much as possible with very quick turnarounds. The cabin crew cleaned the aircraft. In 1973 a young Texan called Herb visited San Diego and saw the Pacific Southwest operation from the inside. There was no competitive threat from the eager visitor since both airlines served different regional markets. It reminds me of a visit a young Irishman called Mick made to Love Field, Texas, in 1990. When it comes to low fares airlines flying around the world, Herb Kelleher, not myself, wrote the book.

Ruinair owes its business model to Southwest. And Southwest only flourished following President Jimmy Carter's deregulation of US air travel in 1978. And Carter only became President when an embarrassing incident at Watergate in 1974 forced the previous incumbent to fall on the sword. So next time you take a cheap Ruinair flight remember that you owe it all to the late great President Richard Nixon.

Luxembourg

Ruinair Flight FR1954 – Thursday @ 6.40pm – DUB-HHN-DUB

Fare €25 plus taxes, fees and charges €40

Luxair fly from Dublin to Luxembourg's Findel airport via a twenty-minute touchdown stop in Manchester but their website quotes a return fare of €748, which is either a private joke or a computer error. There are no low-cost airlines serving Luxembourg so I will travel to the nearest Ruinair destination: Frankfurt. While Frankfurt-am-Main international airport is 3 km and an eleven-minute s-Bahn ride from Frankfurt city centre, Frankfurt-Hahn airport is nearer to Luxembourg than to Frankfurt, being 124 km from Frankfurt but only 112 km from Luxembourg. It should be called Luxembourg-Hahn but I guess they wouldn't sell so many tickets. The airport's name is possible only because Hahn is legally owned by Fraport, the Frankfurt-am-Main airport owner. Hahn is the German word for cock, as in the bird. There are 55 daily flights listed on Hahn airport's official schedule and 45 of these are on Ruinair. So I am flying to Frankfurt-Ryahn airport.

I thought about travelling on LUAS, Dublin's tram system, but it's too dangerous. Today's newspaper tells me LUAS trams were involved in twenty-two road accidents in its first six months. Eighteen accidents happened on the northside and four on the southside, which proves Southsiders are better drivers. LUAS is supposed to take cars out of the city centre and it appears to be successful in that, albeit at four cars per month.

So I leave at 4.10pm to drive to the airport for the 6.40pm flight. It should be plenty of time but traffic on the M50 is stationary. The M50 is once again the safest and cheapest place to park a car in Dublin. I switch on the radio to learn there is a major accident ahead. After ninety minutes of snail-driving at 5 mph I reach the accident, which comprises two shaven skangers in a white builder's van and two other shaven skangers in a Nissan Micra standing in the road, looking at their 1992 vehicles whilst spitting and having a smoke. I must check in by 6pm or Ruinair will certainly decline my custom. I do 100 mph to the toll booth safe in the knowledge I will miss my flight. At 5.50pm I am still on the M50. At 5.55pm I approach the airport. At 5.57pm I abandon the car in short-term and leg it like a criminal athlete. At 5.59pm I arrive at check-in and receive a boarding card. When checking in very late we all feel the need to publicly apologise for our tardiness. 'Accident on the M50,' I wheeze at the girl. She doesn't look up. 'So I heard.' I race through security and departures but our flight is delayed until 7.05pm. If only this airline was as punctual as I am.

We board when the Assistant Ramp Co-ordinator shows the small boy from the cabin crew what to do. One of the cabin crew is a Spanish Kylie look-alike girl and a gang of blokes at the rear are not slow to show their appreciation. When she appears for the safety demonstration one of them announces, 'Jaysus, this is one safety demo which will have my full and undivided attention.' When she finishes she receives a round of applause, cheers and wolf-whistles but she's the colour of a jar of Crosse & Blackwell beetroot. The cabin supervisor makes an announcement: '*Ladies and gentlemen, due to a catering discrepancy, we are unable to provide the following to you today: tea, coffee, hot chocolate, cappuccinos, hot paninis or hot dogs.*' This is a polite way of advising that the kettle and microwave oven are fucked. But it could be worse. '*Ladies and gentlemen, due to a technical discrepancy, we are unable to provide you with an engine today.*' I wonder which is the more difficult to maintain — a water kettle or a General Electric turbofan jet engine?

Ryahn airport is ideally located if you live in Lautzenhausen because that's the nearest village. Much like Stansted, the US Air Force was here but they were genuinely unable to pronounce Lautzenhausen so they named their base after the next nearest village: Hahn. During Desert Storm, fighter squadrons flew from here to the Gulf but on return flew straight back to the USA. The USAF 50th Tactical Fighter Wing left in 1993 and rather worryingly their ammunition dump on the same site closed only two years later. Few could have foreseen in the 1960s that the end of the Cold War and the collapse of the Berlin Wall would provide so many wonderful ex-army facilities with immense B52 runways for use by the low-cost airline industry. The locale is still largely rural and underdeveloped and the surrounding towns within one hour's drive include Simmern, Zell, Morbach and Bad Kreuznach. Precisely. It is worth noting that all road signs to the airport on the surrounding roads refer to Ryahn, and not one refers to Frankfurt-Ryahn. The airport is sufficiently in the middle of nowhere such that the only guidance I can offer is that it is west of Frankfurt.

Ryahn airport is a draw for four million passengers annually plus locals. Judging by the passengers loitering about for connections, Ryahn is a transit hub in the centre of Europe. Mick doesn't offer through connections. 'Code-sharing, alliances, and connections are all about "How do we screw the poor customer for more money?"' There is nothing else to do in these parts so courting couples arrive for a night out on the airside *Flyer One* terrace near the giant picture of a Ruinair aircraft, to sip his and her beers and have a nibble, to neck each other whilst watching a Boeing 737 execute a 25-minute turnaround. The terrace is less populated than the glass windows of Terminal 2 at not-so-nearby Frankfurt-am-Main airport, where I once whiled away an hour watching plane-spotters, wannabe pilots and kerosene heads nod approvingly or squeal anxiously as pilots approach nose down or with a wobble. Nothing compares to the Air China pilot who, rather than landing as is traditional, attempts to physically plant his 747 jumbo into the asphalt in a cloud of rubbery smoke. There's a hootin' and a hollerin' from the Germans. I can't translate but none will ever be flying Air China.

Ryahn is a functional low-frills airport with significant growth potential. Ruinair have announced routes from Ryahn to Morocco. Europe is conquered. Next stop North Africa. Then we take Tobruk, then Al Alamein and we drive the others back into the sands of the Sahara. Second impressions are that reminders of the USAF remain. Outside Ryahn terminal lie rows of disused barracks, bunkers and gun emplacements, bomb shelters and F-14 hangars. Ruinair park one spare aircraft here, in case another 'goes technical', and it sports the slogan *Nein to Lufthansa's Fuel Surcharge*, thus representing the world's first sixty-million-dollar advertising hoarding. And when staying overnight in the Inter-City hotel located at the end of the runway it is worth noting that the first Ruinair flight of the day departs for Rome at 6.25am.

This airport is unique in that passengers are directed to an adult shop on the upper level which sells sex toys, dirty magazines, tasty lubricants, flimsy negligees and much protection. Or so I am told. It is best not to visit this shop before a flight back to Dublin because as you exit, bag in hand, you will usually meet one of your mother's best friends outside the shop. Buying such items is a perpetual hazard such as when Woody Allen went into a New York newsagent, selected a copy of *Time*, *The New Yorker* and *Businessweek* plus a copy of *Big & Busty* hidden discreetly underneath, only to have the shopkeeper shout down the length of the shop, 'Ed, how much is the *Big & Busty* porno mag?' Or like Griff Rhys Jones going into a Soho porn shop on the *Not the Nine O'Clock News* TV show to buy mags, accepting the offer of a bag from the shop assistant and feeling content, yet he failed to notice the bag said '*Porno Filth*'. Some German airports have hair salons but not here. Bremen airport has a barber shop called *Hairport*.

A bus service takes me on a trans-continental journey through two countries to my destination. The fairly tiny 2,500 sq km independent principality of The Grand Duchy of Luxembourg is home to 400,000 inhabitants and is not to be confused with the Belgian province of Luxembourg which lies adjacent to its border. Despite being crammed between the giant neighbourhoods of Belgium, Germany and France, locals speak Luxembourgish, an example of which is the national motto, which is engraved on some public buildings: *Mir wëlle bleiwe wat mir sin,* which roughly translates as *We want to remain what we are.* So the Luxembourgers wish to retain their national identity and are not so keen on wild abandon. It's the sort of place where the immediate visitor attractions include nice woodland, valley walks and walled farms.

I am fortunate that an ex-colleague Matt and his wife Marie allow me to stay again in their home. Luxembourg is centrally positioned in Europe but not a lot happens here. On my first visit Matt and Marie drove to a newsagents in France to buy Christmas cards and drove to a supermarket in Germany to buy bread and milk. They effortlessly cross international borders like I cross Dublin pavements. Matt and Marie are fans of Ruinair. 'We drive to Charleroi or to Ryahn. Those airports are ninety minutes away. Findel airport is ten minutes away but we never use it. People don't choose to fly Ruinair. They only use them because they are cheap.'

Luxembourg is an enigma wrapped up in small European state. It is a democracy, yet you cannot cut your grass on a Sunday nor wash your car in the street. It is a modern economy, yet most shops close on a Sunday. It is exceptionally pro-Europe, yet they do not welcome workers from the new EU accession states in the East. They brew an excellent beer called Bofferding, yet don't export it in case it is discovered. They have one of the highest qualities of life, yet so many citizens jump to their death from the high red bridge in the capital that the area below is known as *Splatter Valley.* It is a gastronomic centre of excellence with more Michelin-starred restaurants per capita than any other country, yet a sumptuous meal out only costs the same price as a bread roll in a Dublin restaurant. I endeavour to meet some locals to find out more. I ask them about the essence of the country but they think I am asking about the French word for petrol. The essence of the locals is that They Just Don't Go Out Very Often. Their homes have heavy metal roller shutters and they like to get home by 6pm and get those shutters down to spend time with their families. I don't know what they do behind the shutters because the local TV station RTL is not all that good.

The Luxembourgers know themselves best. In the *Musée d'Histoire de la Ville* there is a permanent exhibition of cartoons depicting their nation. One cartoon is of a souvenir shop which only sells duty-free alcohol, tobacco, petrol and diesel (Germans cross the border to buy cheap fuel). There is a backpacker with a magnifying glass who examines a tiny dotted square of land called Luxembourg lying in the middle of the road. There is a banker who hoovers up money from passers-by into his bank, washes it in his laundry machine and hangs the notes out to dry on a laundry line. There is a smug Luxembourger sitting on a bigger pile of bank notes than a Swiss citizen. There are the eurocrats on expense accounts with a map who advise that the EU Commission is in Brussels, the auditors are in Strasbourg, the courts are in Luxembourg and the canteen is in Oslo. But perhaps this country is best epitomised by a map of Europe which shows a small dark blob in the centre called The Grand Duchy of Luxembourg, while the rest of Europe is a blurred orange mass without national borders or cities, and simply referred to as *The Petit Rest of Europe.*

It is a quiet morning in the residential suburb of Strassen. 'Let's go to Weiswampach,' I suggest.

Matt has only lived in Luxembourg for seventeen years. 'Where the bloody hell is that?'

'Up north.'

'What's there?'

'A special field.'

'Jesus. You and your book.'

It looks about three inches away on the map but Matt says it's further than that. We set off on the drive to traverse an entire country but this being Luxembourg the distance is a mere 60 km and takes fifty minutes. It's an annoying trip for two reasons. One is that Matt uses his car's satellite navigation so an anonymous woman's voice keeps telling us to take a U-turn or an exit which we don't agree with. Secondly, when abroad I am prone to break into involuntary spasms of French lingo such that I point at each passing Volkswagen and say '*Voila, le Golf*'. Or '*Le Polo.*' At the lesser known village of Weiswampach we take a right down what in retrospect is a wrong turning. We pass a memorial to a downed Lancaster bomber crew, a reminder that we are in Battle of the Bulge territory. Near here the French built the impregnable

Maginot Line to keep out the Germans and keep the concrete industry in business but the Germans rather cunningly, and unfairly in my mind, went around the Maginot Line, thus rendering it utterly useless.

We trundle along a pot-holed dirt track towards misty forests and sunken valleys, encountering a stream of unyielding moto-cross bikers. I am like one of those navigators in a rally car shouting instructions at Matt. 'Left, 100, sharp right, 50, bend.' The *SatNav* woman has lost the run of herself and is screaming at us. 'Destination unknown. Make a U-turn. You bleedin' eejits.' In the valley of the River Our, Matt makes a deduction and he suddenly understands why we came here. 'We are now in Belgium. Look at the registration plates of the cars in the houses.' We turn a corner. 'No, there's a Luxembourg flag so we're still in Luxembourg.' Another bend in the road. 'No, we're in Germany. Look at those road signs. They're in German.' Another bend. 'No, I'm wrong. We're definitely in Belgium. It says so on the wall there. Jesus, I don't know where we are. I don't know which bloody country we are in.' Even the *SatNav* woman is lost.

After the excesses of WWII an idea germinated in the mind of George Wagner, then president of the Association of the European Countries of Eifel-Ardenne, to build a European monument in this unique location at the confluence of the Ribbach and Our Rivers. In 1972 the nations, via the communes of Arzfeld in Germany, Heinerscheid in Luxembourg and Burg-Reuland in Belgium, ceded a piece of sovereign land precisely equal to one third of the size of the field to erect six impressive megaliths, each one symbolising a country of the then European Community. The nations' leaders gathered in this small tranquil park to inaugurate their monument to *entente cordiale* in October 1977. I can't help thinking that the UK would not be as keen on ceding any sovereign territory, especially if the French are involved, notwithstanding the fact that the English Channel lies in the way. I look around at this bland yet unique land. I stand in a foreign field that is forever Europe, the only genuine piece of Europe anywhere on the continent. No single country owns this field. This is what Europe is all about. But the Belgians mow the grass.

I walk over a tiny wooden bridge between Belgium and Luxembourg, then back and forth over another bridge to Germany. There are no border controls between these nations. Here Europe is seamless and instantly accessible. This is the essence of Luxembourg, and why Matt and Marie love to reside here. With a two-hour drive they can be in Brussels or even in Charleroi, or they can be in Frankfurt or even in Ryahn. Grand slam rugby matches in the Stade de France are only a three-hour drive away. A weekend in Amsterdam is a four-hour drive. A few more hours of driving leads to idling in the south of France or skiing in Switzerland. Essential Luxembourg lies in the middle of nowhere yet it is in the middle of everywhere.

The (other) Belgian (B) / German (D) border

Easy

EzJet was founded in 1995 by Sir Stelios Utterly-Unpronounceable-Long-Greek-Surname who made the successful transition from lounging about on various playboy Med yachts to working in a pre-fab office in Lootin' airport. He started the airline with a loan of five million quid from his Dad, two leased aircraft from BA and a large pot of *Pantone 021C*, the latter being a particularly vile shade of bright orange paint. Stelios later handed over the managerial reins to Ray Webster, a Kiwi executive who is, fortunately, colour-blind. Stelios remains in the *Guinness World Records* as the world's youngest international scheduled airline chairman when he launched EzJet at the age of twenty-eight.

Wealth did not come easy to the family. Stelios' father Loucas was a poor hill farmer, the eldest of thirteen children, who left his village in Cyprus to buy and sell used tankers, becoming in time the billionaire owner of *Troodos*, one of the world's biggest tanker operations. His business logic is simple — buy tankers when no one wants them and sell them when there is a shortage. His hard work was almost sunk when the *Haven* exploded in 1991 outside Genoa, killing five and causing a 35,000 ton crude oil slick. The Italian authorities pursued the family with a billion-dollar legal suit which failed in court, not once but twice. Stelios admitted, '*In typical Italian fashion, they have gone after the wealthiest man they could find, and his son.'*

Stelios wished to start his own business and caught the aviation bug in a conversation on a Virgin Airlines flight from London to Athens. European air travel was being deregulated and there were new opportunities. His father gave him the seed capital with a single proviso — not to base the airline in seasonal Athens. The airline's name was not chosen by expensive brand consultants. Rather Stelios slummed it sitting in *Harry's Bar* in Mayfair and scribbled possible names on a napkin, bizarrely copying Herb Kelleher. At the time Stelios was personally worth £100 million with homes in London, Athens and Monaco and a *Porsche* outside. Names such as *CheapJet* and *No-Frillsjet* were rejected but Easy stuck. Job done. Easy.

The airline set up in Easyland, a prefabricated office building at Lootin', thirty miles north of London. The atmosphere in the office remained informal with no ties (*'if anyone turns up for work in a tie, we suspect them of having been for an interview for another job'*) and everyone was on first name terms, largely because no one remembers the boss's surname. In fact the wearing of ties was officially banned for all employees at the airline, except in respect of pilots. Around the small office the jolly Greek giant was known affectionately as Stel Boy or Steli Babes. Stelios wished to operate a paperless office but installed so many paper shredders that staff hid any important paperwork in the Ladies' lavatory, it being the only safe place. In the early days Stelios even answered telephone calls from would-be passengers. One day he says he took a call from a man who had booked two tickets for a honeymoon but had since broken up with his fiancée and called off the wedding. Stelios told him that normally there were no refunds, but in this case ... 'Oh no, I don't want a refund,' replied the man, 'I want to change the name of the other passenger.'

The first flight, EZJ11, took off on 10 November 1995 from Lootin' to Glasgow, the destination being obvious since Scotland was the biggest domestic UK market where flying is an alternative to the train. Fares from £29 each way were a staggering one tenth of that charged by BA from Heathrow to Scotland, and flights were openly advertised in the UK press as *'making flying as affordable as a pair of jeans'*. Many could not understand how EzJet could fly anywhere for so little but time changed public opinion. *'People couldn't believe the prices we were charging. But once they got on to the planes and saw for themselves that they were clean and had the requisite number of wings, they were pleasantly surprised.'*

Stelios believes in no-frills travel. *'The so-called freebies that other airlines offer are not freebies at all. If someone came up to me with a plastic tray of airline food and said, "Will you give me a tenner for this shit?" I would say no. There is no such thing as a free lunch so we don't pretend to provide one.'* Stelios has also visited Southwest Airlines. *'I saw their winning formula — they were carrying more passengers with a cheap and cheerful service. I don't mind admitting but I copied the idea. But I took it one step further. Southwest give away free peanuts — we don't. You can buy them on board for 50p if you want them.'* EzJet make money by selling food and take every opportunity to point out the difference. When BA catering staff go on strike, EzJet run adverts with, *'Our catering staff will never go on strike — because we don't have any.'*

Stelios is fully aware of the commercial realities. He refused to sell tickets through travel agents, thus saving up to 25 per cent on the cost of a ticket. *'I knew nothing about the travel business. I had no allegiances, I had no friends in the travel industry. I just said, this does not make sense, and we will not do it.'* His aircraft have to be in the air for the maximum amount of time each day. *'We have to sweat the assets. I love planes but they're only metal tubes for making money. You can only really fall in love with a boat.'*

EzJet slowly embraced the internet and became one of the first airlines to offer web booking. *'We started off as something very obscure like www.1145678.com. And I said this is never going to fill the planes. It's just for nerds. Then we bought the domain easyjet.com for about £1,000 and put up a proper website. At that time we had the telephone number in big letters on the side of the plane. And we put a different telephone number on the website. Week after week I watched how quickly the numbers were growing and that gave me the confidence to launch a booking site. It is the neatest and simplest way since you outsource the work to the customer. The internet has had a bigger effect on people's ability to fly than the jet engine. The jet engine was an improvement on the propeller, but what really made it a mass market was the ability to fly somewhere for £1.'* The fuselage of each EzJet aircraft still carries the proud claim to be *The Web's Favourite Airline,* a statement designed to annoy BA, then *The World's Favourite Airline.*

No expense was spared either when kitting out the cabin crew of the fledgling airline. Stelios hopped out to a nearby *Benetton* shop to buy the first uniforms: black jeans, orange polo shirts, orange bomber jackets and baseball caps. The crew were the laughing stock of Lootin' in the early days. Some wore a duffel coat with Easy in big letters, jet in small letters and Cabin Crew in big letters, making them the easiest cabin crew of all time, and that's quite some feat considering the social activities of the airline industry.

Their first continental European destination was Amsterdam, a route owned by BA and KLM. Stelios printed coupons in EzJet's in-flight magazine addressed to the head of KLM, complaining about their high fares, and turned up in person to deliver hundreds of signed coupons, albeit without receiving a welcome at an office outside Amsterdam. However, the publicity on Dutch TV was excellent. And free. *Easypublicity.* Next they added Nice, not only so that Stelios could easily visit his bachelor pad in nearby Monaco. Later a Geneva to Barcelona route was a flight too far for Swissair who demanded that EzJet sold holiday charter packages which included accommodation, rather than selling only a flight. Stelios bought five tents and erected them at a campsite 60 miles from Barcelona. *'We got them from Argos at £29.99 each.'* Needless to say they were rarely used by passengers but the tent still hangs in EzJet's Lootin' HQ and remains a potent symbol of Swissair's futile and illegal attempt to block fair competition within the EU.

Stelios is not averse to a good publicity stunt. When Barclays Bank-owned Lootin' airport threatened to increase landing charges by 300 per cent, he led a protest outside the Lootin' branch of Barclays Bank and ceremoniously cut up his own Barclaycard. When the British Airways offshoot Go was formed, Stelios bought ten return tickets at £100 each for the inaugural flight from Stansted to Rome in 1998. The chief executive of Go was wise to his stunt because his surname is not exactly that common and she sent him a note saying, 'Looking forward to welcoming you on board.' Stelios did not disappoint and arrived for the flight with nine other colleagues dressed in orange boiler suits that spelled GO EASYJET. Go retaliated by giving the ten stowaways ridiculous large boarding cards with the word Go in huge letters making them look stupid. Once on the aircraft, the Go CEO thanked Stelios for 'making Go the low cost airline of choice'. Stelios responded by handing out flyers on board which said, 'The unbelievable fare you are enjoying today is the result of a revolution led by EzJet which started in Europe some three years ago.' But both were happy. Next day *The Sun* ran a full page entitled '*Cheap Jet: High-jacked.*' Easy publicity for all concerned.

I watch the 'warts and all' reality TV series *Airline* featuring the odd passengers and staff of EzJet. First aired in 1999, it once ranked third in the UK ratings with ten million viewers, behind Corrie and EastEnders. Up to 40 per cent of the viewing public tuned in. There's the two confused middle-aged ladies, one of whom impossibly tries to check in both, while the other goes off to park a Nissan Micra in the long-stay car park when they are only away for two days but returns from the car park five hours later and they wonder why they have missed their flight? And of course it's not her fault, but the guy who drives the shuttle bus from the car park to the terminal. There's the passenger who fails to arrive on time by one nanosecond before the desk closes, so he fumes and swears away to get on the flight, and it's touch and go until they move him to another same-day flight, but there's enough of a delay to build the tension we need in TV programmes, so he zooms around the airport terminal in a rage from clock to clock until he finds one that's one minute slow, proudly points at it and tells the cameraman he'll be suing EzJet. Somehow, they never do.

There's a Frenchman turned back by Security because he has three live carp in a plastic bag in his luggage, so his solution is to run to the Gents and flush them down the U-bend. He tries but they fail to disappear so famous Leo Jones helps. '*Hello … I've got fish in the toilet*', but as Leo reaches in to rescue the fish, his body sets off a sensor and the carp are flushed away to a new free, but regrettably short, life. There's the lady in Bristol who is off to Provence and in her luggage she carries her father's ashes. There's the Englishman travelling from Lootin' to Inverness who is refused boarding because he doesn't have photo ID such as a passport, and he's baffled since he's not leaving the UK. Like the family who didn't bring their passports, not because they forgot them, but because they don't possess passports and never thought to get them. How far can one travel on a laminated *John Lewis* store card? There's an irate French passenger. '*Er ... zees is not a human business, zees is a cattle business.*' There is always a marriage proposal couple on board where he asks her on bended knee and she always says Yes. I wonder do they do two takes? The crew go stone mad and break out a six-pound snipe of champers. But it all works, not as television of course, but as free advertising. Each time *Airline* is broadcast, bookings for EzJet soar.

Note that celebrity chef Gary Rhodes watches *Airline* yet he refuses to fly on EzJet, because they don't tell passengers where they can sit before they get on the flight. 'I've never been on EzJet or Ruinair and I never will. I'm a chef and I have to be organised, because everything is in the preparation. It all has to be right and that's the way I am in life. When I go on a flight I like to know what seat I've got on a flight. Also, the way they speak to guests is not on. If you look at that programme *Airline*, people arrive five minutes late, it's not their fault because of the traffic, and they're not allowed onto the flight. If someone had a reservation at 8.30pm in one of my restaurants and they turned up at 8.35pm and were refused entry, they would freak out.' Look, Gary, you are not trying to effect a 25-minute turnaround per table.

Ruinair frequently proclaim themselves as Europe's largest low fares airline and that is true in respect of annual passenger numbers. EzJet is very close behind but because of their higher average revenue per passenger, EzJet enjoys greater annual revenues than Ruinair, making it Europe's largest low fares airline by revenue. And while other airlines mouth off, EzJet gets on with the business of flying.

Ruinair refer to EzJet as a '*high fares airline*'. When EzJet halved the number of their flights from Gatwick to Shannon, the immediate celebratory Ruinair press release referred to them as an 'easy come, easy go' airline. But Mick bears some begrudging personal regard for Stelios. *'He's Greek and I'm Irish. The Greeks will never outdo the Irish in anything. We'll even outdo them in drinking. He's the son of a billionaire. He could have been a rich tosser but at least he did something and set up an airline.'*

When EzJet bought the British Airways subsidiary Go in 2002, they overtook Ruinair. Mick was not happy. *'Embarking on an acquisition of another higher fare airline at this time is certainly a ballsy move. I will be taking lessons in humility now that we are, for the time being, Europe's second largest low fares airline.*

'There's scope for EzJet to be a profitable airline competing with the numbnuts in Europe as long as they stay out of our way. EzJet are a convenient target for us to have a go at, but they do what they do, and we do what we do, but we do it that much better. Over the next five to ten years we will see the emergence of three to four large price-gouging carriers and one very large low fares airline. There is only one really powerful low fares airline in Europe and it is called Ruinair. And there is only one in the United States and it is called Southwest Airlines. This is not a great business to be in if you are somebody else.'

Likewise Stelios is entitled to a view on Mick and his cheap airline. *'I'd like to think that, generally, the business I have created is more friendly to consumers. Ruinair has one mission — to be the cheapest possible — with little or no customer service. We position ourselves as value for money but also as caring and convenient. I haven't spoken to Mick for a couple of years. We're in the same industry and inevitably paths cross. But I wouldn't say we are best buddies.'*

Greece

EzJet Flight EZY2001 – Thursday @ 2.25pm
– DUB-LTN-ATH-LTN-DUB

Fare €84 plus taxes, fees and charges €64

I don't care what I promised to do in chapter one; I am not going back there. No way. I have had it with Athens. It's nothing personal, Stelios. I spent two weeks working in Athens a decade ago. My lasting memory is that we almost starved to death in those two weeks. We ate out at the same restaurant in a square in Plaka every night because it was out of season and everywhere else was closed and the waiters were the least openly hostile whom we encountered. We survived on Greek salads with fetid (sic) cheese plus tomato and cucumber. If I ever see a Greek salad again I will be obliged to do something surgically unpleasant with the remnants of the cucumber.

We stayed in allegedly the best hotel in Athens at the time, called *The Grand Bretagne*. Even Hitler, Goering, Himmler and Rommel stayed there in the war, though not at the same time and not whilst on their summer holidays. Churchill was almost assassinated in the hotel when a ton of dynamite was found in an underground sewer and at the time I wished the culprits had demolished this evil bastion. We had box rooms overlooking the glass-roofed main ballroom. On several evenings there were weddings in the ballroom which finished at 7am. I was sorely tempted on some nights to drop a chair from my room through the glass roof. Breakfast was a miserably lean affair, akin to scavenging for rotting carcasses in a barren desert, and of course being continental included cold cuts, tomato, cucumber and more fetid cheese. I still possess some top quality wooden clothes hangers I nicked in modest retribution.

After six days in Athens myself and my colleagues were suicidal. We had to get away for our sanity so we booked a one-day cruise around the Greek islands. Athens has always suffered from being an unnecessary stopover on the way to the sunny charms of the Greek isles. We realised later that day there was some special stop-over deal for Japanese tourists who fly from Tokyo to Europe on Olympic Airways via Athens. Of the one thousand people on the cruise ship that day, we three colleagues were the only non-Japanese passengers. Everyone stared at us. It was like being lost in translation in Tokyo. So whilst waiting for the return BA flight to Heathrow in the aptly named Hellinikon airport, and before the age of the laptop computer or Blackberry, I scribbled some manic thoughts in ink in my *filofax*. Remember those?

'*Athens is undoubtedly one of the worst places I have ever been. The hotel is crap. The restaurants are dire and I wouldn't risk my life having an over-priced Chinese or an Italian in these parts. No matter what you order everything tastes the same. I am sick of Greek salads. Style is non-existent in this city. The people are boorish and are serious fashion victims, so many nasty brown check jackets. Some of the locals here seem so ugly that even a sniper wouldn't take them out. It all seems so poor. Unfinished pavements, leaning cranes, peeling billboards, no lighting, dirty wheezing geriatric cars. Unfriendly locals who stare through you. Everyone's out to shaft you for as much as they can get because no one has any cash. There's no decent nightlife. The driving is horrendous and there are no rules of the road. The TV is rubbish. And so is the 1950s period airport. Nothing has progressed here in hundreds of years. Even the timeless Acropolis is pure 100% Athens: covered in scaffolding, inaccessible, dirty and half-finished.*'

In six years of travelling around Europe, Asia and America for work, it's the only tirade I wrote in that *filofax*. I am in denial as to how the Athenians managed to host a recent Olympics. In typical local fashion the only two Greek athletes of note had a moped accident before the Opening Ceremony. I don't know how the

Greeks won *Euro 2004* when their sole game plan was to venture into the opponents' half only once in ninety minutes, earn a corner kick and score a lucky headed goal against the run of play.

But I have no choice. My publisher insists that I must honour my commitment to visit every country in Europe. If you possess a fondness for Athens and its environs, please look away now. Hey, maybe it's all changed?

Ruinair don't fly to Greece. I have to fork out for an EzJet fare equivalent to one quarter of my entire self-inflicted 300 euros budget on which to visit all of Europe. So I doubt I will succeed within my budget. I have never flown on EzJet before for one simple reason. They do not fly to or from Dublin. If they did commence such flights, Ruinair would likely hire a set of ack-ack guns and shoot them out of the sky. It's worth pointing out that while there is no known Greek low fares airline, the state-owned airline, Olympic Airways, has already adopted a pre-emptive no-frills strategy in its Business Class cabin. There is a regional low fares airline called Helios Airways but I am not keen to try this airline since they were last seen on BBC *News 24* when they deposited 121 passengers on a mountainside near Athens.

I've seen the Pyramids and Sphinx at Giza and the Taj Mahal at Agra, circumnavigated Manhattan and steered a junk into Hong Kong harbour, weekended in Bermuda and Kuala Lumpur, gambled cash in Macau and gambled more in Bangkok's Patpong, posed in LA and roughed it in China but this is my first time connecting at Lootin' airport. We are met at the arrival stand by a bus from the late eighteenth century with wooden seats. Arrivals is a series of long, brightly-lit, advert-and-window-free sterile corridors and blue swing doors, reminiscent of a sanatorium. If I walk far enough and through a sufficient number of swing doors I will likely be able to hand over flowers and *Lucozade* to a terminally ill elderly close relative.

Departures is a darkened bunker with a tin-metal hangar roof, without natural light from the outside world. The only lighting emanates from a few 20-watt bulbs hidden in the eaves way above our heads. The inviting centre-piece of Departures is a *Food Hall* wafting greasy odours in my direction. It takes time to find the check-in desks hidden behind the *Burger King* concession. '*You got it!*' The *Bar des Voyageurs* is frequented not by passengers but by chain-smoking loquacious Lootin' Ladies in uniforms and belt-size skirts who work for BAA. There is a myriad of signs pointing to nowhere. A giant poster advises that if I need a break I should go to Milton Keynes for the day. '*What a difference a day makes.*'

There are few seats so long-haul travellers kip on the floor, upon radiators, on window ledges or on their baggage by garbage bins. The one plate-glass window is blocked by shoulder-to-shoulder plane-spotters with cameras, binoculars, anoraks and ham sandwiches in curly white bread and tin foil. I sit in the Special Assistance Waiting Area with other able-bodied, fully sighted, soft of hearing passengers. Neither of the self-service computer screens work, so today there is no information to be had in Lootin'. The toilet blocks are honking. Even the amusement arcade is not so amusing. I walk around the burger joint several times, certain there must be more to Departures but there is not. I take back everything I said about architects and airports. Stansted had a celebrity architect. Lootin' badly needs any architect.

When I can take no more I walk out to find *Easyland*. It's difficult to miss. There's a giant portakabin cum shoebox shrouded in orange awnings at the end of the runway, surrounded by a challenging spikey eight-foot metal perimeter fence in the style of *Stalag Luft Easyland*. I am reminded that a billion pound corporation operates from these jaded premises. It's not that welcoming. *No entry for spectators.* There are many bright young things coming and going, almost exclusively wearing shades of *Pantone 021C*. In the car park there is an Audi TT which is painted bright orange, being perhaps the ultimate company car.

Back in Departures I check in at the hand baggage desk in double-quick time, an idea other airlines could copy. I loiter at the EzJet customer service desk in the hope of spotting one of the stars of *Airline*. After twenty minutes I am rewarded. A door opens and the wonderful Leo Jones appears and glides across the concourse before disappearing. He wears a white shirt so he has evidently progressed up the career ladder to become senior management. His hair is longer and gelled and he looks three years older, which is unsurprising because all the *Airline* programmes are three-year-old repeats. It happens so fast that I cannot ask him my chosen question. *What's it like being a z-list celebrity?* I wait as long as I can without being bumped off. He never shows. It was a cameo.

In the recently upgraded *Galleria* lounge a glorious Bentley GT is parked centre stage. It's the prize in an expensive draw, with a tan all-leather interior and a body like a supermodel, and the cheeky chappie selling tickets at fifty quid a pop invites me to participate. 'Would you like a car like this?' he asks.

Talk about asking a bleeding obvious question. It's £200,000 plus. 'Nah, I already have one.'

Next I am surveyed in the Departures lounge by a pleasant lady from the Very Civil Aviation Authority. All goes well until she asks the exact purpose of my leisure break.

'I'm writing a book about travelling to every country in Europe on low fares airlines.'

'What a fantastic idea.' At least that's one pre-sold copy. 'I meet a lot of strange people in my job.'

Meaning I am the strangest. 'I plan to spend only three hundred euros on the fares.'

'You'll never do that.'

'I already know that.' We chat and I promise her a brief mention in the finished work. Done.

EzJet aircraft sport the invitation *Come On, Let's Fly*. We're ready. But are they? Boarding is an hour late yet refreshingly agreeable with no hookers being willing to form the front row of a scrum. There are five orderly queues. The passengers are different to Ruinair. The men wear ties and the ladies wear pearl strings. While Ruinair fly Italian students with facial jewellery, EzJet fly middle-aged couples in sensible shoes. Some of the Greek male passengers look like runners-up in a Stelios look-alike competition. A few of the female passengers sport severe black glasses last seen on the singer Nana Moussaka.

On board, the Airbus interior is bright and the grey leather seats are comfy. The crew are in *Bobbsey Twins* mode: smiley happy guys and girls with bouncing pony-tails and hugging black jeans with orange thread on their back pockets. They take their job seriously and rightly tell some passengers to shut up during the safety demo. They maintain great eye contact and exude confidence and assertiveness. I feel safe. Safer than usual. They enjoy their chosen profession. There is no hard sell. Service comes with a smile. If I had a choice of going to the Ruinair or EzJet Christmas party, I would definitely go orange. But one of the crew members believes he is a budding comedian when it comes to cabin announcements. *'We will shortly be leaving the subtropical paradise of Lootin'. Please ensure you turn off electrical items, DVDs, iPods, Nanopods, PCs, Blackberrys and Blueberries. Please turn off your mobile phone now since the captain does not like to hear that annoying ringing sound in his headset.'* I am not a fan of humour in the cabin. Flying is a serious business and badly delivered humour can be as unfunny as any episode of BBC's *Little Britain* programme. Any airline humour is best left to travel books, if that's at all possible.

It's appropriate to use this airline on this route. Stelios inaugurated his airline's London–Athens route in 1998 with an ad campaign that said passengers should cut out travel agents and book direct. Greece's travel agents were not amused, and a war of words erupted as the young millionaire publicly called them a cartel. So they sued. Stelios' next ad promised a free ticket for anyone who came to court to cheer him on. Almost 1,000 Athenians showed up on the court's steps and Stelios and his cheap flights to Greece were splashed across the evening news in a blaze of free and easy publicity.

Last time here we took a late-night taxi from the airport and drove across an army assault course or else down the main road to the city — it was hard to tell. Along the way we passed houses and buildings in a state of total disrepair, with many collapsing into ruins. I assumed these were priceless and historic relics of a bygone era of Greek splendour, but later I learnt they were fully occupied social housing from the present millennium. Upon arrival this time I am directed to the new metro. It's a few euros and 37 minutes to the capital. Athens outdoes Dublin. I alight at Syntagma Square, the heart of the city, and I'm in perhaps the most beautiful train station in the world. On the upper street levels there are reminders of a glorious past with a stratified excavation of the city's progression as centuries were built upon prior centuries. There's a skull from the fourth century BC, with teeth intact. Gravestones, urns, decanters and perfume bottles from centuries ago are exhibited in glass cases, ignored by commuters but highly valued by visitors. Classical music wafts through the cool interior, the music changing daily based upon the mood of the station master.

Reaching my hotel involves outwitting the infamous Greek taxi driver. I hop into a taxi near the metro station and give the name of my hotel. The seasoned conman at the wheel is puzzled and furrows a brow. I show him a map and he seems to recall leading hotel names. Surrounded by empty night-time streets, he powers off at Grand Prix speed to the only grid-locked street in Plaka, grinds to a halt and fumes like a bad actor. I look at his meter and see it shows 22.20, which is either the fare after two minutes, or the time. He asks me where I am from and then garbles away in Greek but the only words I understand are *Roy Keane*. I am not lulled. After five minutes the malleable meter is up to fifty-something euros. I think about doing a runner. We pass policemen and I almost shout for help. I don't know if the door will open to my touch. Then he pulls up at my hotel. The meter has *fallen* to nineteen euros. I laugh, throw him a tenner and run.

Last time Syntagma Square was surrounded by hoardings on all four sides. Behind the hoardings archaeologists toyed about with toothbrushes in the style of Channel 4's *Time Team* programme while engineers waited to sink tunnels for the new metro. Imagine the frustration of trying to build the metro as beardy types in woolly jumpers got excited again over another little piece of pottery as your boring machine gathers dust. As the work progressed at chisel pace, the locals chucked rubbish over the hoardings. But now the square is a revelation. First I dodge into the adjacent Grand Bretagne Hotel and see more change. Starwood Resorts spent seventy million dollars on its refurbishment and I examine the palatial lobby until I am politely asked to leave. This city is certainly cleaner than it was on my prior visit. The last time anything of note was seen lying around on the streets of Athens, it was Paula Radcliffe in the Olympic Marathon.

Speaking of Paula, there is now a golf shot named after her (one that starts well and is a good runner but suddenly stops). Other golf shots named after famous people include an Adolf Hitler (one shot in the bunker), a Maradona (a nasty five-footer), a Salman Rushdie (an impossible read), a Rodney King (over-clubbed), a Jean Marie Le Pen (gone very far right) and a Glenn Miller (didn't make it over the water). There is also a Ruinair golf shot (flies very well but lands a long way from where you expected).

It's a gradual climb past the *Eonikon* outdoor café with ladies on wicker chairs in sunglasses, furs and leathers, with time on their hands, mobile conversations on their minds and *café frappe al fresco* on standing order from aproned waiters, through lush greenery, sprinkling fountains, marble seats and orange trees with real mandarins to the Parliament and the *Tomb of the Unknown Soldier*. I am always worried by such memorials that someone will accidentally stumble across the name of the soldier in a dusty national archive and tell everyone and the mystery of this memorial will be lost for ever. The tomb is guarded by two *Evzones*. They wear wooden-soled shoes with blue pom-poms, white tights with more pom-poms and short pleated skirts and are chosen for this honour by being the best soldiers in the Greek Army.

The plaza is infested with pigeons. Wizened old Greek men sell birdseed for one euro and offer souvenir photographs to tourists, but the men must rue the advent of the in-built camera in today's mobile telephone which surely has adversely affected their business; of course not as much as the digital camera which completely fucked the corporate aspirations of Kodak, Fuji and Agfa. Most of the photographs people take now are of flocks of rabid birds devouring small terrified children as parents look on and laugh. At eleven o'clock two replacement *Evzones* and a sergeant noisily march down the road from the nearby barracks. On the day I was there the stomping soldiers suddenly encountered two dizzy blondes with shopping bags on the street corner so naturally the fierce soldiers gave way. The soldiers change guard in an elaborate ceremony largely reminiscent of the famous *Monthy Python* Ministry of Funny Walks sketch.

There should be less traffic circling these city centre streets. A decade ago the authorities ruled that cars would only be allowed in the city centre on alternate days, based on whether the numbers in their registration were odd or even. However, in the best traditions of Greek rule-bending, the Athenians purchased second alternate cars so they could drive in the city every day, resulting in a zero improvement to congestion and the environment but providing a positive sales boon to the motor trade. Tourists in rental cars are exempt but they have other problems. Unlike any other European capital, there are no parking meters in Athens. Nor can I see any public parking garages. Where do cars go? Locals double and treble park wherever they like, which is acceptable once their hazard lights are flashing. Anywhere will do — bus stops, entrances, zebra crossings and disabled ramps are all fair game.

It is anarchy because parking anywhere for free is an Athenian's right. It's like assuming you could leave the Mondeo at Piccadilly Circus anytime. For free. I watch a law-abiding German who does not know the local practice circle the old city in a stunning Munich-reg SL Merc looking for a parking space which simply does not exist. Walking these tiny car-crammed streets one wonders if Athens has ever had a town planning department. This is the sort of city where people stand in empty spaces and call their friends on their mobile to come and move their car to the free space. If you can find fifty square foot in Athens, then that's a parking space. And if hiring a car, remember that the Greeks drive on the wrong side of the road except on one street I stumble upon near Omonia Square. On *Eolou* the traffic direction is reversed so here, and only here, they drive on the right side, which is the left side. Or on the wrong side, if you are Greek, of course.

I must cross seven lanes of manic traffic to reach the main pedestrian street. This is not a problem to Athenians who walk across, one lane at a time. A green man at a pedestrian crossing in Athens means *Cross If You Think You Can Make It*. It's best to ignore all street crossing signs and walk alongside the locals so at least we will all die together. There is commercial progress on the paved *Ermou*. There is a Gant shop, a Lacoste A Lot shop and even an M&S store. This street is where the beautiful people shop. But there is a problem. I don't wish to generalise but it would not be untrue to say that the Greeks are not the most attractive nation on earth. Try to think of a famous attractive Greek celebrity. Except Stelios. Have you seen that movie *My Big Fat Greek Wedding*? Greeks are dark, short, stocky, squat and hirsute. And that's the ladies. Everyone in Athens wears black or dark grey. Razor blades are not widely used.

Along the next street, *Athinas*, I inhale the rawer edge of the city. This is the ancient Ottoman part of the city but it feels more like commercial Cairo. Beggars display their prosthetic prowess. Dirty six-year-old children sell packs of tissues on the pavement. Bent men vend bent goods from stools and trestle tables. '*Cigarettes? Special price.*' Comatose stray dogs splay on the street, as still as statues. A taxi prangs a Skoda, an argument ensues until the police arrive with a big whistle to blow, there's an argument for no reason since the minuscule dent on the pitted bumper has added character to the Skoda.

Traders in crammed shops invade the pavements, selling the oddest items. How many people need standby generators, power tools, chains, hoes and hose in a city? Clothes cost a fiver. Past the central market where unidentifiable butchered parts of bloody animals hang from metal hooks. Pet shops with puppies crammed into tiny cages. A man with grey stubble exits one pet shop with a snake in a glass case. I recoil. Others admire. The environs are run down, so much so that I also disappear into a grave-sized hole in the pavement, which is a surprise given that the Greeks spent £26 billion on their infrastructure before the last Olympics.

Acropolis now. Last time I climbed a sheer vertical cliff to reach the incomparable *upper city*. Now there is a 2.5 km paved archaeological pedestrian causeway which connects the exhibits of this open air museum. I amble past snack shops, restrooms, guide stalls, seats and water fountains to the ten acre craggy rock perched 300 foot above the plain of Attica until I stand before the ultimate photo opportunity, the Parthenon. Construction work here was commissioned by Pericles in 447 BC and remains ongoing. The official guide to Athens called '*Life in Capital A*' has the following direct quote: '*The Parthenon — An incomplete pile of weather-*

beaten stones sitting on a big bare raggedy old rock. A building cloaked in scaffolding, overhung with cranes, often shrouded in a haze of heat and dust, and forever surrounded by hoards of snap-happy tourists. Surely nothing to write home about.' Honest.

This remains the safest place in the city and is where the olden-day women of Athens barricaded themselves when they grew tired of their menfolk going off to fight against Sparta, depriving their men of care, cooking and sex, a strategy which can be successful in modern times. At the far end the Greek flag flutters freely, but it was not always so. When the Nazis took Athens they instructed an *Evzone* to take down the flag. He did so calmly, wrapped himself in the flag and jumped to his death. Below me 1960s low-rise commercial and residential buildings sprawl to where the eye meets the hills or the smog. Above the din of the hammers of the workers who still restore the Acropolis, the buzz of four million inhabitants rises above tolling church bells, their car horns tooting incessantly as they continue to search for a car parking space.

Nearby is the arousingly named temple of *Erechtheion*. Athens was named here when Athena and Poseidon displayed their best party tricks to see who would become patron of the city. Athena touched the ground with a spear and an olive tree appeared, but Poseidon could only manage to make a spring burst forth from a rock, so Athena was the victor and Poseidon was awarded a tiny village in Syros in the middle of nowhere. There are six replacement maiden statues and I read the inscription. *Five of the original classical statues are in the Acropolis Museum and the sixth one is in the British Museum.* That is, it was nicked. See *Elgin Marbles,* sold to Lord Elgin by the Turks when they were occupying Greece, somewhat akin to a burglar breaking into your home, holding you hostage, selling your best artwork to your neighbours who then refuse afterwards to return your possessions on the grounds that they paid money for what is yours but agreeing to keep them in their own museum for 'safe-keeping' for a few centuries.

On this trip I occasionally refer to my trusty 1995 Berlitz Athens pocket guide book, bought the last time in the days before tourists printed free city guides from the internet. I thumb through the restaurants section when a small card falls out. *Byzantine Restaurant, 18 Kidathineon Street. Traditional Greek Food.* It's the scene of the crime. I wonder is it still there? I climb towards Plaka with its small roads, quirky tavernas and bars, souvenir shops, blind corners and hidden squares until I stumble across a vaguely familiar plaza. It's still there and it might be the same touting *maitre d'* outside but I am sold for old times' sake. I sit outside and order beer, crispy calamari followed by chocolately sweet *Baklava*.

Naturally I start with a Greek salad. It's fantastic: fleshy beef tomatoes, crisp wedges of cucumber, with a drizzle of virgin olive oil and oregano, of truly *Oliveresque* proportions. The feta cheese crumbles like historic remains. Above me the Acropolis is a flood-lit cliff-hanger radiating optimism over this rejuvenated city. Despite significant progress over the past decade, Athens remains a city whose reputation, inevitably, lies in ruins.

Germany ... not quite

HLX Flight HLX7503 – Saturday @ 11.30am
– DUB-HAM-DUB

Fare €11 plus taxes, fees and charges €29

I am not flying with Lufthansa today because they are four hundred euros plus from Dublin. Mick shares my sentiments about that airline, and its chief executive. *'He says Germans don't like low fares. How does he know? He's never offered them any. If €99 is the best Lufthansa can do for the World Cup then they shouldn't bother leaving the changing rooms. Their €99 fares are own goals. Germans will crawl bollock-naked over broken glass to get low fares. The only thing that Lufthansa have not yet got is an injunction from the German courts to prevent Ruinair from calling itself Ruinair. We are stuffing it to Lufty. I feel like the Michael Owen of the airline industry, beating the Germans on their home turf. Lufthansa in Germany makes even British Airways look cheap. I'd like to thank Lufthansa for their help setting us up in Germany.'*

HLX, or Hapag-Lloyd Express, are a German low fares airline. The HLX advertising offers *flights for the price of a taxi* and they're not wrong. A taxi to and from the airport is €60 so it's cheaper to fly to Hamburg and back this weekend. I booked the flights on one of their *Devilish* special night promotions, where the prices are *hellishly cheap*. I'm not unhappy with a return flight for eleven euros but they ripped me off because some of their flights only cost one cent.

Check-in is quick. We have unassigned seating. In the airport bookshop I annoy staff by browsing German guide books but buying none. I contemplate buying a newspaper but change my mind. There's a rumour going around that if you buy a CD on a Sunday morning, you get a free newspaper. I wait at the departure gate. The guy beside me is German because he produces a phallic raw carrot which he proceeds to eat slowly as several hundred *Ruinair* aircraft come and go. There are more Ruinair aircraft over Dublin now than both sides had over London during the Blitz. *WhineAir?*

Our aircraft arrives and a child announces, '*Mummy, look at the big yellow plane.*' They have taken this taxi lark to the extremes. The Boeing 737 on the apron is painted bright yellow with a black and white checker side-stripe. Last time I saw a low fares aircraft like this, it was a New York Chrysler cab. The incoming aircraft is a few minutes late which doesn't bother me but the Germans are pacing up and down in battalion strength by the plate-glass windows, in disbelief that anything emanating from Germany could be late. There's another delay at the gate when one German passenger holds up two boarding cards.

'Are you with someone else, sir?' asks the airport Jobsworth.

'*Nein.*'

'Are you travelling with perhaps some artwork or valuables?' Honest.

'No. I bought two seats.'

I bet he shaves twice every morning, and wears two pairs of underpants, to be sure.

Inside the *Yellow Peril*, the interior is somewhat shabby and tired but the crew make up for it, offering a welcome and a smile. Mandy wears dark trousers, a tight, luminous-yellow, low-cut T-shirt with *hlx.com* on the back and a neck scarf knotted at a jaunty angle, as she sells me a *cappuccino* and cake.

'It's an instant *cappuccino*,' she advises apologetically. 'Is that okay?'

I am bewildered. 'I was hoping for one of those cappuccinos which take ages to arrive.'

I pass the time reading the adverts on the back of headrests. '*New routes to England for €19.99; Fish 'n Cheap.*' Germans remain the nationality most likely to take photographs from aircraft windows. The cheery crew hand out gifts to kiddies and boiled sweets as we disembark. They could teach Ruinair a lot.

Hamburg airport is one of those airports where domestic residences lie very close to the perimeter but it's not as bad as Mumbai airport, where locals live beside the runway. If you leave the landing lights on in your home in Mumbai, you could be in serious trouble with an uninvited jumbo. Passport control is always a serious matter in Germany. A Bundes-something khaki-uniformed guy with receding hair, intimidating eyes and studious metal-rimmed glasses examines me like I'm on ITV's *Prime Suspect*. He scans my passport, checks an unseen *Wanted* screen and nods very slowly. '*You may enter our beloved country but we know about the litter you discarded on Mainzerlandstrasse in Frankfurt on 9th May 1998.*' In general it is not advisable to engage immigration officials in idle banter. There was the Englishman who was questioned at length by Australian immigration officials at Sydney airport. In answer to the question '*Do you have a criminal record?*' he replied, '*I didn't think that was necessary anymore.*'

The last time I visited Hamburg was on company business ten years ago. My employer paid British Airways four hundred pounds for a limp wet prawn salad (four prawns) and a glass of warm Chardonnay. Mick hates British Airways. '*There is too much "we really admire our competitors". All bollocks. Everyone wants to kick the shit out of everyone else. We want to beat the crap out of BA. They mean to kick the crap out of us. We love tilting at the English, they have done it for about 700 years, but we're only getting our own back. Remember they beat the crap out of us for the first 700 years. I have no time for large airlines who say they care and then screw you for six or seven hundred quid almost every time you fly. Businessmen need to be competitive. They need to stop drinking champagne at six o'clock in the morning on British Airways flights. They need to get there on time. Why the hell would anyone fly with BA and pay four or five hundred quid just to be late?*

'*And if BA wants a fares war, they have come to the right place. I know more about flying Concorde than BA knows about low fares. We should outlaw business class traffic. We should pack businessmen into economy class rather than have the fat and overpaid flying around on flat beds after they've all eaten and drunk their fine wines. You'll get crap food and a free drink worth £2 and you'll pay £400 for it.* BA *keep turning passengers away with fuel surcharge after fuel surcharge, high fares, poor punctuality, flight cancellations and no catering. At least on Ruinair, customers can buy a sandwich with £100 they have saved over* BA*'s high fares. A move to the moon might be needed to streamline* BA*'s operations. A Mickey Mouse Irish airline can start in a field in Waterford and in twenty years the self-styled, self-proclaimed world's favourite airline is overtaken by the world's lowest price airline. Now there's a thing. When I have stuffed* BA*, then I'll quit.'* Maybe British Airways will change under its latest chief executive, Willie Walsh. Whoever thought the two largest airlines in Europe would both be run by Irishmen? BA has such a huge pension deficit that it is now described as a large pension fund that happens to own some aircraft.

Last time we stayed at a hotel with a palatial pool and health spa. In those days I travelled so much and so well that I didn't purchase a bar of bath soap for several years. I sat in only my pristine birthday suit inside a steamy oven of a sauna when two elderly stark-naked German gentlemen joined me. I nodded politely and looked upwards. To my amazement two sporty German ladies then joined us. They sat on their towels rather than using them as modesty intends. It was too much for me, an innocent young Catholic Irish boy on my first trip to Germany. Like a *News of the World* reporter, I made my excuses and left. I experienced a culinary disaster in Hamburg in a restaurant by the *Alster* lake where I ordered *steak tartare*. A wiser colleague asked me if I knew what I was ordering and I bluffed with a confident Yes, certain I was in for steak and chips plus all the trimmings. I got a plate of raw red mince beef which tasted like, well, raw red mince beef. But the chopped raw onion and the sprig of parsley on top were very tasty.

German taxis are great. In Germany if you see a gleaming cream Mercedes, you know it's a taxi. In Ireland if you see a filthy bald fifteen-year-old Datsun with 100,000 miles on the clock, you know it's a taxi. But Irish taxis have drivers with considerably more personality. A while ago I was stuck in a taxi at a red light in Dublin for ages but when the lights went green the car in front didn't move. So my rather irate Dubliner taxi driver yelled out the window at the car in front, 'Christ, get a move on. It's not gonna get any fuckin' greener.' But I am not taking a taxi to this city after the last taxi ride I took here. On that trip to the airport we encountered a mega-tailback with serious delays. The driver jabbered away at me in *Deutsch* but I understood nothing. We arrived at the cause of the problem. An Audi A8 was wrapped around a tree and was a total write-off. The driver swore in German at the accident scene and turned back at me for confirmation. On the spur of the moment I pointed at the Audi and replied, '*Vorsprung durch Technik*'. Mark Twain described the German language as follows: The Germans take part of a verb and put it down there, like putting a stake in the ground, then they take the other part of the verb and put it over yonder like another stake, and between these two outer limits they shovel in more and more German.

Without the Germans, we wouldn't have the motor car. As Karl Benz drove his noisy three-wheeled invention around the streets of Mannheim in 1885, Gottlieb Daimler was driving a similar motor car in Stuttgart, and although the two lived only a few hundred miles apart, they never met. A friend's daughter had the interesting and catchy Christian name of Mercedes. Robert Bosch was the bright spark who invented the spark plug, the magneto and probably your dishwasher, and Rudolf Diesel made an engine. Adam Opel built a few cars too but never forget Ferdinand Porsche designed the first *Volkswagen*.

The *Jasper* bus takes me to the main train station and I walk through the concourse towards my hotel. Inside, two crew-cut blokes with beer bottles are accosted by *Polizei*. Both police officers are female, with long blonde pony-tails, khaki trousers, leather jackets and big truncheons. They can arrest me any day.

I am stopped in my tracks by a set of red pedestrian lights. There isn't a car for miles but we all wait for the green man. Jaywalking is not the done thing here. I edge forward. A girl cycles towards me and she's smiling at me. What friendly people. She cycles nearer. Her smile becomes a stare, but then a glare. Something's not right. She points at my feet, shouts something. I am standing one millimetre over the solid white line that is her cycle lane. I step back, aware that I have committed a capital federal offence.

The town hall is a magnificent neo-Renaissance building, with a tall clock tower, perfect symmetry, shining gilt edges, pristine brickwork and 647 rooms, being six more rooms than Buckingham Palace, which is important information for Germans to know. Hamburg is a long-established Hanseatic trading city, Germany's second largest city, the richest city in the EU on a per capita basis and home to two million people. It's an independent place, bereft of a cathedral, but a town hall like this sends out a definite message to original trading partners and latter day pretenders. *Don't fuck with us.* When the town hall was built, the city fathers removed a mural of a man kneeling in prayer. Hamburg's citizens kneel to no one. There's a rumour that a German only became Pope because he got his towel over the balcony first.

I can recall part of the city from my first visit but *Ballindamm* is always a shock. The *Binnenalster* inner lake has placid waters surrounded by majestic buildings on three sides. There are private banks and stockbrokers, and grand hotels I cannot afford where the penthouses cost thousands, and that's without breakfast. It's the sort of street where I watch a guy in a blazer double-park his Aston Martin to hop into a goldsmith's, in the same way you or I would hop into the Spar for a loaf of bread.

It's my duty in the interests of great literary endeavour to explore the *Reeperbahn*. Going to Hamburg and not visiting the *Reeperbahn* is like going to a major European port and not going to check out a notorious red-light district of ill-repute and wanton vice. I set out for the *Sündenmeile*, the Mile of Sin.

The Germans have the most bizarre sex laws. Prostitution is legal in Germany and brothel owners, who must pay tax and employee health insurance, have access to the official databases of jobseekers. I read on the web about a 25-year-old waitress who turned down a job offer in a brothel in Berlin and so faced cuts to her unemployment benefit. The waitress, an unemployed IT professional, said in her CV she was willing to work in a bar. She received a letter from the job centre telling her that an employer was interested in her *profile*. Only on contacting the employer did she realise that she was calling a brothel. Under German labour law any woman under fifty-five who has been out of work for more than a year can be forced to take an available job, including in the sex industry, or lose her unemployment benefit. Unemployment at 12 per cent is the highest since reunification in 1990. The government had considered making brothels an exception on moral grounds, but decided that it would be too difficult to distinguish them from bars. '*I'll have a beer, whatever you're having, two packets of crisps and of course full blown sex, dear.*'

The *Reeperbahn* in the early evening is not what I expect. It's a wide street jammed with traffic. There's a hardcore Lidl store selling low fare groceries. There's an XXX stall selling fruit and vegetables, although some are rude in shape. There is an adults-only kebab shop. The *Dollyland Diner* sells ... food. It is all so tacky. I don't feel threatened at all except by the phalanxes of tourists who threaten to run me over. I decline kind offers by members of the Russian mafia to enter their clubs where the entrance fee of five euros is dwarfed by the one hundred euro price for a beer. Allegedly. I mean, if I had to pay one hundred euros for a beer, I'd be writing a letter to the German Ministry of Consumer Affairs post haste.

But there are a few sex shops, and for research purposes only, I enter one. The *Emporia Erotica* is huge, with glitzy window displays, two floors, bright lights, row upon row of pervy goods, and staff everywhere. There are changing rooms downstairs where locals try on black leather gear and check how they look in mirrors. Only the Germans could build a sex shop with all the facilities of a Tesco out-of-town superstore. The customers are either wandering couples and tourists, or else sad and solitary blokes in long coats. I suddenly realise I am a solitary bloke. *Honest folks, I'm only here because I'm writing a book.*

They sell the most amazingly named products. There's the Black Mamba, the Beginner's Bondage Kit, the Big Jelly, the Golden

Nugget, the Venus Butterfly Trap, the Classic Bender (up to 18 inches), Horny Hooters Love Oil in Exciting Lemonade flavour and the Inflatable Swiss Love Ball, the last of which I suspect is a contradiction in terms. There are videos with *Russian Amateurs* when I would expect to see professionals and don't ask about *Hairy Miffs*. The saddest aspect is some worker must come in to work every Monday morning at some sleazy manufacturer to think up these weird and whacky names. I worry that this product expert may take his work home. He might refer to his dear wife Bertha as Big Busty Breasty Bertha. He might refer to his modest home as a multi-roomed multi-themed pleasure palace. He might refer to his Volvo estate as the newest comfortable Swedish model with easily accessible rear-entry. I dread to think what he tells others about his three children Helmut, Virginia and Labia.

People walk towards what seems to me to be a dead end but *Herbertstrasse* is where the working ladies, work. Entry is *Verboten* to other women and to children. There are warning signs and a barrier with advertisements for *West* cigarettes. Only the Germans could find a corporate sponsor for their red-light district. I venture past to see ladies sitting in windows in their finest lingerie. As I pass at speed they knock on glass, call out and open the windows. The small rooms have spotlights to accentuate the white lingerie, which glows like Luke Skywalker's sabre. I walk faster, conscious that the lights are having the same effect on my white sneakers. A guy takes two Japanese tourists down a side passage, so to speak. I don't know what they do but I hear him say '*One Hundred Euros*'. I suspect he does not operate a *Bureau de Change*. At a street corner I naively stop to check a map to find the nearest u-Bahn station to safety. A girl approaches and asks me something in German. I ignore her. She asks me in English and I make the mistake of saying 'No'. She says 'Can I ask you a question?' Somehow I know it's not going to be '*What's the fastest land animal?*' or '*How did my Deutsche Bank shares perform today on the stock market?*' I love meeting new and interesting people on my travels and not all of them are working girls on street corners.

There are more ladies. Fifty of them are lined up along *David-strasse*, every yard or so, clutching at passing males. They are identical, twenty-something, bleached blonde with fake tans, dressed in shocking bright colours of orange, lemon and lime, like some sexual fruit salad. They wear jumpsuits, tracksuits, hoodies and trousers, more suited to the ski piste than on the make. They are the world's fittest prostitutes. Some wear short greyhound skirts, so called because they are only an inch away from the hare. A few of the ladies wear brighter high-visibility garments which I suspect may also be a traffic-calming measure.

There's a shop called the *Condomerie* which sells nothing but assorted condoms. A few rubbery samples are on display in the window. One condom is in the shape of a kangaroo and has all the required protruding body parts, which I assume is primarily for homesick Australians. A huge white condom, the sort of thing you could hold a circus in, hangs in the middle of the window with a sign announcing that the shop owner offers one hundred euros to anyone who can comfortably fill the condom. I debate his kind offer for a moment but decline, solely on the grounds of hygiene rather than personal inferiority.

I face a dilemma in St Pauli U-Bahn station. A man in a wheelchair at the foot of an escalator needs help and I am the only person within sight. Up close he is pale and ill. He holds out an open hand and I offer to help him move but he prefers hard cash. He's a beggar but I don't care for his modus operandi. I am unconvinced and walk past and turn to watch him from afar. He motions with his hand to others, suddenly rises up out of the wheelchair and drags it up the escalator with ease. It's a bloody miracle.

Next morning I take an early train to the harbour area, keen to see the *Fischmarkt* which opens at the ungodly hour of 5am. Nearby tall-masted schooners are moored, seaplanes land and tour boats begin their round trips. Locals sell antiques, collectables and trinkets and there's hardly a soused herring or smoked mackerel in sight. It finishes at 9am. I am amazed at the crowds. If this market was held in Dublin no one would turn up until 2pm and even then we would all suffer from the mother of all hangovers. But something else is afoot. Roads are cordoned off, police mingle and helicopters hover overhead. Now I know why it was so difficult to reserve my hotel room. I hear cheers as thousands of runners hove into view along the *Landungsbrücke*. The Hamburg Marathon is being run, so to speak. I see the look of the long-distance runner etched on strained faces. '*I'm never running in this bleedin' race again.*' The crowd save a special cheer for the fat fifty-year-old blokes in spandex. Six Kenyans gambol along effortlessly, destined to triumph with ease, Kenya being the sort of place where folks jog sixty miles to get a morning newspaper.

I check out, grab the airport bus opposite my hotel and twenty minutes later mistakenly walk into Terminal 4 to learn it's the posh terminal for people who fly full-service Lufty and BA. I am herded to the darkened gothic pit that is Terminal 3 where I queue for HLX. The security checks at the X-ray machines are tight, so tight the new shift of security staff are frisked repeatedly by the departing shift. On board I have what every flyer craves — a row of three seats with only me by the window, until a hippy couple lands alongside. He spends five minutes ramming his guitar into the overhead bin beside my backpack. She has a pointy pixie face and viciously cropped red hair and sits beside me, then turns to me like an old family friend and asks me the flight time to Dublin. Do I look like the pilot? I advise her it's nine hours.

I could live in Hamburg; in a handy-walkabout, photo-opportunity, city-yachting, BMW soft-top, integrated-transport, alfresco-dining, cappuccino-imbibing, polarised-eyewear, Teutonic blonde sort of way. But eleven euros is way too much to pay for a return flight to Germany. There must be a cheaper flight.

Germany ... again

Germanwings Flight 4U397 – Saturday @ 12.00
– DUB-CGN-DUS-DUB

Fare €0.01 plus taxes, fees and charges €23

I never heard of Germanwings until I saw their advertisement in Dublin airport. They promised fares from as low as €19 to the heart of Germany. Their motto is *Fly High, Pay Low*. It sounds like my sort of airline. I register online for their newsletter and receive an email about a *Crazy Night* planned for Thursday. I don't know how they got to know about my social life and why they told all their email subscribers.

On the crazy Thursday evening I check flights and worry I'm seeing things on my PC screen. Some offers are from nineteen euros *including* fees and taxes. I pay one tiny cent for a one-way trip. I am feeling rather pleased. To the best of my knowledge one cent is as good as it gets and no one has yet successfully sold an airline seat to a punter for half a cent. Suddenly Ruinair seems sort of ... expensive.

The departure time of midday on Saturday is a civilised time for a low fares bargain. We will travel to an airport called Cologne-Bonn, which is either reflective of urban indecision or brilliant marketing to double the airport's catchment area. Behind me are some American friends on their way home to JFK and LAX.

'We did it all this time round. We even went North.'

'You mean you crossed the border?'

'Sure did.'

'You see any guns?'

'Nah.'

'You see any soldiers?'

'We saw *Gardai*.'

'They're everywhere.'

'We saw the hunger strikers' prison called H where they starved themselves to death.'

'Gee. That's cool.'

At 11.30am an aircraft pulls up at our gate. It's silver and gleaming, with a purple and yellow tail. A few of the usual Ruinair contingent are already up on their feet to queue since we have unassigned seats. A child beside me asks her mother why some people are queuing. Her mother looks up from a newspaper and slowly casts a disinterested glance in the direction of the gate. '*Don't worry, dear … they're German.*'

Germanwings are new to me. They are mostly owned by Lufthansa so they must be all right; safe and all that matters. I assume they have the rest of the essential body parts, such as Germanfuselage, Germanwheels and Germanengines required to get me to the heart of *Nordrhein-Westfalen*. The Airbus A319 has an all-leather interior, and is clean and bright. The crew sport immaculate, smartly tailored purple uniforms with white blouses and neat neck scarves. They smile at us and help mothers with children, later heating up bottles of milk and goo-gooing at the children without terrifying them into tears.

The flight has an 80 per cent load factor today. First impressions are great. This is well worth one cent. After we take off I suffer the ultimate embarrassment for the male traveller stuck in a tiny seat for an hour or more. I am, how should I say, dressed on the wrong side. I shift in my seat several times. Now, that's much better. I offer the crew my custom and ask for a sandwich and coffee. They advise I can have the *Happy Snack* with a free chocolate bar. I am happy despite it costing five hundred times the price of the flight.

There is a *Euro-Quiz* in their in-flight magazine. I learn that Kleinmaischeid (where?) in Germany is the geographical centre of Europe, Estonia is obliged by law to provide free internet access to its citizens (my sort of country to book flights online), in Bulgaria shaking your head means 'yes' and nodding your head means 'no', and mobile telephone throwing is a recognised sport in Finland. Finland holds the World Air Guitar Playing Contest where the winner receives an imaginary cheque for one million euros.

We all jolt back. Another aircraft passes so close I can see the passengers on it and some of them are now close personal friends. Their jet trail fills my view. Beforehand our aircraft had banked slightly right, away from the oncoming aircraft. It feels like two boy racers going in opposite directions down a country lane and our guy up front blinked first. In the business they call it a near-miss. I think it's more of a near-hit. We land and this time I have some trouble at immigration. I always leave a fifty euro note inside the flap of my passport cover in case some local street entrepreneur lifts my wallet from my person whilst travelling. The immigration officer accidentally finds the note in my passport and holds it up to me.

'Ah, I zink dis is fur me?' he smiles. In Germany, this is what is known as a joke.

There are no dodgy bus excursions or connections here. I stride to the train station to catch the S-Bahn to Cologne. The station is a destination in itself, an immense multi-platform concrete construction sunk into the ground yet topped by a vaulted glass roof which arches over us plebeians below. Sunlight beams down. It's marble and chrome and clean enough to have been first opened yesterday. We Irish people walk around in amazement and look up with awe. So this is what a proper train station looks like. I try to buy a ticket at the vending machines but they all have stickers on them with a word 'DEF'. I am not sure what this stands for, but I can guess. The locals might call it *Kaputt*. I think we call it *Fucked*.

It sort of all began here. I knew I had a travel book in me but I feared that every destination was done. Other authors have enjoyed olive oil and virgins in Tuscany, converted rustic farmhouses in Provence and driven over citrus fruit in Spain. Travel in Ireland has been done by authors who never pass a bar with their surname on it and by others who pull fridges around the country (although the latter strikes me as a pointless undertaking).

The UK has been penned by that famous US travel writer who a decade ago took trains around the UK, arrived at dead seaside towns, walked the High Street of M&S and Boots, found a mouldy guest house, ordered a meal off a laminated menu at a Chinese restaurant called *Fook Yu*, got drenched on the way back and locked out of his guesthouse and spent the night alone reading a book by a 20-watt bulb with oncoming pneumonia. So for some time I toyed with the idea of a book about Germany, possibly seeing it all by train. I sent a few early chapters to my then literary agent who told me to cease and desist and that it was too bloody boring, which was a reflection on the subject matter rather than on myself. Then fortunately a cheap Irish airline left me for a day in an airport in Spain and the topic of my travel book was crystal clear. (Much like men gone fishin', the length of my delay in Malaga increases each time I recount the tale.)

I stand on *Gleis 1*. I sometimes feel self-conscious when alone on German train station platforms, aware that I do not blend in with the locals. What I fear most is some chap in uniform approaching me and saying something in German which I don't understand, and then asking me for my identity papers which I don't have, and I blurt out something involuntarily in English and the game is up and I'm rushed back to the *Stalag Luft* to spend the rest of the war with Donald Pleasance, James Garner and Dickie Attenborough.

According to the display the next S-Bahn train departs for the city centre at 2.50pm. I wait with others, mostly tanned locals from the inbound flights from the Med and other hot spots.

2.50 comes and goes. But the train doesn't. There is some consternation.

2.51. Still no sign of the train. The locals get up off their seats and walk the platform, chat to each other, stare into the underground tunnel as if the very act will make a train appear instantaneously.

2.52. The locals are on their mobile phones to loved ones. I don't speak much German but I can decipher enough. They're telling wives and husbands, sons and daughters that they're going to be late, that the entire planned schedule for the first day back home needs to be moved back by two minutes.

2.53. Still on the mobiles. Now they're telling wives they love them dearly and if they never see them again, they'll always remember the way they were before they left for that fated holiday. A guy calls his girlfriend and tells her he loves her, wishes he had proposed earlier and asks her if she'll marry him. Someone else calls home and ends their conversation with *Natürlich*. German, I think, for *Shit Happens*.

2.54. There's an announcement on the PA overhead. Again it's hard to translate but the locals visibly relax. They look at their watches and nod to each other reassuringly. I sense the train is on the way.

2.55. The PA announcer resigns from his job in disgrace and moves to live in a Black Forest cabin.

3.00. The train arrives. Gleaming, empty and cheap enough at two euros to the *Hauptbahnhof*.

Choosing a hotel room is like buying a new home. Location, location, location. My hotel is in the city centre and the modest room has a view onto the *Hauptbahnhof*. I can see a succession of arriving trains. My bed is as close to being in the train station as it's possible to be without actually having to sleep rough on platform 1. The room is a box room on the fourth floor, set into the eaves so that the space is cut in half by ugly diagonal roof beams. The room is airless and leaves me gasping. The air-conditioning has two levels, Gale Force and Maximum Tornado Force. I open a window to get some sleep. My room also overlooks the bus terminus and taxi rank, so it's nice and quiet. I hear the train announcements on Tannoy in the station. The announcements continue past midnight. By 2am I know the German rail timetable verbatim.

I set out early the next morning. Cologne is the oldest of the major German cities and its name goes back to the Romans who gave their city the name Colonia. In the Middle Ages it was the most populous city in Germany. Universities and churches thrived. The city waned when the low fares travellers of the time discovered the New World. In 1794 the French occupied the city, followed by the Prussians in 1815, since followed by tourists like me.

As I progress towards the famous cathedral, a mass of people are penned in by crash barriers and wire fences. People are falling over on their backsides around me like a dose of repeats of *You've Been Framed*. I assume it's a pedestrianisation experiment which has gone horribly wrong. The Germans have a secret plan to cover all the country in marble slabs, starting with this city centre which cries out for a single blade of grass. I struggle towards the *Domplatz*, the main city square. There is a vast open-air market underway beside the cathedral. There are one million plus living in Cologne but two million more come here at this very special time of year. It is Christmas.

Being Germany, there is not one Christmas market in Cologne: there are six. The market stalls are identical sequentially numbered wooden garden sheds arranged in neat ordered rows. They sell lotions and soaps, hats and scarves, candles and mirrors, wood carvings and stone sculptures, glasswork and jewellery: all items you would enjoy receiving as a Christmas present but which you don't need. There is a heady aroma of fruit punch and *Glühwein*, roast chestnuts and fresh crêpes, and the *Bratwurst* is selling like hot cakes, which coincidentally are also selling well. Some of the sausages are two foot long and the size of something you would put under a door with a draught. My favourite stall is called *Schmuck Metallobjekte*.

Glühwein is dispensed in pleasing ceramic mugs. If this was Ireland, everyone would nick the mugs as free presents for close relatives, but this being Germany everyone queues to deposit empty mugs back on the counters. The lethal *Glühwein* has gone to people's heads. Gangs of blokes in flashing Santa hats are hammered. Bevies of girls wear pointy reindeer antlers. Middle-aged ladies sing in unison badly. I catch a breather by a crib in the centre of the fair. There is some space only here. No one came to see the crib. One stall is doing good business selling small figurine characters for cribs. They are sold individually or in box sets. I assume purchasing the box set is the best option in order to avoid nasty surprises on Christmas morning in front of the assembled kiddies. *'Hey Helga, did you buy the little baby guy, or not?'*

Neumarkt is another dense conurbation of retail opportunity if you crave items whose primary purpose is to collect dust. There is a *Unicef* gift shop so I purchase some Christmas cards. I do a lot of good work for charity. Two psychopaths at another stall sell ten-inch hunting knives, meat cleavers, pen knives, serrated blades, handcuffs and Walther and Beretta *Luftpistolen*; basically all the items I am unlikely to successfully bring home in my carry-on baggage. The guy on the waffle stall talks and talks. The highlight for me occurs when an over-enthusiastic chestnut roaster self-combusts his entire flaming stall.

There are many superlatives to describe the 157-metre-high Dom cathedral: the city's landmark, a UNESCO World Heritage Site, the best example of high gothic architecture in Europe, the most visited building in Germany, or a five-aisled basilica with a triple-aisled transept, and that's not effortless to say after a few mugs of *Glühwein*. I look up but all I can see is an oppressive hulking mass. It's no coincidence this epic building survived the night of 30 May 1942 when Bomber Harris sent 1,047 RAF planes to drop 1,455 tons of explosives here. The Allied crews spared the cathedral as a navigation and bombing aid. The Dom cathedral was started in 1248 and finished in 1842. These are not times on the twenty-four-hour clock. Six hundred years to finish the Dom is a feat since unequalled in the history of the German construction industry. Apparently the plans were lost but I find this hard to believe. Did some jaded labourer suddenly announce after six hundred years to his bewildered colleagues, *'It's okay guys, I found those plans. Sure I had them on me all the time. Now let's get stuck in and finish this thing off.'*

The Dom is covered with scaffolding and hoardings. It is also pitch black. If I came here in the dead of night, I would be hard pressed to pick it out from the night sky. Up close the stone is layered with aeons of grime. I wonder if there is a work crew which appears in the off-season with pots of black paint and bags of soot which they daub liberally. Now and again there is a wild panic when stone becomes visible. The vaulted roof towers but sadly it's not impressive inside. It should inspire me and draw me closer to the celestial heavens but it's gloomy and badly lit and there doesn't seem to be much to see. A prayer service is about to commence so a guy in a big red robe blocks my way up the aisle. He has a chunky wooden box hanging around his neck with some words about a

Church Collection. He is what I would call an optimist. There's a decent crowd assembled in a corner who admire a substantial multi-tiered nativity crib with scenes of basic carpentry, much peasantry and general sheep worrying. It's evidently a labour of love but there are no Ferraris, swimming pools or plasma TV screens, so it is one crib that won't feature on MTV.

It's difficult to walk along the main pedestrian shopping street, called *Hohe Strasse*. I am buffeted by people who glare back until I see what's wrong. Those on the right-hand side of the street move in my direction and those on the left-hand side move in the oncoming direction. In Germany, chaos is organised. They are so efficient that they celebrate Christmas a day before everyone else on the 24th of December, dining sumptuously in the evening not on turkey, but on carp. December 25th is a quiet day in contrast. I read a survey in the papers. Germans prefer to spend Christmas with a tree, rather than with their families.

Along this shopping street is a shocking red outlet of the *Beate Uhse* sex shop chain. Founded by a former female pilot who was unable to continue flying with the *Luftwaffe*, or indeed any other airline, post-WWII, she turned to selling advice on the rhythm method by mail order. She opened the world's first sex shop in Germany in 1962 and ultimately floated her valuable company on the Frankfurt Stock Exchange. The shares are in demand, partly because the certificates feature nearly naked women. A group of middle-aged ladies emerge from the shop with scandalous gifts so I stare until they grow mortally embarrassed.

It's disconcerting to hear so many English accents. I assume they come for the Christmas shopping. I hear two couples up-front chatting away in broad Essex accents. '*We were going to go to Lakeside Thurrock but you know, with the traffic and all that, we decided to come here. It's so much easier.*'

There's a window with a stack of perfumes proudly sporting the *4711 Eau de Cologne* logo. So this is where the ghastly stuff comes from. I don't venture inside because 50% of the price of a bottle goes to manufacturing the phallic phial, 49% goes to pay a supermodel to walk on a beach in a moody black and white TV advertisement and the balance goes to make the coloured smelly water. Still, without Cologne, Henry Cooper would never have had much of a career after the boxing ring. Such a *Brut* of a fighter.

On *Schildergasse* there are novelty fun rides for children. Some locals offer placid Shetland ponies, another has a nice ass, so to speak, but the flashiest bastard in Cologne has a llama. This intelligent and inquisitive beast stands proudly, watching shoppers with bulging bags, thinking, '*I should really be in Peru.*'

That evening I eat in a Maredo steakhouse and break several rules of international travel. Never eat in a restaurant with a multi-lingual menu. Never eat in a restaurant with pictures of the food on the place mats. Never eat in a restaurant with numbered dishes on the menu. Never eat in a restaurant with a written definition of a rare, medium and well-done steak. Never eat in a restaurant largely populated by Japanese tourists. Never eat in a restaurant with an '*All You Can Eat*' salad buffet to ruin your main course appetite.

There is nothing on this week in the vast *KolnMesse* on the far side of the river. It's where they hold thirty annual trade fairs, events such as the *International Enamel-Plated Cutlery Exhibition,* the *Annual Widget Manufacturing Convention* and most likely the *Not Very Exciting Oily Industrial Bits 'n Bobs Fair.* So I walk the Rhine. It's 1,320 km long but I only manage two kilometres between the bridges. I bypass another market, this time of the floating variety; the MS *Wappen von Mainz* is moored conveniently. I encounter middle-aged couples in brown leather jackets, arm in arm, enjoying the bracing air. The only out-of-place people I see are a guy with bright green hair and a pit-bull terrier, and a very obvious transvestite.

Why is it that German males of a certain age all wear identical sleeveless beige or cream-coloured short coats with dozens of outside pockets? These coats are better suited to pitch-side photographers or beardy, crusty, rural ornithologists like Bill Oddie (I once watched a BBC TV programme called *Bill Oddie's Top Ten Birds* but I was very disappointed). The coats have zips at the shoulders to attach sleeves for winter wear and the more advanced models have pockets sewn onto pockets, plus epaulets and buckles and even pockets around their backside which are only accessible to the triple-jointed. I see the coats everywhere along the streets, and see them later on TV as German tour groups invade Majorca in high summer and 90 degrees plus, still wearing their little coats. I expect many males are passed a soft sixtieth birthday present by their wives only to reply, having torn apart the wrapping paper, 'Oh ... you got me one of those little coats. Lovely.' This manner of dress, however, is preferable to that of the English male on his holidays who dresses as if he is about to receive a call up to the national soccer squad.

On the Rhine peninsula lies Cologne's sweetest temptation. The Chocolate Museum is the main attraction on this stunning peninsula, which juts out into the river like a moored ship of the future. Here you can learn all about the 3,000 year history of chocolate, from the humble cocoa bean to the posh praline. I don't wish to visit. It's not worth the risk because I like chocolate too much. I have visions of a museum guide pointing at a mouldy, furry piece of green chocolate in a glass case and telling me it's the oldest known surviving piece in the Western world.

Outside is the last market I can endure. The *Medieval Christmas Market* is a run-down, lean-to collection of outlets manned by hideous witches and guys in Robin Hood costumes with pointy hoods. Everything about this place is medieval except the entrance fee of two euros, which I refuse to pay. There is free entertainment since I can watch two peasants baking bread in traditional brick ovens. When they open the doors to check progress, the Germans take photographs of the trays of bread. There is much grime, soot, flour, smoke and dust about. An English guy behind me wearing a Leicester City FC jacket by the name of Killjoy does not approve. 'If the Health and Safety people saw this, they would shut it down immediately.'

I have this nagging doubt since I landed at Cologne-Bonn airport. Maybe I went to the wrong city. I need reassurance so I catch a regional express train from Cologne southwards to Bonn *Hauptbahnhof*. It's freezing cold when I arrive, which may have something to do with several inches of snow on the ground. Bonn is only famous for three things. First, in 1949 it was arbitrarily chosen as the federal capital and the bureaucrats had a wonderfully civil life until 1991 when the government moved the goalposts, and them, to Berlin. Haribo is its second claim to fame. They're the little packets of fruit gum bear sweets that everyone eats but doesn't know where they come from. The name is composed of parts of founder Hans Riegel and the city where the company is based. The factory in Bonn makes 70 million of the sweets every day. So much sugar, so many children, so much work for the dental profession. That leaves only Ludo.

Ludo's house is difficult to locate. I walk to *Beethovenstrasse* and to *Beethovenplatz*. Nearby is *Handelstrasse*, *Wagnerstrasse* and *Haydnstrasse*. There's also a *Malteserstrasse*. But it's all a ruse. Ludo was born in 1770 in a house ten minutes walk away near the town hall. Ludwig is out so that's another famous celebrity I have missed when calling to their home in person. He will be livid when he returns to find they have stuck a museum in his living room and kitchen, and hundreds of strangers traipsing through his place to emerge with nothing more than a plaster bust of the great man and a CD from the shop.

Ludo was a bit of a player when young. He dropped out of university and frequented the home of the widow Madame Helene von Breuning, who was still a fine-looking woman given that it was, after all, the eighteenth century. Ludo gave '*piano lessons*' to her daughter Eleonore. Nice one, Ludo. Say no more. Ludo's father had pushed his young son to perform in public, blatantly marketing him as another Mozart, even falsifying Ludo's age as six years in what surely must be a forerunner of today's Pop Idol contests. No matter how good the kid was, I cannot imagine ever enjoying a concert given by a whiz-kid six-year-old.

Ludo's artefacts are in the house. There are grand pianos and fine violins, plus a collection of ear trumpets. I need constant reminding that one of the world's greatest composers was deaf. It's profoundly sad that someone bought him an ear trumpet and told him, 'Put that up to your ear, Ludo. You'll be able to hear a lot better.' There's a shopping receipt for one of Ludo's ear trumpets. Did he settle the bill or merely sign it and advise: 'You'd do well to keep this receipt. It'll be worth good money someday when I'm dead.'

I walk to my hotel, starving but sadly not brave enough to dine in an authentic German restaurant. The menus displayed outside have *Schweineschnitzel* and *Speckpfannkuchen,* which may also be medical ailments. Dishes come with *Kräuter,* which I learn are herbs and not Germans at large. And I will not be having the *Senfrostbraten,* unless I walk around in Bonn's arctic conditions without my woolly winter gloves.

The Amber Hotel is fantastic, a four-star place for €44, a sort of low fares hotel. It is located in the leafy up-market suburb of Poppelsdorf, if Bonn is big enough to possess a suburb. I power up the TV and chance upon a typical Saturday evening German cabaret show. It's held in a huge *Toys-R-Us* style warehouse. Thousands of affluent middle-aged couples sit at trestle tables, engaging in mass thigh-clapping. The host is about ninety-nine years old with a tan suit and boot polish hair. Various acts come on in succession, mostly minstrels in lederhosen with accordions, all sporting waistcoats and mullets with centre partings. It's widely believed that many Germans, realising the difficulty of using their own language, have given up on it entirely and instead communicate to each other via large brass bands.

Next on is a reality programme where a presenter in overalls shows viewers how to use a *Parkhaus,* a multi-storey car park to you and me. He drives his MPV past the barriers and finds a space. This is a German car park so all the cars are parked upon polished marble in neat lines, facing the same way and they are all Mercedes. I think the presenter is pretending to be a nerd, but he doesn't have to try hard. I don't understand German TV and it's not only the language barrier. Later on there is a WWII movie where the brave British POWs incarcerated in some Stalag speak in German, which doesn't really work for me.

The TV news features the former German Chancellor. This is the same man who took a court case against a German news agency which reported that he dyed his hair. This makes him the vainest world leader and also somewhat lacking in personal confidence. Even his own personal barber was asked to make a sworn statement to the court denying any dyeing. *Hair* Schroeder won the case. But German TV is still better than NTL digital TV with its

Hollywood's Best Kept Secrets (right), *Bodyshock — the 140 Stone Man, Drastic Gastric Surgery, Soapstar Superstar, Skinniest Celebrity Mums, The World's Scariest Police Chases part 37* and *Jerry Springer's 'I'm sterile so I can't be the father of our five children.'* At home I like to watch the Bulmer's TV channel; an RTE channel which broadcasts mostly Bulmer's cider advertisements featuring orchards and pub interiors, interspersed with the occasional TV programme.

I awake suddenly at midnight. Throbbing euro-techno-dance-floor-bass-acid-house booms outside my window. It shows no sign of abating. I telephone reception. *'That's a student party. It's not part of the hotel. There is nothing we can do. Have a good night. Goodbye.'* So if you want to go clubbing in the wonderful convenience of your own hotel room until 3am, I can heartily recommend the Amber Hotel, Bonn. I am feeling fractious in the morning, much like a laboratory rat after a nasty white noise experiment, one involving prolonged sleep deprivation. Things don't get better as the hot water in the shower lasts precisely two minutes when I am mid-shampoo. I have stayed in hotels in New Delhi, Mumbai, Calcutta and Cork and they all had cornflakes at breakfast but none are evident at the buffet in the Amber Hotel.

'Do you have cornflakes?' I ask two different members of staff in the restaurant.

They stare at the breakfast buffet, examine the items, scratch their heads and reply, 'No.'

I am certain this four-star hotel has purloined two of its stars from a nearby fellow establishment. The humble cornflake is sometimes maligned. Someone once told me that there is more nutrition and fibre in the cardboard box than in the cereal but nevertheless I still prefer to eat the flakes rather than the box.

Now is the time to confront the issue of the continental breakfast, in every sense. I was brought up to believe that cereals, juice, toast and a monster Irish fry-up make the perfect breakfast. So why do the continentals differ? Why do the Dutch eat twenty different varieties of cheese at seven in the morning? Why do the French have nothing but tiny cups of strong coffee, over and over, and that's all? Why do the Germans eat slices of cucumber, tomato and cold luncheon meat roll when I eat that for lunch? Why do the Italians eat frosted chocolate cakes when I eat that for dessert? And why do the Scandinavians even bother to get up in the morning to eat small pieces of dead soused fish laid to rest on thin Ryvita crackers?

As I leave my room for the last time I engage in my favourite hobby in hotels which are unsatisfactory. I walk along the corridor and turn the 'Do Not Disturb' signs hanging on each door around to display 'Please Make up my Room'.

'I got half a night's sleep so can you charge me half the room rate?' I enquire politely at check-out.

A stare. 'That's a student party. It's not part of the hotel. There is nothing we can do, sir.'

'Do you have noise pollution laws for the early hours of the morning in a leafy suburb?' I ask.

'We have no such laws, sir.'

I don't believe the receptionist. The Germans have laws on everything. They are particularly keen on documenting matters on paper so that they can tear it all up and never tell Neville Chamberlain about it. I am about to really get stuck in here, to suggest they accommodate guests on the quiet side of the hotel or ask the *Polizei* to do a student drugs bust. I want to have an excellent verbal spat. I read my bill slowly.

'I have given you a discount on the room rate, sir.' Drat.

I leave Bonn with a heavy heart, safe in the knowledge there will never be a room again for me at the Amber. Ludo left Bonn aged twenty-two in 1792, never to return to his native city. Did he too stay at the Amber?

Berlin

The Jewish Museum depicts two millennia of German Jewish history: Moses, Mendelssohn, the Enlightenment, Ashkenaz, Judaism, Persecution, Resistance and Extermination. It's highly recommended when in the German capital but some memories make me nauseous. The Holocaust is not for tourists.

The *Axis of the Holocaust* is a long, indoor, concrete corridor with an uphill pathway. Along the way are cameos of the lives of those who were lost. The small glass displays feature personal traumas. One is a pianist who never played again. Another is Levi Strauss, who went on to make jeans in the USA. Once half-way up the incline there's no turning back, no diversion along the route, no avoiding the only door at the far end. Other visitors walk close behind and they would see me run away at the fear of the unknown. A solo museum guide guards the steel door. I look at him for assistance but he stares back blankly. I am about to ask him something, anything, whether he will open the door for me, but it's a stupid question to ask. He leans over and pulls the door open, without words or eye contact, for me to enter the *Holocaust Tower*.

Inside it's black until my eyes slowly adjust. The triangular room is half the size of a squash court, with walls perhaps thirty or forty feet high. The walls are bare concrete. Light falls inside through a single high, thin window slit. The noise from the exciting city is audible, but the outside world is out of reach. I walk about slowly, feeling my way to the edges. There is nothing here. It's sunny out but in here it's cold, neither heated nor insulated, feeling cool and damp. The sun never permeates this space hidden to those on the outside. I am not sure what to think. I stumble around the walls, examining the outer boundaries of my limited existence. I gingerly touch the walls, to prove they are real, to determine if I am missing something obvious. The walls are cold to the touch. It's so quiet. When I stop, the enticing bustle of *Lindenstrasse* trickles through the gap in the roof. Does it ever rain in this forsaken place? I wish I was not alone here.

Any initial curious desire to be here fades rapidly. There's no immediate point to the room. It's bewildering but it's not terrifying and I don't know why it is designed to be like this. I wonder how long can I stay here without it being impolite if I walk past the guide outside in some premature anti-climactic exit. Five minutes later and I need to leave for my sanity's sake. I walk back to the door, which has one metal handle, and I pull it open. But it doesn't budge. I grab the handle with both hands and lean back and give it a firm pull. Again it remains shut tight. I look closer to see if there is a lock but there's not. I am trapped. I am undecided. Maybe I'm supposed to do something now, to call out to the guide guarding me so he will let me out. What do I say? 'Help?' 'Let me out?' 'I'm locked in.' 'There's been a terrible mistake. Please.'

There must be more to this. This is a personal challenge. How to get out once you're inside? I step back and look around. A world-class architect like Daniel Liebeskind is creative and introspective. Suddenly in the dark I see a ladder set into the wall but it's so high up I can never hope to reach it. I pace around the walls again looking for another way out, a hidden door or an unseen recess. There's nothing. Still trapped.

I've been inside for ten minutes but it feels like hours. I cannot remember what daylight looks like. Back at the door I need to make that decision. Do I cry out for help, or not? Will he even hear me? The door opens and light floods in. The door opens outwards. The handle on the inside is there to confuse me. I was so disoriented as I climbed towards the door that I forgot that the guide had pulled the door open.

I walk past the guide without words. None are needed. I am not the first nor the last. We know how I feel. Plus six million others. I have only experienced an infinitesimally small amount of what they endured.

Austria

Niki Flight AB8374 – Monday @ 8.00am – NUE-VIE

Fare €22 plus taxes, fees and charges €17

Nuremberg is the second city of Bavaria and lies 100 miles north-west of Munich. Half a million residents live here in comfortable suburban bliss. The city's motto is *Stadt der Menschenrechte*, the City of Human Rights. I catch a 9 tram from *Marktplatz*, formerly known as *Adolf-Hitler-Platz* for a decade or so. They say there's a programme on British TV every night about Hitler. Check today's TV listings. There is.

Three miles south from the city centre I alight at the expansive *Luitpoldhain*. Nuremberg was always an ideal location to host a party. Its distinguished past as part of the Holy Roman Empire lent historical credence to lesser, more contemporary undertakings. It was geographically central within the Third Reich and became a national shrine under the National Socialist German Workers Party. It is deserted today but in the 1930s half a million people would arrive on an annual basis for a *Reichsparteitag*, a party congress and rally. Each annual rally had a programmatic title relating to recent national events. In 1933 the rally was called the Rally of Victory, followed by the 1934 Rally of Unity and Strength, the 1935 Rally of Freedom, the 1936 Rally of Honour, and so on. All went well on an annual basis until 1939 when the Rally of Peace, due to start on 2 September, was cancelled at short notice because the day before that, Germany had invaded Poland.

I am in the largest open-air museum of Nazi architecture and they didn't do things by half. Within eleven square kilometres there was a parade arena, a congress hall, a stadium, a two-kilometre-long Great Road, a marching field, barracks and camp. Much of the natural stone underfoot was quarried by slave labour at Flossenbürg and Mauthausen. The parade arena is designed to be impressive and momentous and makes me feel small and insignificant, so I will do what I am told to do by the great leader up there on the steps. I contemplate matters alone. If events had transpired differently, they would still visit once a year.

The principal preoccupations at these week-long rallies were standing about, flag-waving, boot stomping, torchlight parades, wearing of smart uniforms and widespread swearing, mostly of allegiances. The organisational reality was somewhat different, as documented in reports by officials at the time:

'The torchlight parade of the political leaders was nothing less than a disaster. Most were totally unaware they had marched past the Führer. Pushing people onwards all the time and the non-stop marching we see every year causes total confusion. It was, in plain and simple German – embarrassing.'

'Experience gained at prior rallies led to the Nuremberg red light district being cordoned off. One couldn't help noticing the political leaders, who enjoy more freedom of movement at rallies, repeatedly tried to get into these streets despite the latter being conspicuously cordoned off by SS guards day and night.'

'The public toilets to the right and left of the War Memorial are hopelessly inadequate. As a result the participants used the walls of the War Memorial itself.'

'It is noticeable that Congress speeches cannot be heard anywhere despite being transmitted.'

The Documentation Centre is located in the Congress Hall, built to hold 50,000 but never completed. I climb the suspended glass and steel walkway, a 130-metre long shaft piercing the heart of the granite building, a permanent demonstration of the fatal disabling of the National Socialists. Inside, the powerful exhibition is upon walls of unrendered brick, another break with the past; black and white photographs of the public queuing to buy tickets to attend like some modern day rock concert, Hess in full flight before he bottled it and fled to Scotland, postcard sets and nice souvenirs to take home from the rally for the wife.

It's the aftermath that impresses. With deep irony, Courtroom 600 of the Palace of Justice in Nuremberg was chosen by the Allies for the post-mortem. Over 218 days 240 witnesses faced 21 accused as 300,000 statements were admitted in evidence. There's an open page from a US magazine featuring twelve pictures of the hanged, their names on the bodies, eyes bloodied, pictures never printed in the UK. The courtroom is still in use today, albeit for much lesser offences. I exit this museum of unnatural history. The return trip takes me along a pedestrian boulevard, with the distraction of on-coming roller bladers and the pleasure boaters at ease in the man-made lake. Today remnants of a fun-fair linger in the *Nürnberger Volkspark*. A circus of a different sort is now in town. The party animals are long gone.

Next morning I expect to take an Air Berlin flight but outside the terminal is a Niki Air Airbus 320. Air Berlin own a 24 per cent stake in Niki, the only low fares airline to date founded by a former Formula One racing driver. He is suffering from an identity crisis since his other aircraft sport the Lauda Air logos on their tails. Mick is not impressed at rumours of the two airlines merging. '*If you put two expensive, loss-making airlines together, then you just get another even more expensive and even greater loss-making airline.*'

The Niki cabin crew sport amazing in-flight uniforms. I am in disbelief. I am one of the first to board and initially I was under the impression that the contract cleaners had yet to leave. The happy young girls wear a silver one-piece sleeveless house coat down to the knee, with wide red shoulder flashes and loose red belts hanging free. Underneath anything goes, that is, they wear what they want. Some prefer plain T-shirts, others favour tops of all colours. They wear jeans, and fashionably distressed ones at that. Shoes are flat and are mostly sneakers. Smart Casual has gone too far. Last time I saw a flashy shiny uniform like this the eager crew were refuelling an F1 car at Monaco (have I used that line before?).

We have assigned seating so no cattle herding is required. The F1 girls breeze through the cabin offering a choice of free newspapers.

After we take off there's a video overhead with cartoons, sports, Nicole Kidman and Mr Bean, which surely addresses everyone's tastes. There's something amazingly comforting about watching Mr Bean clean his ears with an electric toothbrush in the midst of chortling Germans.

The F1 girls dispense food and drink. I watch again in disbelief. No one seems to be paying for the food and drink. The passengers ahead of me are the biggest bunch of low fares freeloaders I have ever encountered. Soon it's my turn. I risk all and ask for an orange juice and sandwich. Both are free. More disbelief. I check the menu card. Only the beers and spirits cost us. And all this in a forty-minute flight. The world has gone mad. Free food and drink are nice. I mean I don't expect free food and drink if I take a one-hour bus or train trip. Niki's motto is *Double Satisfaction*. So it can indeed be better to travel than to arrive.

I am grateful to be landing at Vienna's international airport. If I flew on Ruinair they would deposit me at Vienna (Bratislava). That's their brackets, not mine. I mean Bratislava is not even in Austria. But Vienna airport is chaos, with smoky hazes and cramped Arrivals halls, looking much like a poor man's Germany. I've been to Vienna before, fifteen years ago. Myself and a colleague were working in Frankfurt for a few weeks and went bank-insane in Bankfurt and needed a change. We flew for a weekend on Lufthansa for three hundred quid return for a forty-minute flight plus more ruddy prawns and warm wine.

It was soon after the Berlin Wall tumbled and the city was invaded by Eastern Europeans making their first touristic forays into the West. Matching stone-washed denim jackets and jeans were big behind the Curtain. They arrived by road in beat-up, diesel-spewing Czech and Hungarian coaches salvaged from the last war and they parked in snaking rows along side-streets. The strength of the *Schilling* proved too much for their pockets so they lived in the coaches, brewing steamy stews on gas stoves on the pavement, drinking from crates of giant Budvar bottles and sleeping inside the coaches. They were the first low fares tourists. Ourselves plus ten thousand denim fashion victims went to the Prater amusement park, only I didn't find it so amusing. I wished to ride the Ferris wheel as seen in *The Third Man* movie. But my colleague made me take a ride in an amusement torture instrument that churned my guts for ten minutes and spat me out as green as the grass on which I deposited my lunch. I have not experienced such violent turbulence since.

Last time I saw all the traditional city sights. The *Stephansdom* cathedral is still maintained by the same folks who clean Cologne's cathedral. At the *Lipizzaner* riding school the horses pranced like they had something itchy up their behinds. I checked out the *Staatsoper*, Vienna's opera house, built by Sicardsburg and Null in the 1860s, which received such appalling reviews from the general public that Null soon committed suicide and Sicardsburg died shortly afterwards. Mozart is big here, but even bigger are Mozart liqueurs, Mozart busts, Mozart CDs, Mozart cameos and Mozart mugs. The latter are the folks who buy these souvenirs. One does not go to Vienna for the culture, art, music, shopping and history since one would be here for weeks, if not months. So this time I have decided that I'm going to do basically fuck all in Vienna. I don't feel so bad about this since the locals don't do much either, but sit about all day drinking coffee in cafés.

The Turkish army arrived at Vienna in 1683 without a formal invitation. Besieged and desperate, the Viennese needed a volunteer who could pass through Turkish lines to get a message to nearby Polish troops. Franz George Kolshitsky, who spoke fairly good Turkish and Arabic lingo, took on the assignment disguised in a Turkish uniform. Kolshitsky (and what a great surname he has because I would never mess with a guy called Kolshitsky) completed his valiant deed, returning to give the Viennese the news of the Poles' imminent rescue of their city. The Turks were ejected from Vienna, leaving everything they brought: camels, tents, honey, and bags of brown beans which were first thought to be camel feed.

Kolshitsky, having lived in the Arab world for several years, knew these were bags of coffee. Using the money bestowed on him by the mayor for his heroic deed, Kolshitsky bought the Turks' coffee, opened Central Europe's first coffee house, *The Blue Bottle* (since swatted), and brought coffee to a suspicious Vienna. His first efforts were foul but later others accidentally added sugar, and milk. Once the Viennese mastered the process of filtering, coffee houses appeared everywhere. Painters went to one, politicians went to another. Kurt Tucholsky, whoever he is, said a coffee house is a place where you feel at home, even though you're not at home. By 1900 there were 600 coffee houses in Vienna.

Coffee here is, like perfume, an obsession. The Austrian poet Tallyerand, a household name to his friends and a legend in his own coffee break, opined that coffee *has to be hot like hell, dark as the devil, pure like an angel and sweet as love.* Another local said that the Viennese coffee house is an institution without parallel anywhere else in the world, a democratic club where the cost of admission is no more than the price of a cup of coffee. I am about to find out as I walk the *Herrengasse* to the most famous café.

Stepping inside *Café Central* is like walking onto a stage. All eyes turn to look at me, then refocus on a cup, a newspaper or a conversation. I have walked through an open door yet there is no welcome. It feels like an old gentlemen's club. It seems as old as time, like some movie set. There are isolated white marble tables and long red drapes in the vaulted room. The walls are off-white and drab. A piano is audible from somewhere. Everyone has seen me except any of the staff. I walk around the room. There are no spare tables. No one moves to leave. I am in no man's land. The psychologist Alfred Adler took coffee here while working on his new theory of the 'inferiority complex' so presumably he too waited to be seated.

It was in *Café Central* that the Mayor of Vienna Karl Lueger met a young Russian emigrant called Laib Bronstein, better known as Mr Trotsky. A civil servant of the Austrian Ministry of Foreign Affairs chatting to a colleague in the café about the possibility of a revolution in Russia once pointed over at the idle Trotsky and shrugged his shoulders, 'Who do you think is going to lead a revolution? Him over there?' Inside the door is a life-size figure of the bohemian Peter Altenberg who drank here so often that he gave friends the café address as his own. Felix Salten came here. He wrote books called *Bambi* and the *Memoirs of Josephine Mutzenbacher* (the latter being a classic Austrian erotic tale of a

high-priced Viennese courtesan aka prostitute which includes the
memorable line '*He rubbed his rugged little plough against my
untilled furrows*'.) Walt Disney later made one of Salten's books
into a kiddies' cartoon movie.

The waiters in white shirts, aprons and bow-ties pivot about the
tables like ballerinas. They can do amazing things like balancing
trays of ten cups on each arm but they have rubbish eyesight. Or
maybe they saw through me two streets away. There's no point
trying to attract their attention. The more I might wave and holler
or stand on the table and fornicate, the more they will ignore me.
They will assist me when they are good and ready. I might as well
wear a large sign around my neck: '*I am a bloody tourist.*' One local
has described the waiters here as prison warders who tolerate the
prisoners' escapades. The waiters in *Café Central* could work as
cabin crew on Ruinair. They have all passed the *Post Graduate
Diploma Course in Rudeness, Disinterest and Naked Customer
Hostility*. I am still no nearer to finding a seat until I see a space at
the rear but it's marked 'Reserved'. I don't feel at home here.
Suddenly the door bursts open and forty tourists led by a woman
with a brolly and a flag arrive en masse. I am outta here *espresso*
fast.

Café Hawalka on *Dorotheergasse* is more my cup of coffee. It's
off the beaten track. Inside the door a genial old gent aged 100
points me to a vacant table. The room is dark, lit only by five light
bulbs. Old posters hang on musty peeling walls. The solo waiter is
superbly rude and hostile, barging past people but taking orders
from no one. He must have a Masters degree. So I play his game
and don't look like I want to order. Soon he comes over to me,
perhaps out of curiosity, and asks me what I want. I win.

The coffee menus are extensive. In the 1920s the *Café Herrenhof*
had a waiter who brought around a colour chart with twenty
variations of the colour brown from which you ordered a number
and he delivered the brew as ordered. The worst mistake I could
make here is to simply order a coffee. I would be laughed out of
town. It's important to know there's a strong *Mokka*, a coffee *mit
Schlag* (whipped cream), a frothy *Melange*, a *Fiaker* with brandy
and a cherry on top, or a sweet *Turkish* brought in a copper pot.

'*Ein Kapuziner.*' That's cappuccino in Austrian but I'm showing him I am well-versed in local matters.

'Eh?' he retorts.

'*Kapuziner, bitte.*'

'Eh?' He's about to leave me to slowly die of thirst in a dark corner. I must relent. He wins.

'A cappuccino, please.'

With each *Kapuziner* the waiter insists on also bringing me a small glass of water on the silver tray. The water is free and cleanses my palate but it serves another purpose. When the cafés are busy an empty glass means that I am ready to order again. I test the theory. I down the water. The waiter soon reappears. A guy at the next table scribbles in a journal. This place must be for us writers. I am among my own. I read a newspaper. Others come and go. As some regulars leave, the genial gent shakes their hands in gratitude at their custom. Soon I am the longest serving customer in residence. I nod to the old gent as I leave. Maybe, if I come here every day for the next ten years, he might shake my hand one day as I leave.

Flushed with success I am ready for the top end of the market. Ten minutes' stroll along the gracious and stylish *Kärntnerstrasse* brings me to the Hotel Sacher and its café, famed the world over, or at least in Vienna. Here's a tip. Turn up at five minutes to midday like I did when it's closed, grab the best corner table under the outside awning, order when they open at midday and watch the others fight for a space. I order a coffee plus a slice of *Sacher-Torte* cake, which arrives with a blob of cream on the side. In this cake rests the proud history of Café Sacher. A prince called Metternich gave a posh dinner party one night in 1832 and told his chef to make a damn fine dessert. 'Be sure not to bring shame on me tonight.' The chef fell ill, so his apprentice, Franz Sacher, made the dessert that was to found a café dynasty. It's good.

I linger awhile as I watch couples close by, often amazed at how two people can converse so little. The bill for a coffee and cake comes to eight euro and forty cents. I fall off my cushion and chair. As I pay, a German couple muscles in to grab my table before I have even stood up. I tell them as politely as I can to clear off since what I have paid amounts to a short-term rental of prime real estate and I'm not budging.

Unsurprisingly these institutional cafés are under threat with only two hundred left and it's not only because of their prices. Along a side-street a *McCafé* serves coffee and cakes to a younger generation for half the price but they throw in yellow plastic seats and the lingering aroma of a greasy Big Mac. Workmen on the other side of the street hang a new sign for another branch of Starbucks as they cannibalise Vienna. It seems the more established premises are only frequented by us aging has-beans of this coffee society.

My last stop is the grand *Café Landtmann* on the *Ringstrasse* at the Burgtheatre. It's packed outside with the beautiful people in black and makes the Sacher look cheap. I dare not venture inside unless I first call *MasterCard* and inquire as to their current interest rates. Sigmund Freud used to take his coffee here, giving rise to what later became known as a Freudian sip. Freud founded the theory of psycho-analysis which is expounded simply as follows: '*If anything bad happens to you in life, you can blame your mother.*'

Vienna is a city where people like to be watched, rather than to watch. No one is in a hurry to work, or to even leave a café. I read there is one café with a sign saying: '*Sorry we do not cater for people who are in a hurry*'. I have gleaned much about Vienna's population of 1,600,000: 38% are alabaster Japanese tourists in sun hats, taking odd photographs as Asians do, in awkward positions; 22% are rushing Russians having a bad hair day, still in stone-washed denim; 11% are trainee cartographers working on a better city map of Vienna; 9% are ladies who lunch on the *Kärntnerstrasse* but alas ignore me; 3% are suited businessmen evidently in the wrong city; 2% are locals in traditional Strauss and Mozart garb with white powdered wigs and dandy costumes of pattered gilded designs, neat waistcoats and ruffled shirts.

The latter category of folk harass me most. They are everywhere selling nightly trips to the opera at *Schloss Schönbrunn* outside Vienna and other grand venues. If you sit on the wall by the Opera House for any length of time you will be outnumbered by these tourist to tourist salesmen, so much so that small passing children turn to their parents as they point at me. 'Mummy, why is that Irishman over there wearing chinos and a shirt?'

One of the vendors approaches me with a clipboard. 'Would you like to go to a concert tonight?'

'That's very kind, and I am here on my own, but I hardly know you. Let's go for a coffee first.'

Germany ... more

Air Berlin Flight AB8181 – Wednesday @ 8.10am
– VIE-DUS

Fare €1 plus taxes, fees and charges €28

Austrian Airlines is fucked. This is evident when you arrive in Terminal 1 of Vienna's airport at 7am to view their Departures hall with rows of waiting check-in staff and miles of red ropes for passengers. The only problem is that there are no passengers checking in. This coupled with the fact that their staff wear jaded red uniforms including red stockings for the ladies, making them appear like waiting storks on a day off from the zoo. Did I omit to mention Austrian Airlines lost a staggering €930 million in the first six months of a recent year? Mick is amazed at Austrian Airlines' decision to reintroduce free meals for its economy class passengers. *'Nothing's for free on Ruinair flights, we sell everything. Not like these idiots in Austrian.'*

All the action is happening across the road in Terminal 2 where Air Berlin are packing them in. I am not even sure I will be flying on a German airline today. After the Second World War, only aircraft from the Allied powers were allowed to land in Berlin, so for this reason, Air Berlin Inc. was founded in 1978 in Oregon, USA, by a former PanAm captain from Portland, USA, called Kim Lundgren. The first aircraft had Air Berlin USA plastered on the side. So they are not some German *Hans-come-lately* low fares airline.

In April 1979 the first Herr Berlin flight took off from Berlin-

Tegel, their home base, to Mallorca. Germany's favourite holiday island is still the prime destination of their route network, with 360 flights per week there in the summer months, earning the airline the rather unenviable title of the *Mallorca Shuttle.* Today 36 per cent of all passengers who step off an aircraft at Palma airport in Mallorca do so from Herr Berlin, and their appetite is whetted and sated by the pages of Mallorca property adverts in the in-flight magazine.

More flights to the Med were followed by others to European cities such that they connect 20 German places, such as the well-known Paderborn-Lippstadt and Munster-Osnabrück airports, to 67 destinations in Europe and North Africa. Their advertisements proclaim they cut fares, not service, and fares include taxes and charges. '*And a smile.*' First impressions are good in my close encounters with their staff. Twenty million passengers annually cannot be wrong. And they're German. They're the fussiest of all passengers.

We are greeted at the foot of the steps to the B737 aircraft by a tall male crew member in a dark uniform. Unlike Ruinair cabin crew he shaved this morning and washed his hair this week. He welcomes each passenger. '*Morgen*'. It costs nothing but it's priceless. I can't tell if he's a flight attendant or the pilot. Inside, the blonde in a burgundy jacket could be on the cover of the in-flight magazine. As it happens they have Claudia Schiffer on the cover instead, which suffices perfectly for the eighty-minute flight north-east. Staff uniforms are designed by the famous Jette Joop, whilst George at ASDA still designs the Ruinair staff uniforms? Like Niki there are free newspapers, sweeties, soft drinks and food, plus more videos. There must be some catch here. There's a chance they'll ask me for more money as I deplane. But they don't.

Herr Berlin began life with two old B707 aircraft serving the West Berlin holiday market to the sun, has grown organically, and bought DBA (the old Deutsche British Airways airline) and TUI (a German charter airline) to become the third largest low fares carrier in Europe, after Ruinair and EzJet. Germany is the low fares capital of Europe with three excellent domestic low fares airlines. Ruinair only fly to a small number of destinations in Germany, but they fly to many more in France and Italy, all three countries having a similar-sized population. The message from Herr Berlin to Ruinair is clear. *Stay out of our back yard.*

Last year Herr Berlin was voted the world's best low fares airline by the industry's leading passenger survey, Skytrax. More than 13 million passengers in 94 countries took part in the survey and most agree with me. I don't know why any German national would choose Ruinair over a domestic low fares carrier. Flying Ruinair in Germany is like shopping in Aldi but knowing there is a Marks & Spencer or a Sainsbury store nearby where the prices are also Lidl. *Herr Berlin, bitte fly direct to Dublin very soon. Danke. Paul.*

Ireland

Aer Lingus Flight EI699 – Sunday @ 8.30pm – DUS-DUB

Fare €0 plus taxes, fees and charges €33

Herr Berlin do not fly to Dublin, nor anywhere west of Stansted, so the flight from Vienna deposits me in Düsseldorf. I pray that I'm at the correct airport. I read a web tale about the confusion of Ruinair passengers so I test the theory as I approach the guy at the information desk at Düsseldorf International airport.

'Hi, do Ruinair fly from this airport?'

'Nein, sir, very sorry to say, they do not. Weeze.'

It's been a long walk with heavy luggage. 'Yes, I know. I'm a bit unfit.'

'No. Weeze. They go from Weeze airport.' He advises Düsseldorf airport welcomes people each day who ask for the Ruinair check-in desk only to be told that Ruinair fly from the airport of Weeze, a former RAF base seventy kilometres and one hour's drive from Düsseldorf on the autobahn.

'How do I get there?' I wheeze.

'Do you have a car?'

'No. Can I take a train?'

'There's no train. There's a bus.'

'Excellent. From here?'

'From Düsseldorf train station. You must go back into the city to catch the bus.' He hands me a photocopied A4 map with hand-drawn arrows and two airport logos. 'So many passengers find themselves at the wrong airport that we have a map to give out explaining how to get to Weeze.'

From the moment of my arrival at the Aer Lingus desk in Düsseldorf airport this is a different experience. There are two queues at my check-in. One queue is long and is called *Economy*. The other queue consists of one Suit and is called *Premier / Gold Circle*. I chance my luck and join the shorter queue. I am checked in within a minute and receive a boarding card for seat 17c. They assign seats. Nice touch.

The check-in lady is most welcoming. 'Flying by yourself today, sir?'

'Yes, I'm a big boy now. And I've been on an airplane before on my own.'

Aer Lingus has been turned around by management. They used to lose a hundred million euro per year, now they make that much. Their motto is *Low Fares, Way Better*. And they are not wrong. They erred a few years ago when they hired international brand consultants to advise on a new logo for the airline. After several months' work and a few million punts, the consultants reverted with one suggestion. '*Er, why don't we get the big green shamrock on the tail to lean a bit to the right?*' The airline, however, does have a propensity for industrial action and can strike faster than a safety match. When they do strike the Chief Executive of the Labour Relations Commission is none too impressed when Mick offers sincere advice to Aer Lingus. '*The kind of Monty Pythonesque slapstick he engages in, I don't think can be taken seriously.*'

The airline is prone to the odd PR gaffe such as when a 40-page Human Resources strategic plan was leaked to the press, outlining 'environmental push factors', nice words for measures to get rid of staff and encourage them to avail of a voluntary redundancy programme. The push factors listed in the plan ranged from changes to shift patterns which would be unsuitable for employees with families, to tedious training programmes for surplus pilots and telling two hundred supervisors they had no future. The plan suggested changing the cabin crew uniform to encourage cabin crew to leave, specifically that cabin crew, including older cabin crew, would have to abandon their current uniform for tight jumpsuits and clinging т-shirts.

But Aer Lingus remain my favourite Irish airline, the nation's national airline, and they have an increasingly winning proposition and here's why. If I wanted to fly one-way to Frankfurt five years ago, I had a choice of a 100 euro fare on Aer Lingus or a 10 euro fare on Ruinair. I know that I would have chosen Ruinair and saved 90 euros in the process. But today Aer Lingus have flights to Frankfurt for a mere 19 euros and Ruinair have flights for one cent. Saving 19 euros is of little interest to me. It's the price of a round, or at least it was the price of four beers last time I bought a round in a pub in 2003. In the future Aer Lingus' fares will go even lower, but Ruinair fares are unlikely to go lower than one cent. So now I choose Aer Lingus and fly to an airport actually close to Frankfurt on an Irish airline staffed by significantly friendlier cabin crew.

And as we grow older and wiser, the bottom line matters less, and convenience matters more. If I want to take a trip to Berlin I choose Aer Lingus, which departs Dublin at 11.40am. It will be dearer than Ruinair's fare but no one could pay me enough money to take Ruinair's flight at 6.05am.

My most memorable trip on Aer Lingus was made over a decade ago. It was in the good old days when Ireland won the Eurovision Song Contest annually because every other country wanted to come party next year in Europe's then hippest capital. I took a flight from Heathrow to Dublin two days before the contest only to find Terry Wogan sitting a few seats away from me. He cracked jokes non-stop. Before we landed he got up and disappeared from our view into the cockpit to see the landing up close. It was a truly horrendous touchdown, a sort of a *nul points* for the two wobbly pilots. As we taxied to the terminal Terry reappeared, all smiles, rubbing his hands. 'Now that wasn't too bad for my first time ever landing a plane.'

At the departure gate I am further assured this is not a low fares airline. There is an aircraft with a tilting shamrock on the tail. I hear the voices of Irish passengers who arrive before we depart. Three crew members in their Paul Costelloe designed uniforms are here too but they speed past me on their way to the duty-free shop. Sure, there's no hurry here for a quick turnaround. *Let's go shopping.* On their return two of the crew stop for a ciggy break in the smoking area. Very professional. Come to think of it you never see Ruinair crew smoking between flights, what with all that aviation fuel about. I wonder do Ruinair even hire smokers? Twenty ciggies per day at five minutes each is a lot of down time. Next the pilot passes by with two bulging duty-free carrier bags. Evidently he has a second job running an off-licence in Dublin. But the ever-efficient German ground handling staff are a step ahead of them all and cunningly announce a boarding call while the last crew member is still swiping her plastic in duty free. Passengers queue in the gangway as she pushes past to reach the cabin to greet them, bottles clanking as she gets back to work.

One of the airport officials at the counter suddenly makes an announcement and calls out a passenger name. Mine. *Would I make myself known please?*

I look up from my paperback. What have I done wrong? *Crimewatch* here I come.

'Your boarding card please, sir.' I hand it over like some guilty suspect. 'You were in 17C, sir.'

He's used the past tense. He's bumping me off? 'I certainly am.'

He tears my boarding card in two, slowly and deliberately. I am in big trouble. I assume that ranks of police armed with Uzis will now descend upon us. I don't look like *that* much of a terrorist suspect on a good day, except when I don't shave for a few days and wear those torn jeans and white sneakers.

'Not anymore, sir.' I am deflated. He produces a new boarding card as if by magic. 'Seat 1C, sir.'

A gang of gougers from Dublin board the aircraft and pass by. There's about twenty of them, maybe it's a soccer team plus coaching staff, not Celtic FC despite their gear. They are the worse for *Holsten Pils.*

'Now folks, next stop Terenure. Any more for Terenuuuuuure now, pleeeeaaaaaase?'

We depart Düsseldorf on time. Fifteen years ago an aircraft left a German airport five minutes after its scheduled departure time but it hasn't happened since. They shot the pilot, all the ground handling staff resigned en masse, the departure gate was permanently closed and shrouded in a black silk awning and a small bronze plaque was placed on a nearby wall to commemorate the terrible event that blights a nation.

I sit in the best seat in the aircraft. The cabin crew always smile at me except once when they caught me reading Mick's autobiography on a flight. I am close to the cabin crew and it's good fun. They talk to each other out of sight. I eavesdrop. It's slightly boring stuff, upcoming weddings, who's seeing who, scandal, where they have been and where they will go to next. There's a minor crisis when the gaggle of four crew can't all fit into the curtained area at the same time. On this airline they hire budding chat show hosts as cabin crew. We Irish do like a good old chat. German O_2 mobile phone customers spend on average 118 minutes on their mobiles per month while UK customers spend 137 minutes. The Irish spend 209 minutes. Being a flight attendant is truly a wonderful job. You get paid to see all the globe and all you have to do is serve drinks and peanuts and pull a little luggage trolley around the world's airports in a nice smart uniform. Note you will never see any Ruinair flight attendants pulling luggage in airports. They are too busy working.

I read the incredibly exciting *Business Traveller* magazine, nicked from a hotel lobby, where there's a letter from a reader about the time he was at the coffee stand in a major carrier lounge at Heathrow when he encountered an elderly American lady who was wandering about with two cups of black coffee.

'Do you know where there's some cream?' she asked.

He didn't so he watched her in turn approach a city gentleman in a sombre suit.

'Do you know how I can get cream?' she asked.

He replied, 'Madam, I believe it's part of the pasteurisation process of cow's milk.' And he left.

Across the aisle a female passenger opens up a monster 500-page Sudoku book and she begins to fill in the numbers, repetitive grid by repetitive grid. There is no greater waste of time or brain matter known to man. She would do far better to read a book and expand her mind. Buy a book dear, preferably this one. But I see the light. She reveals herself to be a nervous flyer as her speed and mental focus improve once we hit bad turbulence. There's a guy sitting to my right reading a rather boring cycling magazine. I assume in all likelihood based on my extensive European research to date he must be Dutch. He turns the next page to the regular monthly feature. It's called *Great Rides*. I twist to read more. Now that's my sort of magazine. I accept a chilled drink from the bar and select a complimentary *Sunday Independent* to read. I smell hot food. I dine on twirly pasta shells with roast chicken and veggies and it's very edible, complemented by cheese and bikkies and *Lir* chocolates. The best thing is no one asks me to pay a cent.

Back behind the curtain a German with a suit and laptop pays for his coffee and food. Unbelievably he asks the crew for a receipt. I turn around. He repeats the request insistently. Yes, he needs a receipt. They have no alternative but to go forward and write something down for him to pocket. It's not their phone numbers. I'm tempted to ask him who he works for. They must be the tightest company in Europe. And he must be their tightest employee. I hope his Accounts Department accepts expenses on paper napkins.

There is a hot towel service before we begin to descend. I am refreshed and relaxed. We make our approach as the cabin crew announce we will be *on the ground* in ten minutes. I wish they wouldn't make such alarmist announcements. I prefer to *land* than to be *on the ground*. A final cabin announcement is delivered after we touch down and taxi towards the terminal. '*If any passenger has been on a farm or in contact with livestock or live poultry, would they please make themselves known to an official from the Department of Agriculture inside the terminal building.*' This was a reasonable request during the Foot and Mouth emergency but now it's frankly embarrassing. Do I look like the sort to spend my summer holidays frolicking about with sheep? I am arriving from one of the biggest urban conurbations in Western Europe and I am not wearing my wellies or Barbour. Sometimes I feel like going up to the civil servants who sit at their desks reading the *Evening Herald* and telling them I had bacon, egg and sausage for breakfast.

Over the years I've heard some good one-liners from fellow EI passengers sitting a few seats back when landing in Dublin. It's what we do best. Once when a pilot subjected us to a fairly horrendous landing, a guy behind exclaimed, *'Jaysus, did we land or were we shot down?'* and another time when a female pilot subjected us to an equally truly horrendous landing (on the basis that anything a man can do a woman can do equally well), a Dub piped up from row 21, *'I'd hate to see her parking her car.'*

Nothing beats the exchange on a US airline after another very bad landing. A passenger leant into the cockpit as he was getting off and asked, 'Now that we have stopped, did one of you guys check to see if the wheels were ever lowered?' The savvy pilot expertly and instantly replied, 'We were pretty sure the wheels were down, otherwise it would have taken full power to taxi the plane to the terminal building.'

Today's flight cost me nothing. Mick has a view on claims that Ireland is expensive for tourists: *'That's a lot of shite. Ireland is expensive to get to but we are changing that.'* Flights for nothing are rare but not impossible. We can enjoy them if we work hard. A few months earlier I went on a work trip to LA, San Diego and New York. The trip, like the American Express card, had its benefits — a chunk of airmiles.

But take care because these business perks can be abused. A Middle Eastern airline once offered free flights to wives who accompanied their husbands when they booked First Class. It was a huge success, so much so that the publicity department of the airline wrote to many of the wives asking for a valuable testimonial on how much they enjoyed their trip. Most of the replies were short and to the point. 'What trip?'

This airline seems to like my custom because they sent me a *Gold Circle* card in the post soon after. It was enough to garner the upgrade from *Economy* to *Premier* (when they used to have a Premier cabin to Europe). This is the lowest fares airline of all. Zilch Air. I love Aer Lingus. *'Enjoy your flight.'* Mick has a view, as ever. *'If anyone thinks Aer Lingus is a low fares airline, they are smoking dope.'*

Switzerland

Helvetic Flight 2L009 – Friday @ 7.00pm
– DUB-LTN-ZRH-LTN-DUB

Fare €38 plus taxes, fees and charges €144

When the first Swiss 'low fares' airline opened for business, the more established airlines in Europe had already claimed the optimal liveries: yellow, blue, white, red, green and other primary colours. Helvetic Airlines' only option was thus to paint its aircraft shocking pink, earning it the nickname in the Swiss media of *The Barbie Airline*. Barbie's maiden flight was grounded due to an engine failure on their sole aircraft, leaving eighty Vienna-bound passengers marooned at their Zurich home base. Barbie uses Fokker 100 aircraft to fly to fifteen European destinations, but a few weeks before I fly, they terminate four routes, fire pilots and cabin crew and reduce their fleet to a mere four aircraft. On this airline every eleventh flight is free but I will never stay the course to claim my freebie trip. The odds are that by the time you read this they will have gone the way of many other low fares start-up upstarts and have only zero aircraft. I use the term 'low fare' loosely since nothing Swiss can ever be considered cheap, except perhaps their chocolate.

On board we are in the pink. The seats have pink headrests. The immaculate and smart crew sport pink name badges, pink neck scarves and pink ties. A male passenger removes his salmon pink tie. A female passenger wishes she hadn't worn her pink sweater in case we ask her for a G&T. A crew member demonstrates Swiss efficiency by using a hand-held counter to count the passengers but it's unnecessary because there are only forty of us on board, which is further proof this airline won't be flying in a year's time.

There are complimentary newspapers and a pink in-flight magazine. Inside the latter is an article on a holiday weekend in Nottingham which in itself is no mean feat. I read Nottingham was previously called Snottingham. In line with Swiss tradition the menu is focused on health and wellness, with half the menu devoted to *Carpe Diem* botanic water, mixed fruit bowls, cheeses and fresh seasonal salads. The detail is pure Swiss so we learn the salmon comes from Norway but the chicken and beef from Switzerland and Brazil. Unlike Ruinair the drinks we purchase come with a napkin, ice, lemon, a plastic stirrer and a smile. We swoop over the Alps, all chocolate-box hills and valleys. Switzerland is the neatest country in the world. We traverse Europe's longest river. If I founded a Swiss low fares airline, I would call it *RhineAir*. It would be sure to generate another storm of controversy and legal action, plus many accidental bookings.

The aircraft at Zurich international airport are mostly local. The Swiss are a shrewd bunch. They had a national airline called SwissAir which had red livery and a fleet of Airbuses but it went bankrupt, the staff lost their jobs and the creditors' bills went unpaid, so the Swiss formed a new airline called Swiss with red livery and a fleet of Airbuses, rehired all the same staff but left the bills unpaid. How very Swiss. The other three planes in the Barbie fleet are parked alongside for the night. It's 9.30pm. This is a worry. If this was Ruinair they would be setting off for a midnight run to some outpost near Barcelona or Stockholm.

We disembark and the captain stands at the door to the cockpit and thanks us for flying today. A crew member offers pink luggage stickers, postcards of pink planes, pink souvenirs and pink chocolates. I can't help thinking that this is what is meant by customer service, rather than meaningless statistics about lost baggage and the speed of replying to all the complaints.

I check in to a city centre hotel but cause consternation when I complete their extensive paperwork.

'Can you write your ZIP code please?' the receptionist requests, unimpressed with my handiwork.

'We don't have ZIP codes in Ireland.'

'You don't have ZIPS in Ireland?'

ZIPS are what I use to keep myself decent when out in public. 'We don't.'

'Are you sure?' she persists.

I have only lived there for forty years. 'I'm sure.'

She turns to her colleague. 'They don't have ZIP codes in Ireland.' Swiss tourism grinds to a halt.

There's nothing better than flying on a new airline and arriving in a new city. Well, nothing apart from mutually climactic orgasmic sex or a large-size *Mars* bar all to oneself, but travel comes a close second. If Switzerland is viewed as a large blot with its outer margins leaking into eastern France, southern Germany and northern Italy, then Zurich lies in the north of the world's biggest pen and ink disaster. It's fantastic to be here because this is the best place to live in the world. And that's not my opinion but that of the experts who compile the annual *Mercer Quality of Life Survey*.

Once again Zurich is tops, tied with glorious Geneva and ahead of venerable Vancouver and Vienna. Frankfurt is in fifth place. The survey is based on several quality determinants including healthcare, infrastructure, culture, housing, traffic congestion, pollution, sanitation and safety. The nice men at Zurich tourism, *Downtown Switzerland*, rarely mention this is the seventh most expensive city in the world. The worst place to live in the world according to the survey is sunny Baghdad. The tourist office also provides a wonderful guide to Swiss cities in which you have to thumb through countless cities in alphabetical order before turning to what you think is almost the last page with Zurich. But it's bloody Zug.

No one can argue that Switzerland is not safe. Despite being eternally neutral, it has one of the largest armies per capita in the world. Every male citizen keeps a gas mask in his house, along with a rifle and a box of ammunition sealed by the government for emergency use. Every male citizen undergoes seventeen weeks of military training and returns yearly for a three-week refresher course until aged thirty-six, after which it is only two weeks, and so on until retirement. In the rail station I see proof that the conscripts are allowed to bring sub-machine-guns home for the weekend. The Swiss skilfully dealt with both sides in all world wars, despite the shock of the US Air Force accidentally bombing Zurich on 4 March 1945, traded with both sides and permitted German trains to run from Germany to Italy across their border. They have not seen war for 500 years yet possess mountain fortifications and keep jets in Alpine caves.

Switzerland does not *have* an army; rather it *is* an army, and one so successful that its pen-knives can be purchased worldwide. The Swiss army has a somewhat chequered past such as in 1292 when Zurich was about to be overrun by the imperial Habsburgs after the menfolk were soundly beaten. The women of Zurich donned the body armour of their men and scared the invaders away by convincing them they had to face yet another army. Swiss males like to spend weekends practising marksmanship, much like the Swiss citizen William Tell. It's safe too to cross streets here. When I step within ten feet of a zebra crossing, irrespective of whether I intend to use it or not, all cars within a five-mile radius grind to a screeching halt. Zurchers spend hours every day standing on deserted streets, looking at a red man yet to turn envious green. My white sneakers get dirty stares again. I don't know why because I'm flying the flag here. These shoes are *K-Swiss*.

Housing is of a high quality but don't ever try to rent a communal apartment around these parts. When you sign the contract, a list of the house rules, *Hausordnung,* will be attached. There are many rules in life but nothing compares to life in Switzerland. You may not make any loud noise from 10pm to 6am, and this includes music or using the shower, dishwasher or washing machine, and you may not flush the toilet, and in some instances gentlemen are asked to sit down to avoid any offensive splashing noise. Net curtains at the windows are often required. No children playing at the playground between noon and 2pm. No washing your car on a Sunday. No laundry or vacuuming after 9pm or on a Sunday. If you all share a communal laundry room you will have an assigned washing day and will be required to clean and dry the washing machine and its ruddy filter after use. All this in a country where women could not vote until 1972 and the women of Alpenzell only won the right in 1991 to stand beside their husbands in the town square to vote by hand. Switzerland only joined the UN in 2004, along with East Timor, and still refuses to join the EU.

Experience has demonstrated that in European cities the street leading from the main railway station is lined with xxx video cabins and flea-shops flogging clothes for five euros, but not here. This is Zu-Rich. Shopping on the *Bahnhofstrasse*, a mile-long street of luxury boutiques, is for the absolutely fabulously wealthy. I pass Gucci, Prada, Tiffany's, Zegna, Boss, Louis Vuitton, Chanel, Dior and Montblanc. Inside Cartier a high-heeled, high-brow, high-end lady in fur examines watches while her micro-dog with dog coat tears around the shop on an extendable leash. I could join them but I would never get past the bouncer on the door. Every second outlet is a bank with a difference. Inside UBS, Credit Suisse, Julius Baer and Bank Leu there are neither cashiers nor cash. Instead there is corporate art, marble floors, ming vases, eastern rugs, big busts and lounge chairs. This is a rare street that is paved with gold since underfoot are the safe deposit boxes of these elite private banks. There is an Adidas retro store which I avoid because once one item is purchased here I will be on the slippery slope to having every garment in my wardrobe sporting three stripes. There is space near the Globus store where a small park marks the spot where felons were once hanged. At the far end the *Confiserie Sprüngli* has towering window displays of chocolates. Inside this uber-confectioner's is an overpowering heady rush of cocoa powder air, enough to induce an involuntary sneeze. This street represents all that the Swiss hold dear: banks and chocolate.

It's clean here, as clean as the alpine spring water that is available from the various public water fountains, of which there are 1,030. A skilled medical practitioner could most likely perform open heart surgery on these polished streets without any fear of contamination. The other Irish writer James Joyce once advised that he could safely eat minestrone off the pavements. After a day

I long to see some abandoned rubbish or a boarded-up shop. When you leave rented accommodation here, landlords can send in inspectors with latex gloves to check for dirt and grime behind the back of the toilet and you can lose your deposit if they find an offensive speck. Swiss cleanliness is exemplified by the Swiss rail employee who approaches me on a deserted platform late one evening. He has a look of firm determination and clenches a large metal blade in his right hand. I am half worried he's out to get me but instead he's looking for chewing gum on the platform and scraping it off. I look about my feet but I cannot find a piece of gum anywhere. He is passionate about his job, and successful too.

The restaurant with the longest waiting list here is called *Blindekuh*. Diners eat in total darkness and the staff are blind. There is no menu. Their website has no pictures. The most commonly asked question from the public is whether there are lights in the toilets? There are. It is perhaps the ultimate restaurant to take a blind date. The bars in the oldest part of the city, the *Neiderdorf*, a place of narrow, tumbling, winding Gothic streets, are surprisingly crammed with attractive people. Alain de Botton, the philosopher of life and a significantly more accomplished travel writer than I, is Swiss and he was born in Zurich. His view is that attractive girls who are born outside of Switzerland are particularly averse to going to Zurich, preferring to go to LA or Sydney; or if they are Protestant or homebirds, they go to Antwerp or Copenhagen. Alain always tries to interest girls in Zurich because he is convinced that if a girl likes Zurich, then she may well find the rather cerebral, intellectual and professorial Alain quite attractive. The bars are buzzy and inviting but I don't wish to nurse a beer inside any of them because I am here on my *Tobler-Own*.

I remain confused after my first day. I don't know what language they speak. When I use German, they reply in French. When I try French, they reply in English. When I use English, they reply in German. And the younger Swiss all speak such perfect English that my attempts at French are firstly met with surprise but then they switch to English to show how much better they are at foreign languages. And they are. Their post office vans have both *Die Post* and *La Poste* on the side so they are as confused as I am. The multi-linguality is best demonstrated by an encounter on an inter-city train when passing the suburb of Berne-Wankdorf, where an English couple seek help from a local reading a French language newspaper.

'Excuse moi,' they ask. 'Pouvez vous ou est the car pour le dining sur le train.' Or close to that. At the same time the couple make some exaggerated and animated knife and fork movements, bringing their hands repeatedly to their mouths, and chomping and guzzling like two individuals starved for weeks.

'The dining car is located at the centre of the train,' replies the Swiss in perfect English. *Parfait.*

The English make such good international travellers. Like at breakfast time in a hotel when presented with a choice of finest Ceylon, Assam, camomile, lemon or peppermint tea sachets, the visiting girl in the broadest Essex accent asked the local waitress, *'Like, do you have, like, any normal sort'ah tea?'*

I do feel safe here, largely due to the police in military gear, with peaked caps and guns in holsters. Occasionally fleets of police cars scream past across the *Bahnhof* bridge on their way to a heinous crime, such as someone discarding more chewing gum on a railway platform. Outside a police station two blue water cannon trucks are parked as a gentle reminder not to try anything funny, such as writing about Zurich.

It's all a sham. On my last night I am awoken by loud noises outside in the *Hirschenplatz*. Zurich has 360,000 inhabitants and tonight its 100 ardent anarchists are out in force. They march behind a red banner which I cannot decipher, shout slogans through loud hailers, whistle shrilly in unison and let off fire crackers. The hooded hoodlums use cans of spray paint to daub the walls of the old city with hammer and sickle logos and slogans. *No* WEF. I deduce the latter to be the World Economic Forum, commencing next week in nearby Davos. I think of slipping out of my pyjamas and joining them for the experience but I am a chartered accountant. An hour later the crowd returns on their round trip, more vocal, more agitated and more of them. There is not a policeman in sight which is surprising because this mob represents ideal target practice for a water cannon. Next morning the offensive graffiti is painted over by 9am.

After a bad night's sleep I settle my account at reception. The bill for a two-night stay is equivalent to the annual gross domestic product of a small African nation.

'You had a good stay?' asks the receptionist, now happily having put the ZIP code issue behind us.

'It was okay except for the riot.' A pause while the Central Bank of Ireland confirms I can pay my bill.

'Sorry about that. It's the Forum. It happens every year.'

It's not her fault. 'Where were the police?' I ask.

'It's always the same. The police are everywhere but never where you need them to be. They don't get involved.' She hands back a seriously dented *MasterCard*. 'But they are very, very strict on car parking.'

The Swiss are conscientious and fussy. I do not wish to descend to lavatory humour but the lavatory in my hotel room had a flush button and also a stop button so that in the event that I over-flushed the lavatory and unilaterally depleted a nation's reservoirs, I could stop the wanton excess at any time. When using the conveniences at Zurich's airport, one can be surprised by the little puff when standing at the urinals. A sensor expels a waft of air-freshener which coincidentally coincides with a tinkle.

The Swiss like to be significantly over-manned. I watched six cashiers sit inside Zurich airport's Union Bank of Switzerland *Bureau de Change* and do nothing for thirty minutes but chat amongst themselves and polish their nails. This is not dissimilar to the check-in desks at Terminal 2 in Frankfurt-am-Main airport where two staff X-ray hold luggage, one staff member directs passengers to a check-in desk (not a difficult job in itself since there are two desks per flight) and there are usually two staff per each check-in desk (one doing on-the-job training) such that I suspect Frankfurt airport (not Ryahn) is over-manned by a factor of four.

Orson Welles noted that in Italy for thirty years under the ruthless Borgias, there was warfare, terror, murder and bloodshed, yet they produced Michelangelo, Leonardo da Vinci and the

Renaissance. In Switzerland they enjoyed five hundred years of peace, democracy and brotherly love yet all the Swiss produced was the cuckoo clock, although even this invention is now claimed by the Germans. Just when you think you know the Swiss, you are reminded that they won the *America's Cup*, the world's most coveted yachting prize, and all this from a country that is landlocked and lies hundreds of miles from the ocean.

The Swiss like to hang lines across their country, especially power lines from giant pylons, chair lifts up and down valleys for lazy skiers, or power lines to drive trams. The more scenic the location, the more likely the Swiss are to hang their lines. They also like to build wooden lean-to's adjacent to their homes in which to store logs for the winter, all logs being of an identical size and length as per some cantonal law.

The Swiss like everything to be left in its rightful place, such that outside the shops in Zurich there are small metal hooks on the walls, saying *Hunde*, on which to attach your dog leash while you shop inside. The Swiss prefer to build tunnels for railways and roads, so if presented with a mountain standing in the way of a new route, rather than circumnavigating the obstacle, the Swiss, invariably, prefer to bore.

Liechtenstein

I wish to first address the *Ten Most Ludicrous Things About Liechtenstein*:

1. The place is ridiculously small, measuring only 16 miles long by 4 miles wide. In the time I drove from my home to the airport, I could have driven across this entire country, with time to spare. In addition to being tiny, two-thirds of the country comprises uninhabitable Tyrolean Alps and one fifth comprises dense forests, which means the entire population must huddle along the Rhine Valley. It's so small that the official country map provided to me by the tourist office shows tiny individual alpine huts and children's playgrounds.

2. The population of the country is a mere 35,000, of whom 28,000 work, making this the most industrialised country per capita in the world. In addition, 13,000 people commute from Germany, Austria and Switzerland to work. So between 9am and 5pm, only on weekdays, the population soars by 30 per cent.

3. Liechtenstein is loaded. It has a zero national debt. Unemployment is 1 per cent and those 350 people who are unemployed are all on first-name terms with the social welfare

folks who dole out their weekly benefits. The maximum tax rate is only 20 per cent and quick incorporation rules have induced many dodgy post office box shell companies to establish nominal offices in Liechtenstein, providing 30 per cent of all state revenues. This is the only country in the world with more registered companies than people. The biggest industries are repetitive postage stamp printing, denture and sausage skin manufacture and alleged money-laundering.

4. Politics here are odd. Women in Liechtenstein received the right to vote in 1984. The government is a hereditary constitutional monarchy on a democratic and parliamentary basis, which means nothing to me. Crown Prince Hans Adam II is one of the richest men in Europe but no one has ever heard of him, except Prince Charles and family who pop over to Malbun for a spot of on-piste activity. The Crown Prince runs the country, rather than parliament, so when parliamentary reforms were rumoured he threatened to move lock, stock and crown up the road to Vienna and 'to no longer provide the country with a monarchy'.

5. In 1976 Liechtenstein was refused entry to the Eurovision Song Contest, its zippy tune being *Little Cowboy* by Biggi Bachman, not because the country is so ludicrously small or because the song was crap (that's never stopped any nation in the past, e.g. Norway) but because it is without a national TV station.

6. The Liechtenstein national soccer team is the world's most spectacularly unsuccessful team, having played thirty World Cup and European Championship qualifying games and winning only one, whilst scoring six goals and conceding 132 goals. A good defeat is a good result for Liechtenstein. When England play away matches here, authorities worry if they will have enough cell space for the travelling hooligans since the country has only one jail with space for twenty-two people. Such hooligans are often confused since the Liechtenstein national anthem is sung to the exact same tune as *God Save the Queen*.

7. So insecure are the locals about their country that in 2004 they commissioned a London brand agency, Wolff Olins, to brand Liechtenstein. After many months of detailed research the agency came up with the unique branding idea of … the colour purple. And so today everything official is coloured purple.

8. Liechtenstein is notoriously difficult to spell correctly. If it wasn't for Bill Gates's *Spellchecker* and an army of publishing proofreaders, I would have spent all of this chapter working out how many 'i's I need.

9. Speaking of armies, Liechtenstein has none. The last war they fought was in 1866 when eighty soldiers went off to fight and a few months later eighty-one men returned because a guy joined their army along the way.

10. It's impossible to get to Liechtenstein. Along with Uzbekistan, it is one of only two doubly-landlocked countries in the world. No low fares airlines fly to Liechtenstein. In fact no airlines at all fly there, not because there isn't any demand, but because there isn't an airport, possibly because a runway would not fit. A railway line conveniently runs from Switzerland to Austria through Liechtenstein; there is one stop at Schaan at which passengers could alight, but for some unknown reason trains do not stop at this station. If you try to book a train from Zurich to Schaan, the Swiss Rail website tells you to take a bus instead.

So I take a train from Zurich to Sargans, seven miles from the capital Vaduz, population 5,000. At the rail station I offer the huge sum of a hundred Swiss franc note and am laughed out of the booking office with derision at this paltry monetary offering. Swiss trains display the lengthy initials SBB CFF FFS, which is surely six initials too many. On the way I set my Swiss Tissot watch to the correct time using Swiss railway timetables and their actual departure times, this being far more accurate than listening to the pips on any telephone call. Swiss trains make German trains seem late. The train runs east along the southern shore of Lake Zurich, providing views of snowy peaks, mountain valleys, jaunty yachting, para-gliding, hot-air balloons and dazzling sunlight. Rolling manicured hills merge with sandy inlets, tall fir trees and water features. Switzerland may be the world's biggest public golf course.

At Sargans the number 1 bus goes to Vaduz. A little lady joins from the train, carrying groceries in *Mövenpick* bags from Zurich. If folks around these parts take a three-hour round trip to Zurich to get their weekly foodstuffs, I am going to seriously struggle in Liechtenstein. The trip takes thirty minutes because the bus meanders along the route and stops at every residence along the way. Around these parts you can ring the bus company any day and ask them to wait for you outside your own front door. And you know, they likely will. Along the way passers-by wave at others in the bus. The driver gives new passengers a friendly *Grüsse Gott*. Everyone knows everyone else it seems, but me. It already feels a bit incestuous. I am beginning to think everyone looks the same. All I need is a cross-eyed blonde kid plucking a banjo, *Deliverance* style. We cross a bridge after Trubbach and I see a sign for Switzerland, and then one for Liechtenstein. There are no border controls here. We don't so much arrive, as accidentally stumble across another country.

Liechtenstein reminds me of that movie *The Mouse That Roared*, starring Peter Sellars, where the tiny and broke European Duchy of Grand Fenwick declared war on the mighty USA. There are parallels. The Duchy of Grand Fenwick was located in the Alps and occupied fifteen square miles. The army of Grand Fenwick consisted of twenty volunteers. Their weapon was the longbow and their uniforms were made from trusty chain mail. It's a well-proven fact that there are few more profitable undertakings for a country in need of serious cash than to declare war on the US, be quickly defeated and enjoy the war reparations.

I booked accommodation online in advance. On offer were the usual accommodations, plus *huttes*. These are wooden chalets (i.e. huts) perched several thousand feet up in the mountains where guests who have hiked for days up sheer icy precipices can sleep for €7 a night in dormitories of fifty people, boots and all. Not being one to ever slum it, I instead selected the four-star Residence Hotel in Vaduz city centre. They replied to my email reservation request within ten minutes. These folks are keen.

Vaduz is so small that if you miss your bus stop, the next stop could be in another country. I ask a lady on the bus to advise me when to alight for the hotel. She is most helpful to the nation's only tourist. At the reception desk of my hotel, a girl looks up and immediately opens with '*Hello, Paul.*' She's been expecting me. I know what happened. The lady on the bus rang her up excitedly and advised her of the new tourist in town. The hotel is deadly quiet. I fear I am the only guest in the hotel this weekend. I risk all and ask if I am the only guest? She smiles and laughs. 'Oh no, of course not, we have another guest.' Visitors need not worry if their hotel is well located, because here in Vaduz everything is in the city centre.

It's a nice touch when hotel staff know you by name, except when I stayed on the executive floor of the Excelsior Hotel in Hong Kong a decade ago. An efficient Cantonese guest services manager took my photograph with a *Polaroid Instamatic* (yes it's that long ago). 'We will place your photograph and name on our staff notice board so everyone will know who you are.' Nice except she evidently got the guest names mixed up. So I had three weeks of '*Good morning, Mr Edwards. How are you today, Mr Edwards? Welcome back, Mr Edwards. Sleep well, Mr Edwards.*' I hadn't the heart to advise her of her error, and I guess Mr Edwards never did either. I wasn't even convinced that the idea would ever work. Sure, don't we all look the same?

There are great capital cities of the world; places you go where you worry about not having enough time to see everything; places where you can think of oodles of things to do and see before you even arrive: New York, Paris, London. Unfortunately Vaduz is not such a place. I have allowed the best part of two days to explore Vaduz. Upon early inspection I have overestimated matters by possibly forty-seven hours. That's the trouble with international travel. One minute you're sweeping through the majestic Swiss Alps with a growing sense of speed, excitement and anticipation, and the next minute you're in Vaduz.

The city centre, if that's not a contradiction in terms, radiates from a roundabout with five exits. Each exit has a few closed shops, offices, bars and cafés. Further on down one road are the highlights: the post office building, government offices and a graffitied multi-storey car park. I walk for ten minutes, mostly along two adjoining streets called *Stadtlestrasse* and *Aulestrasse*, which enclose the centre of town. The streets are lined with private banks where absent rich Germans and Swiss hide hot money. I have done all of Vaduz. I am half thinking of buying a newspaper to pass the time. If I could find a shop that is open.

There are few restaurants, and those that are open are empty inside. I retreat to the restaurant in the hotel where I am the first guest of the evening. And the only. The bastards give me a table by the window, possibly to drum up more business from the passing trade, which I can confirm does not exist in Vaduz. A dour waiter in black who looks like the lead singer from Level 42 brings me a cremated steak. Two kids outside see me eating on my own and think it's hilarious to wave, stare and grimace at me. I think I can see one of them mouth back at me, '*You're that tourist we heard about from the lady on the bus.*'

Everything was expensive in Switzerland, but Liechtenstein makes Switzerland look cheap. I am stunned at the bill after a modest dinner with one beer. Around these parts, one can either dine out or take out a mortgage, but not both. I have a few more Warsteiner beers back in my room. The night is still hot so I leave my window wide open. I am on the first floor of the hotel. My room overlooks the main pedestrian street and it's ten o'clock on a Saturday night. There isn't a sound outside. Liechtenstein is a great country in which to wake up late and have a long lazy breakfast, safe in the knowledge that you are not missing anything. My hotel is central, a stone's throw from the attractions, but everything is a stone's throw from everything else around here. Wish I had a stone.

It costs two euros in the tourist office for a souvenir stamp of Liechtenstein to adorn my passport. Some 40,000 people ask for this unique memento annually. Instantly I regret my impulsive decision. It's going to cause me grief sometime; specifically I sense there's some trouble ahead the next time I go through hostile immigration at JFK: *'Hey guys, this fella here has a stamp for Lye-chin-steen. Anyone ever heard of that?'*

Close by is the Quick Tourist Shop which one moment is quiet and then invaded with the arrival of two tour buses. Loud Americans in red Stanford sweatshirts and extra-large denims disgorge from the bus, pillage the shop and buy tack. On offer inside are cuckoo clocks, beer mugs, cow bells, stamps, and particularly nice laminated table mats featuring various Alpine cows in provocative poses. The Americans pronounce that a rather useless letter opener with a red Swiss cross (Swiss?) is *really neat.* One hour later they are gone. If you are on the *One Country per Day Europe* tour, Liechtenstein represents the ideal stop.

It's wise to make for the cultural venues since the Americans won't be there. The *Landesmuseum* features impressive displays about the nation's origin and history, much of it being pottery and most of it broken. There is a particularly small room to display the various exploits of the National Army, which last comprised one Spike Milligan look-alike. There's a movie featuring cows coming down from the mountain pastures to Vaduz, a sort of cow marathon. What impresses me most is the request at the entrance for my nationality. *'We need it for statistical purposes.'* The Swiss have always been very good at gathering data.

The *Kunstmuseum* is new but it's an eyesore, a three-storey cube of black granite. The architect who designed it had the brief finished before he had eaten his cornflakes one morning. The Prince's private art collection is not here. He has a Da Vinci (that's the painter, not the paperback) and a few Rubens but he is unwilling to share them with the great unwashed peasant populace like moi. The best part is the ground floor café where a real Japanese chef creates sushi for ten million francs per each wet sticky blob.

The locals print huge amounts of stamps and for some reason collectors buy them for their albums. Vaduz has a Postage Stamp Museum. Inside I learn that the first mail delivery around these parts was in 1219, which was before they guaranteed next-day delivery. There are 300 grim metal frames by a wall. I pull a few out one by one like library books. And one word of warning here, if you visit the Postage Museum don't ask the woman at the entrance, as I did, if she has any stamps for postcards. She doesn't think it's funny.

There is also a Calculator Museum at Schaan but it's too far to visit — the term *far* being relative in a country this size. In any event the calculator museum only features old 1970s models such as the notorious programmable *Casio 710LX*, which is the size of today's portable laptop, has keys the size of seat cushions and possesses such crap unreliability that every fourth calculation would simply be *wrong*.

Vaduz Castle overlooks the city and has the foreboding presence of Colditz Castle. At night it is lit by yellow floodlights and, set above the jet-black hill, it looks like a spaceship hovering over a terrified population. The Princely family do not encourage nosey tourists dropping in of an afternoon for tea and bikkies, yet their regal home is signposted as a twenty-minute walk up the hill. I set off and ascend the peak. A walk of twenty minutes' duration is correct if you have previously scaled Everest. Along the way I pass the frozen entombed bodies of other climbers who failed to overcome the elements. Bring oxygen. Pack rations.

On the descent the *Engel Café* is ideal for coffee and cake. The Black Forest gateau is excellent but I guess that's to be expected since it only comes from a few miles up the road. I am amazed that one of the waiters is the same Level 42 singer from last night's restaurant. Back outside the Quick Tourist Shop, the American and Japanese tourists linger uneasily, then their spewing buses rev and we locals are left in peace. I am not the only tourist in Liechtenstein, but I am the only one who stays for more than one hour. It's like being locked into Disneyland overnight when everyone else has gone home to sanity.

Despite the large number of American visitors, I remain optimistic that the nation's food reserves have not been depleted, yet for my last evening meal I have little choice but to return to the *Engel Café*. The manager remembers me from my afternoon snack. 'You were here earlier today. We've been expecting you.' He's not joking. The same dour singer appears and takes my order. I wonder if he's following me from restaurant to restaurant? I ask, 'Do you work in *all* the restaurants?' but he laughs it off. Am I single-handedly keeping the hospitality industry in work? I order. Amazingly a chef walks into the restaurant, past me and into the kitchen. The chef is Japanese. I'm sure he's the same chef from the sushi bar at the museum. How many Japanese chefs can there be in Vaduz? I am keeping him in a job too. The staff in the hotels around here are likely running a lucrative sweepstake on where I will eat next.

Liechtenstein is the sort of place where people walk around with a somewhat expectant air, hoping that perhaps something exciting or unusual will occur, but safe in the knowledge that it never will. An example is the local FL *Landeskanal*, which is a channel that shows slides about what's on in Liechtenstein. There are only nine slides, which loop endlessly. One of the slides is about an upcoming civil defence exhibition, featuring a real fire extinguisher. Another slide concerns the opening of a kindergarten.

I have not seen a police station here, nor a police car, nor even a police officer. Liechtenstein doesn't seem to possess a national police force. The last recorded crime was in 1956 when someone working in a government taxation department took a single paper clip home from the office without permission. Before I came here I read a travel book about Liechtenstein. I have great admiration for the author who managed to pen a book about the place. I have struggled to complete one chapter. Another book I could have read in advance is called *Firearms from the Collections of the Prince of Liechtenstein*.

Nod off and you might miss Liechtenstein. It's more like a big ski run, an Austro-Swiss sandwich, than a European country. I am beginning to have very fond memories of visiting Beauvais and Charleroi. As a parting gesture I send a few postcards home from the hotel, safe in the knowledge they will never arrive. The local post office censor reads all postcards from tourists and he will surely bin mine along with many others. *'Here's another foreigner making fun of our beloved country and how very small it is.'*

I didn't even visit Liechtenstein because I had to. It's not a recognised state within Europe. It's a Principality, much like San

Marino, Andorra or Monaco. It slumbers. I came because I was curious about the place. Now I know there's only ever one reason to visit Liechtenstein. That's to write a chapter about it. So here's a final reminder. Liechtenstein is small, very small. Vaduz is even smaller. If you take your children here on a family motoring holiday, and one of the little darlings suddenly pipes up plaintively from the rear seat of the car, 'Are we there yet, Daddy?' your answer will invariably be a very confident … 'Yes.'

United Kingdom ... again

EUjet Flight VE402 – Tuesday @ 8.45am – DUB-MSE-DUB

Fare €6 plus taxes, fees and charges €54

I have done something rather impulsive. I saw a new airline at Dublin airport and wondered if they could take me somewhere, since I am increasingly addicted to the smell of aviation fuel. Their aircraft is tiny, a narrow-bodied jet with a blue logo on a white body. It's not a Boeing, nor an Airbus. It's a little Fokker. EUjet fly from Dublin to Manston. I have a vague idea Manston is somewhere in south-east England. I tell a colleague I will fly to Manston. He replies: 'Where the bloody hell is that?' And he's English. EUjet fly to eighteen destinations in Europe using five 108-seat Fokker 100s and are headquartered in Shannon, Co. Clare. Their Irish founder and CEO was formerly CEO of a low fares airline called Ruinair.

On board the three cabin stunners are immaculately kitted out in navy uniforms and neck scarves. They have perfect diction and are in full command of the flight. The overall impression is that of an elite business jet: a small cabin with leather seats and lots of leg room. I sit on the Port side on the Outward trip and the Starboard side on the way Home. EUjet is Posh.

I sit in the emergency row 14 so Alexandra (a posh cabin girl) comes to sit alongside to debrief me, so to speak. She is tall with high cheekbones and gathered hair and instructs me to remove the window in the event of an emergency, telling me how to pull the window inside and how to throw it back outside.

'It's a heavy door but you'll be able to do it because I have tried and I can do it,' she advises.

'Ah, yes,' I reply. 'But you're a big girl.'

Sadly there are only thirty passengers on the flight and three of them are Ground Operations staff in suits who work for the airline and are travelling to a meeting. They sit in row 3 receiving complimentary drinks and pass the time looking around at the rest of us, wondering why we are so few. After we land, the crew play the first ever low fares airline song: 'Get on my eujet.com, when you've got to get away.'

Manston aka Kent International Airport is a low-rise pre-fab, like something secondary schools put up for extra classroom space when they have no money for bricks and mortar. The fire tender outside aspirationally says *London* Manston Airport, London being only eighty miles away. We deplane through a line of red plastic cones reminiscent of a major motorway accident. Inside, posters advise EUjet is '*The Weald's Favourite Airline.*' This airport owes its existence to war. The Royal Navy arrived with seaplanes in 1916, the Dam Busters tested their bouncing bombs nearby in 1943, the Americans arrived with B52s in 1950 but left in 1958 (they always leave eventually) and Bob Geldof's Band Aid flew from here to Africa to Feed the *Weald* in 1985. Manston is not the centre of the universe, let alone the centre of Kent. It lies rather precariously on the north-east coast. Any further east and EUjet would likely use seaplanes. Trains run to London Victoria and Charing Cross in two hours but I am on a day-trip so that would give me six minutes to enjoy London. A local taxi costs a fiver but I am tight so I prefer to spend 75 pence to hop onto the red number 38 *Hoppabus*. I tell the shaven driver I wish to go to the town centre. He looks up in amazement.

'You sure you don't mean the train station, mate? You really want to go to the town centre?'

On the bus I am the only person under eighty years old. Six old dears are heading into town with their shopping bags. We trundle along winding pot-holed country lanes and through Manston village, which is a signpost and nothing more. Today I am going to *Iceland*. That's where the bus stops near the High Street.

Ramsgate lies on the Isle of Thanet in East Kent. Population 38,000. Main industries are fishing and tourism (that's me then). Ramsgate has the only Royal Harbour in the UK because King George IV got a bit carried away when he visited in 1821. Ramsgate's other claim to fame was in 596 AD when Augustine, the first Archbishop of Canterbury, got off a boat and announced, *'I've brought Christianity with me.'* After a dinner party once I was asked to recommend a good port, to which I flippantly replied, *'Ramsgate.'*

The town is quintessential Little Britain, criss-crossed streets with a few banks, pharmacies and tailors, Rook's family butchers and the Red Lion pub. It's not an unattractive town, yet there's a waft of salty sea air mixed with frying oil from nearby fish bars and most of the locals speak Polish, but it's the sort of seaside town Captain Mainwaring and the Home Guard protected in 1940, a la Warmington-on-Sea.

It's June but this is England so it's twelve degrees, cloudy and windy and the time-warped Esplanade is deserted. The kiddies' fun fair is dormant, the deckchairs and windbreakers stacked up, the ice lolly and slush vendor is close to liquidation and no one's digging the bucket and spade sets. Waves crash against the shore and there are more buoys than boys. The beach is golden yet small, occupied sparsely by clusters of optimistic families having an early lunch. Killer dive-bombing seagulls outnumber shivering sunbathers.

Offshore lie the treacherous Goodwin Sands which have claimed many a passing ship, deemed inhospitable until 1824 when the Harbour Master at Ramsgate arranged a cricket match there at low tide. To this day brave local mariners make the annual trip to the Sands to play cricket before sea stops play. The view of the town is dominated by high red-brick arches set into the cliffs, topped by rows of Edwardian four-storey piles, now converted to

B&BS, guest houses and fairly naff restaurants. There is an Obelisk to George IV's visit and I learn the truth. The King returned safely from his Kingdom of Hanover. If he made the trip several generations later he would have got a hostile reception from the Royal Navy.

In the harbour rests the *Sundowner*, a quaint gleaming motor yacht built in 1912 and one of 4,200 *little ships* used to snatch British soldiers from the Dunkirk beaches in 1940. At the helm was a C. H. Lightoller, which is not alarming in itself, until I learn he was Second Officer on the *Titanic*, and thus is not the first person I would choose to take me back to Blighty, although a hail of lethal lead would have been a salient factor. At the time he was sixty-six and took his son Roger and an eighteen-year-old Sea-Scout named Gerald. 'If anyone's going to take my boat to Dunkirk, then it's going to be me and my son,' he said. On one of these trips Lightoller crammed 130 men into the *little ship*, a feat remaining unequalled in the history of compact transportation until Ruinair changed the standard seating configuration on a Boeing 737-800.

When peckish I briefly toy with the idea of going to nearby Sandwich for a sandwich. But the Ocean Lounge is closer and offers a row of outdoor tables along the harbour front. It's empty when I sit down but others follow suit. I find myself eavesdropping on the conversations of the retired folk who enjoy the tranquillity.

'I was twenty-one when I met Daisy and we've been together ever since.'

'I remember Bill pulling up in a gold-coloured Ford Capri.'

'Have you been on that internet thingy?'

The sun breaks through, skies clear to blue and we begin to toast nicely. The salmon and cucumber granary sandwiches sate my appetite. Smooth R&B tunes waft outside from the café. One of the older citizens nods off in the heat. The *Sundowner* bobs at ease in the harbour, its lifetime's work complete, its life-saving contribution acknowledged and its retirement well-deserved. Ramsgate was worth fighting for.

A few months later I see an announcement on the airline's website.

Dear Customer,

Following recent developments and due to circumstances beyond our control, EUjet with deep regret wish to inform you that with immediate effect the airline has ceased all operations and flights. Alternative airlines are helping stranded passengers and offering economical fares home. From all the staff at EUjet we regret the inconvenience and distress this has caused and wish to thank you for your support.

Yours Sincerely,
The EUjet Team

Pity. I wonder what posh Alexandra is doing these days. Beauty can often be life's passport.

Spain ... again

Vueling Flight VL1231 – Monday @ 3.40pm – BRU-BCN

Fare €30 plus taxes, fees and charges €29

A suspicious-looking man stands behind me at check-in at Brussels airport. He wears a brown suit but it's badly creased and ill-fitting and he stands too close to me as he plays with a mobile phone, but he doesn't send a text or make a call. I am already on a heightened state of alert. The oddest aspect is that he only has a newspaper in his hand, no luggage is in sight for this flight. I'm not convinced he's here to check in. I shift my wallet to my front pocket. Then he changes queues to stand behind a tiny Japanese girl with a zippy backpack. I observe him closely from a distance. Today I am on Code Red, DEFCON 1 and all that.

Having booked this flight three months ago it is a pleasant surprise to that find Vueling Airlines is still flying to its native Spain. You can never be too sure with the minnows of the low fares industry. One minute they're selling you seats for thirty euros and the next you're in email refund discussions with the liquidator. Vueling is a Barcelona-based airline, and partly owned by JetBlue Airlines of the US. It flies to Spain, Italy, France, Portugal, Netherlands and Belgium. They have the oddest name of any known airline. It's more Anglo-Iberian-Spanglish: *vuel* (from Spanish *vuelo* meaning flight) and 'ing' (an ending such as flying)? They have christened their aircraft in a similarly odd manner, *Barceloning, Parising, Palming* etc.

Mick knows that Vueling just lost 50 million euros. '*If Vueling was losing money with oil at $65 per barrel, then it's bankrupt with oil at $95!*'

The Airbus A320 aircraft is an artistic creation, a gleaming white body with ochre on the engines and grey dots splattered on the tail. On board the beautiful crew wear white shirts with yellow scarves and grey skirts with micro-belts. Scarves tied at jaunty angles are often big in-flight. The crew sway to the piped music before we take off. The birdlike Jade leads the crew and delivers an exquisite safety announcement in dulcet tones last heard perhaps on *Playboy* TV, pronouncing the airline's name as *Welling*. We are offered newspapers in Spanish, all of which are devoted solely to Barcelona FC. It must be great to come from Barcelona, to support the best football team on earth, to be even better than the Real Madrid thing.

There is no in-flight magazine but there are free newsagent magazines in the seat pockets. Mine is called *Woman* and has Angelina Jolie on the cover and inside there are beauty tips and graphic advertisements for intimate feminine hygiene products. I nick a magazine from across the aisle, *Cinema* with Cameron Diaz. The guy in the brown suit sits close by. He has magically found some luggage. I still have my wallet.

We land at the wonderfully named *El Prat* airport. It could be worse. I am increasingly worried that, like the USA, all European airports will be soon named after famous people. We already have George Best airport in Belfast, Robin Hood airport in Nottingham and John Lennon airport in Liverpool. Watch out in a few decades time for Dublin's Bono airport. El Prat is Barcelona's main airport and only eight miles from the beating city heart, not to be confused with southern Reus (Barcelona), a desolate outpost in deepest Catalonia where Ruinair deposit passengers 90 km and one hour and thirty minutes away by bus from Barcelona, nor with Girona (Barcelona), another 'nearly but not quite there' Ruinair destination.

You push your luggage trolley out of the arrivals hall. A man walks past in front and you rattle his ankles with your trolley. He turns around and you expect the worst but he accepts it's an accident.

When you go to lift your luggage into the bus, you are missing your
backpack. You never saw his accomplice.

Reus's most famous son met an early demise under the
number 30 tram on 7 June 1926 as he crossed the *Gran Via* on his
way to the Church of St Philipp-Neri. Mistaking him for a beardy
tramp, onlookers sent him to the city's charitable hospital. A
priest recognised him but Antonio Gaudi refused to move to
another hospital. Three days after the accident he died and
thousands paid their respects at his funeral. For the last fifteen
years of his life he had devoted himself to the church, working
and sleeping in the church, existing only on bread and water. The
locals have asked the Vatican to beatify him as a saint. He's going
to have trouble because there are 4,000 other saintly types ahead
of him in the queue, including some significant do-gooders such
as Mother Teresa. But sure wasn't he going to mass when he was
run over?

The A1 Aeropuerto bus takes thirty minutes to reach the city
centre. This is a Spanish bus so the driver does 140 kmh in the
outside lane, overtaking Porsches with ease.

You wait at the airport bus stop in the mass transit hub of Plaza de
Catalunya when a man comes up and starts to jabber away at you in
Spanish rather excitedly. You say you don't speak Spanish and can't
help and back away from him until he moves on. When the bus
arrives you find you are missing some luggage. You never saw his
accomplice.

It was in this Barcelona square that a promotion for Ruinair
went badly wrong. The company had offered free plane tickets to
those who went to *Plaza de Catalunya* carrying banners or
placards against the national airline Iberia, but the airline
obviously did not expect the large numbers who attended. The
single woman present from Ruinair had finally to be rescued by
the police as the crowd grabbed her free vouchers between them.
The Catalan Consumers Organisation opened an investigation
into the promotion following complaints from more than 150
people who failed to get their tickets. Some people even went as far
as re-writing their placards changing their slogans away from
Iberia and against Ruinair.

Directly across the street from my hotel is the *Palau Guell*, a substantial home which was built for an industrial tycoon and patron. It's an impressive residence built on only 200 square metres. But this is Spain so the palace is closed for renovations which will take two years to complete. The architect's name was Antonio Placido Guillermo Gaudi i Cornet.

The Hotel Gaudi is off *Las Ramblas* and room 520 has a balcony. I step outside and am twenty feet from the roof of the *Palau*. Fifteen chimneys decorated in glazed ceramics and brightly coloured glass dazzle me. Rumour has it that included in the jigsaw are the shattered remains of a Limoges dinner set hated by Snr Guell. Personally I trace Gaudi's life-long interest in using tiles for decoration to his construction of *Casa Vicens* in 1888 which was built for the owner of a tile factory, so Gaudi must have got the tiles at a good trade price. In the roof centre is a minaret decorated with pebbles and stones topped by a gold dome and a weather vane pointing at me. It's a private viewing of perhaps his greatest work for nothing. I am half-thinking of a money spinner; going back downstairs and offering trips to room 520 to Americans from the cruise ships for ten euros a shot.

Gaudi designed the street lights in *Plaça Reial*. The ornate lamps have six arms, crowned by a winged helmet to symbolise the commercial power of the city at the time. It's not a stunning achievement for any architect to win a public commission from the city fathers but he was only twenty-six at the time. Others too had spotted his early potential for greatness. When the student with blond hair and blue eyes received his degree from the School of Architecture of Barcelona University his professor told him, '*I don't know whether we are graduating a genius or a fool.*' Today this tired square smells of stale beer and pigeons as his lights illuminate vagrants, two police cars, five police officers and paella-selling restaurants where three or four waiters tout for business. I never dine in any restaurant which craves my modest custom so badly.

A polite lady approaches you on Las Ramblas. She is well dressed and speaks broken English. She has been robbed and needs money to get home. She is in tears. You feel sorry for her and give her money. She is in tears very often. This is her day job. Her name is Susan. She is famous in this part of town. She has been sighted in Madrid and Palma too. She is, like myself, a jetsetter. Some take photographs of her.

I ramble down *Las Ramblas*. They are a collection of inter-connecting *Rambla*, meaning torrent, since centuries before, sea water would run up and down here at will. Today it is a paved pedestrian thoroughfare lined with bird stalls and pizza cafés, shaded by trees and surrounded by incessant traffic. There are council signs on lamp posts advising the pea and shell game played by locals is a trick to deceive tourists. It's important not to look too much like a tourist here, not to carry cameras and maps, not to stand about looking lost, not to carry a thousand euros and your passport in your back pocket, not to wear *sombreros*.

Further along Las Ramblas a few youths come close to you. One wears a Barca soccer strip and plays an imaginary game of football with you, comes close to dribble around you, leans closer to you. It's all good clean fun and he goes off with his mates. Next time you reach for it, your wallet is missing.

The harbour end of *Las Ramblas* is seedy with peep shows, con artists, fake street theatre, ladies who work and an air of decay. It terminates at a vicious traffic roundabout with a tall statue of Christopher Columbus, except that he is not a son of this city (he was born in Genoa) and he points eastwards to his home and not westwards to America, indicating perhaps that he didn't like to travel so much.

Amidst the swooping seagulls near the harbourside Port Olimpico, a local points at your shirt. The birds have crapped on your best clothes. He helps you wipe it off with a tissue. You move on. Later you discover your wallet is gone. Suntan cream splashed onto your clothes can look like bird dropping.

The *Casa Batlló* house on *Passeig de Grácia* is made from skulls and bones, the skulls being protruding balconies and the bones being crooked exterior pillars. Gaudi maintained that nothing in nature is perfectly straight so neither should his buildings be straight. Inside it's like being underwater with scaly walls, coloured doors, curvy windows, wavy lines and winding stairs. I'm not sure I could live here. It's true that if you wanted to annoy the hell out of Gaudi, all you had to do was to draw him a straight line.

Casa Milá is a monumental six-storey house on a corner of *Passeig de Grácia,* and also a UNESCO world heritage site. It was built by Gaudi for Snr Milá, who married a rich widow, always a smart move, and wanted a landmark home. Its undulating walls have no straight lines but instead, like a glamorous 1950s movie star, have curves in all the right places. It is lunar in appearance, a dirty white flowing construction, with dents and intrusions like some planet's surface. Gaudi never finished the work because he had a row with the owners and went over budget. When it was first built it was reviled by citizens and nick-named *La Pedrera,* the quarry. I am not convinced either, and wonder if its construction is equivalent to what a small boy might construct given a day off school, a free hand, broken tiles and a giant tub of malleable plasticene.

El Temple Expiatori de la Sagrada Familia is instantly recognisable to us all since the work–in-progress basilica was the backdrop to Ian McCaskill's advertisements for Thomson on the Sky TV weather forecast. Every year 2.5 million visitors come here, making it Spain's biggest attraction, ahead of the Prado Museum in Madrid, *The Alhambra* in Granada and the footie stars playing in the *Nou Camp.* I am not an architectural expert but the hyperbolic parabloids and convex vault helicoids do impress. George Orwell did not feel the same way, however, and said he wished Civil War partisans had blown this church to smithereens.

You wait in line at the entrance ticket booth and a few gypsy ladies come up offering lucky heather. You resist their kind attentions until they ask for only ten cents. As you open a purse or a wallet they gather around and help you find the coin. An hour later you discover you are missing a few €20 notes.

The iconic church exterior is over the top, like confectionery over-baked by a mad chocolatier. Gaudi's plan was to have three facades — for birth, death and the resurrection — along with eighteen towers for the twelve Apostles, the four Evangelists and the Virgin Mary and Christ. He laboured on this final project for forty-two years. When asked about the extremely long construction period, he replied his client 'was not in a hurry'. He used the same construction crew who built Cologne cathedral. And had a go at Beauvais.

For all *Da Vinci Code* fans, there are a series of puzzling
numbers on the front facade of *Sagrada Familia*:

1	14	14	4
11	7	6	9
8	10	10	5
13	2	3	15

I wonder what do they mean? Answers on a postcard to me
please, care of the Ruinair head office.

Inside it's a building site. Scaffolding rises to the apse, the latter
being unfinished. I can see the blue sky. Pieces of Gaudi-style
plasterwork lie on wooden pallets, like something you'd find at
Homebase. Workers drill inside the church. Cement mixers churn
away. A guy reverses a forklift truck at me. Hoists go up and down.
I take the elevator to the top of one of the towers and look down
inside the tower. The walls curve away. This tower is not at all
straight. How can such a great architect get it all so crooked?

Following the tram incident, construction continued on despite
the plans being destroyed in Civil War shelling. They still build
what he would have wanted. It's part of the attraction. The tourist
board's worst nightmare is that some day the basilica might be
finished. There's no fear of that. There are black and white photos
of what the church looked like in 1904. I step outside. To be honest,
it's not changed much. Gaudi still keeps a close eye upon the
workers, having found his final resting place in the Basilica's crypt.

I take an outside table on *Passeig de Grácia* and watch the talent
emerging from Zara. There are many very cool, laid back people
about in Barcelona so fortunately I am able to blend in effortlessly.
But I will never succumb to the Spanish custom of eating late into
the evenings. You could walk into a restaurant here at 11.30pm and
they would look oddly at you because you're so early. You could
call up to make a reservation for 1am to be told you can have a
table for 3am. It's almost breakfast.

You sit at a café table when a youth approaches selling postcards.
He spreads ten of them out on the table and encourages you to buy all
ten for a few euros. You decline and eventually he gets the message,

gathers them up and moves on. Soon you search for your mobile phone which was on the table.

I relax, satisfied that I have picked my way through some of the finest architectural sights, knowing anything less would have been criminal. An English family sits alongside me and orders dinner. The father places his camera in view on the table. The waiter walks over to him and is stern. 'Don't leave your camera on the table, sir.'

I am *gaudi'd* out. I *gaudi*. You *gaudi*. We *gaudi*. They *gaudi*. The verb *to gaudi — to be over-exposed to modernist bendy architecture for several days in a large Iberian city in thirty degrees Celsius of heat.*

P.S. *The numbers are a magic square created by the sculptor Subirachs. The rows, columns, diagonals, and 300 other combinations, all add up to 33, being the age of Christ at his death. Easy, Dan.*

Spain ... more

Clickair Flight XG1065 – Wednesday @ 4.10pm
– BCN-SVQ-BCN

Fare €26 plus taxes, fees and charges €26

I need to see a doctor or psychologist soon since I am increasingly addicted to low fares airlines. In fact I am addicted to low fares everything such that I only buy clothes with big price reductions and I only buy the cheapest petrol on the forecourt. And worse still, I am beginning to believe that the airline I use is more important than the destination. Like when I saw some smart blue and silver Airbus aircraft taxiing about another European airport, so I clicked on their website. The aptly named Spanish Clickair airline is the baby of the low fares industry, only conceived in 2006. They had a promotion which featured a movie trailer called '*This is the Click Invasion*' with their aircraft passing in waves over Westminster's Big Ben, canal-side homes in Amsterdam and the Eyeful Tour in Paris, like the Luftwaffe flying over in old war footage. Click fly to forty major airports and their philosophy is based on *destinos, servicio, precio. Vuela inteligente.*

I booked a day trip but they failed to email my itinerary so I was left in a void of uncertainty until I called the telephone number of their service centre in Spain. I got through immediately to a pleasant Spanish girl who spoke perfect English, rather than *Spanglish,* and who re-sent the email itinerary, which appeared in my inbox as we chatted and who asked if everything was now satisfactory and if she could help in any other way, which left me with a warm positive feeling about this airline even before I stepped onto one of their aircraft. Now that is customer service. Click promises to be a cheap, and not so nasty, airline. Click are partly owned by Iberia Airlines and they do not make a secret of the fact. Check-in is at a row of Iberia desks manned by Iberia staff, my flight has a code share with Iberia and on board the food trolleys are emblazoned with the name of their parent national airline. In all other respects, Iberia it is not.

We have assigned seating yet passengers voluntarily stand to queue at gate 29 with thirty minutes to departure time. This used to be known as the herd mentality. Now it's simply known as the Ruinair effect. We are very warmly welcomed by the Click crew. She wears an aquamarine suit with silver buttons and piping, along with a neat skirt or trousers, plus a T-shirt underneath of varying shades of sea blue, like something you'd wear to the beach, the whole ensemble screaming of sun, sand and summer. He wears a navy suit with an open-neck shirt in the same blue, no tie, reminiscent of an office worker in a corporate head office on dress-down Friday. The A320 interior is calming white and grey and I sit in a reclining seat made from real leather by Recaro, who are the same people who make the seats for the VW Golf Gti. The flight is perfect: on time, agreeable and the only mild shock is the *sandwich de roast-beef* at eight euros.

As we disembark, the beaming crew wish us a sincere fond *Adios*. If you saw a Click girl in Barcelona airport, you would think, 'Wow!' If you saw a Ruinair girl in the same airport, you would think, 'Poor thing', apart from the fact that she is most likely lost because she should be in Reus or Girona. The difference between all other low fares airlines and Ruinair is simple. The difference is one word. Pride.

Incidentally, civil Seville represents Europe's optimal summer-time city break destination: a small, efficient and navigable airport with zero delays, a fifteen-minute public bus ride to the city centre for two euros, shopping in *Zara Home* at Nervion Plaza at a fraction of any Dublin prices, the four-star Novotel next door with a rooftop pool to savour guaranteed blue skies and thirty degrees plus, open-air dining and mazes of tapas bars, a *La Liga* topping and UEFA Cup winning Sevilla soccer team, new two-bed townhouses for only €150,000, an open-top bus tour which fortunately speeds through the barren remnants of the Sevilla 1992 Expo but lingers amongst the fine international residences of the 1929 Ibero-American Expo, a street tram system so new that it glisten, tourists from Spain rather than from Essex, the heady aroma of orange blossom, the biggest gothic cathedral on God's earth with a landmark Giralda minaret tower, a mesh of Islam, Jew, Gypsy and Christianity, horse and carriage rides through the religious grandeur, a river cruise from the Torre del Oro down the Gaudalquiver River made famous by that Chris de Burgh song, and a two-hour walking tour of the achingly photogenic Barrio Santa Cruz old town where the only information imparted by the guide which I dispute is that Seville is most famous for sending all its oranges to the UK to make into marmalade.

It's easy to see why so many operas are set in romantic Seville (Don Juan and Carmen attend the Marriage of Figaro?). But after twenty-four hours it's back to BCN on Click, because there is always another country.

| Andorra

Landlocked between giant French and Spanish neighbours, 210 kilometres north of Barcelona via the long and winding road, lies a tiny mountainous principality of 468 square kilometres and 77,000 residents. The road has more u-turns than a Labour government, more S-bends than a Parazone advertisement, more hairpins than a Jeremy Clarkson road test and more sheer precipices than the last ten minutes of *The Italian Job*. I crash and burn the car at every bend until it *Hertz*, one of the joys of driving a crappy rental car rather than your own. At times the route over the Pyrenees Mountains disappears and I cruise through puffy clouds. It is so high that, much like on a Ruinair flight, my ears pop and I yawn to ease the discomfort. I know I am drawing closer to the enclave when the oncoming traffic includes Porsches and a red Ferrari with *Principat* registrations. Crossing the border into Andorra is quick and hassle-free, but there is a lofty tailback of traffic leaving the country as Spanish customs officials zealously stop and search cars. We can visit but can we ever leave?

The major national CG1 route traversing the country has one lane in each direction except when I wait at make-shift alternate traffic lights while two blokes rebuild a stone wall at the roadside and stall the entire country's road network. The nation's construction industry is engaged in a competition to build the tallest building as close as possible to this road. Development is everywhere, such that the national bird of this country may be the red rusted crane. Three hours' driving from Barcelona brings me to Europe's highest capital city of Andorra La Vella (pop 32,000). The capital rests below steep 2,300 metre high mountains, as a drop of sweat clings underneath an armpit. Andorra has survived intact over the centuries because it has zero strategic importance, so no one bothered about it much, if at all.

As expected, the *Principat de les Valles de Andorra* has a quirky history. Andorra has two co-princes, the President of France and the Bishop of Seu d'Urgell, and according to an agreement in 1278, in odd-numbered years the French co-prince is sent 1,920 francs in tribute, while in even-numbered years the Spanish co-prince receives 900 pesetas, twelve chickens, six hams and twelve cheeses; an archaic feudal arrangement overtaken by the demise of the currencies. At the end of the First World War, Andorra, which had been on the Allied side, was not invited to attend the signing of the peace treaty and so remained at war with Germany until 25 September 1939. Having been exhausted by two and a half decades of phoney war with Germany, Andorra chose to be neutral in World War Two, thus continuing 800 years without a direct war. But there was a close call in 1934 in the midst of the accidental war with the Germans, when a Russian opportunist Count called Boris Skossyreff arrived and seized power in Andorra. He titled himself King Boris I of Andorra, declared war on the Bishop of Urgell and was in power for several days until the Spanish sent along four *Guardia Civils* to see what was happening and Boris surrendered without a fight.

When I step out of my hotel a number of females immediately whistle at me, which is always a pleasant surprise in a foreign city. They wave their hands at me in some indecipherable manner. They are in uniform and I do like girls in uniform. I step off the pavement and one lets out a vicious blast at me. Traffic cops behave like this. Andorra is not run by a legislative assembly. It is run by a gang of glamorous ladies in blue uniforms with orange flashes who tell us what to do and where to go. They are essential, since the narrow hilly circling streets are crammed with fuming gridlocked cars. The traffic snakes up and down and combats the pedestrians at every opportunity. On Avenue Meritxell the traffic triumphs since the street has no pavements and only plastic bollards separate man and Audi SUV. The honking air is foul, like sucking on a belching exhaust pipe. There is an open-air restaurant here where you can order pizza with a local topping called extra lead oxide emissions. I search for respite in the *Barri Antic*, the Old City, where the narrow streets are cobbled and pedestrianised but locals still speed up and down the one-way streets with a millimetre of clearance between wing mirror and historic stone building, and me somewhere in between. I don't know where all these people are going? What is happening in Andorra that I don't know about?

In my quest I walk down to the *Casa de la Vall*, the seat of the Parliament, which is an ancient stone building with a slate roof, no bigger than the average family home. Politics are almost embryonic; the written Andorran Constitution was only passed in 1993. Inside is the only courtroom in the country, plus the Cupboard of the Seven Keys, where the most important national documents were held and which could only be opened by the simultaneous presence of councillors from all of the seven parishes. I want to take the guided tour but the girl at the door advises I must reserve a tour in advance. Then a stroke of luck because there's a tour commencing at 10am, in thirty minutes time, and I can join.

At ten minutes to ten, which is the first giveaway, a battalion size tour party approaches, one hundred strong and led by a loud lady with a brolly in the air. My heart sinks as I hear the voices. They're speaking German. The tour is in *Deutsche* today. *Do you speak German, sir? Nein.* Half the tour are middle-aged males who wear those natty sleeveless khaki jackets. Exit Kilduff towards the communal *Place del Poble*, which is the main town square but which turns out to be a concrete wasteland built six storeys up atop a car park and municipal offices. I am now peckish and there are plenty of official signs on the streets to the most prominent restaurants. The signs include *Big Ben Restaurant 50 metres, Pizza Hut 25 metres* and *Kentucky Fried Chicken 50 metres.*

Andorra has never had much. It never had its own currency and used francs and pesetas before the euro. It never had an army, and defence is the responsibility of France and Spain. It never had an airline, an airport (see Pyrenees Mountains), or a TV station, and only 2 per cent of land can be farmed. It never had a postal service; instead French and Spanish post offices issue Andorra's stamps. It never had visa requirements or taxes. It hardly even has a government since the elected representatives take most of the year off. You cannot buy a guidebook on Andorra because none exist. If they did, they would be more like a leaflet. It has one national resource called snow, which provides a wintertime skiing industry. In the absence of snow on a year round basis, they invented an attraction for the summer. Tax-free shopping.

Twelve million visitors visit the 2,000 specialised shops annually. Yes, in Andorra the Tourist Office kindly counts the number of shops. I am in a neon sprawl where every window display is identical: watches, clothes, perfumes, alcohol, cigarettes, CDs, DVDs, MP3s, spectacles, radios, binoculars, plasmas, hard drives, soft drives. It's an airport without a runway but with duty free, a capital consumed by conspicuous consumption. Here the *Pyrenees* is not a spectacular mountain range, it's the name of a shopping mall in the centre of town. The Andorran Tourist Board literature features photographs of locals in feudal costumes with red aprons and sashes, white stockings and pointy goblin hats so it's a relief to see that the locals are in fact all Spaniards who are all very well-dressed, and why not with this range of clothing outlets? Spaniards are at home here because this is the only country in the world where the official language is Catalan.

The assorted *perfumerias* pump out the aroma of their products onto the street so walking past is like going through the ground floor of Brown Thomas or Selfridges, but without the female glamour. Everyone smokes because cancer sticks are so cheap and the *Big Swinging Dicks* smoke Big Swinging cigars. You can buy most things. Self-defence shops sell CS gas sprays, Glock air pistols and thousand-volt stun-guns. The *Safari Master* shop sells sporting ammunition and nitro-express cartridges. But there are no supermarkets, newsagents or bookshops. It's easy to buy the latest Tag Heuer model or a bottle of CK1, but try finding an apple or a newspaper on Avenue Meritxell. Postcards are easy to obtain since every electrical outlet has racks of them outside for next to nothing prices to lure the retail punters inside.

I refuse to succumb to the hard sell and only purchase two postcards plus two stamps. *Yes, I'll take these two postcards, and no, I don't need a 50-inch wide-screen HD-ready TV set with 1,000 channels, which in any event won't fit into my carry-on baggage.* I don't know what the attraction is, because half the items in the windows are unpriced and 70 euros for a Ralph Lauren Polo shirt is not that cheap, and anyway we have shops too where I live. If I desired a *Krups Nespresso* coffee maker in anthracite metal and anodised aluminium with a high-pressure 19-bar pump and removable steam nozzle I would go out and buy one rather than driving 210 kilometres to save ten euros in the factory outlet that is Andorra.

I want to flee to the countryside where the Tourist Office says there is flora and fauna, gastronomy, spas, a surprising variety of wild mushrooms in the woods and twenty-seven high mountain huts open all year round. Instead I search for air near the *Gran Valira River* which runs through the capital but in best local traditions they have concreted the river bank and the river bed, making it look like a grandiose effluent sewer.

I join the elderly folk in starchy shirts and sensible slacks who sit by the streets in the shade with a seasoned wisdom and together we wonder what the hell is going on here in Europe's highest car park? The answer is emblazoned on all the cars going nowhere in this cloud of lead. The SUVs all display their national stickers of 'AND'. 'AND' what? Cars 'AND' shops.

Italy

MyAir Flight 812511 – Wednesday @ 2.50pm
– BCN-VCE-TSF-STN

Fare €40 plus taxes, fees and charges €54

When checking in for a flight Italians are obliged to bring their entire extended family, usually fifteen to twenty people. They position themselves in each queue and so can lane hop in the same manner as when they drive Fiat automobiles at home, where pedestrians are expendable and wearing a seatbelt shows a lack of personal confidence, and where driving everywhere is acceptable, although officially they're meant to keep to the right side of the road. So one minute you're in a queue of two and the next there are twenty people ahead of you. Italians at check-in are prone to bouts of heavy mutual petting, amorous lovemaking short of full intercourse and fond embraces more usually observed between loved ones and troops returning from significant overseas military conflicts. And don't Italians love to talk. Loudly. Excitedly. All the time. I am looking forward to returning to Italy. Last time I went to Pisa. That tower definitely looks crooked to me.

MyAir operate a covert check-in facility hidden in a side annex in the bowels of Barcelona's Terminal A. Today's queue presents some trouble ahead, principally surfers with towering fin boards and some amateur travellers who paid five euros to have their luggage shrink-wrapped for security purposes only to remember at the check-in desk that they left their tickets and passports inside the same sealed suitcase. We are also delayed by a woman who has taped three bags together onto a large trolley with a mile of duct tape only to find it is too large to pass along the conveyor belt so she unwinds all the tape and discards the giant wheelie device, presumably stolen from either Tiger Woods' caddy or men who move grand pianos.

MyHair is an Italian low fares airline with a suspicious pedigree, being run by the former management of Volare, another low fares airline which collapsed with huge euro debts. I once tried to book a ticket with Volare but I was too late. They went bust. Their ex-website said they were '*Low Cost Made in Italy.*' Undeterred by this commercial disaster the management rapidly formed another airline and took off again. MyHair is based at Milan Orio al Serio airport and flies Airbus A320-200s and some MD82 aircraft within Italy and to Spain, France and Romania. Being Italian, the aircraft are painted in nationalistic red, green and white. Flights are booked online but take care with using www.myair.it since this is an entirely different website concerned with air quality in Europe.

Unfortunately we fly on an old MD82 today. Whilst the eminent McDonnell Douglas Corporation were building long, narrow, pointy 5-seats-per-row jets with engines rear-mounted on the tails, other aircraft manufacturers were building short, squat 6-seat-per-row aircraft with engines on the wings. And where are McDonnell Douglas now? That's right, they're part of Boeing Corporation. This aircraft's nose sports a handpainted one-liner like some motto a crew would scribble on a war-time Memphis Belle: '*No guts, no glory,*' which is surprising since we are flying to Venice rather than going on a night-time bombing run.

On board I am confused. Four of the cabin crew wear red uniforms, almost military, with flares and flair, plus gold piping and big shoulders. They work for Air Adriatic, from whom this aircraft is on loan. Only one girl in a black jacket and skirt works for MyHair but she has lovely hair. She leads the team with a commanding attitude. If I could bottle it and sell it in duty-free it would be called '*Don't Even Think About It.*' All the cabin crew are six foot and love to stride up and down the aisle, but I guess they're being Italian and wish they were on a catwalk.

The flight is on time, the service is excellent, the food and drink are value for money and I can relax. I note Italians remain the only nation on earth to wear sunglasses whilst on aircraft. So they can look cool. And they remain the nationality most likely to burst into spontaneous applause upon a safe landing. Today some of the passengers behind break into a few lines of that New York song, '*I did it my way.*' Honest.

Henry James said the best way to arrive in Venice is by boat, but I disagree. As MyHair swoops to land at *Marco Polo* airport, a magical island hovers in a glistening lagoon off to starboard, connected to the mainland by a ribbon of causeway I will shortly cross. Pink and terracotta buildings emit a welcoming glow. There are spires, towers, palaces and domes. Boats ferry back and forth. Is it real?

Navigation is impossible in Venice. The few streets twist and wind and often lead to dead ends of brick walls and hidden gardens. Some streets are only four or five feet wide, are blind and shaded and if you meet an American you have to give way. The residences have impossibly high street numbers such as 8878N. Being a postman here must be a lifetime's vocation. It takes twenty minutes to find my hotel, which is a two-minute walk from the bus terminal, and that's after annoying about ten citizens for directions. Streets here are called *Calle*. My hotel is on a street called *Calle Bloody Hard to Find Even When Sober*. Once checked in I am inclined not to leave my hotel for fear of never locating it again. Eventually I head out to explore, advising the duty manager that if I am not back in two hours he should call *National Ordinance.*

I accept his advice and catch the number 82 from Piazzale de Roma, crammed together with other highly expectant passengers. The 82 is not a bus. We go under the first of the three bridges, the lesser known *Ponte degli Scalzi*. I am on possibly the most perfect stretch of waterway in the world. It is two miles long, averages a depth of nine feet and is only 130 to 230 feet wide. It follows an ancient riverbed and snakes in an inverted s-shape, cutting this city of 118 islands and 450 bridges into two unequal parts, running from the terminal railway station in the north-west to the vital *Piazza San Marco* in the south-east. This is the world's greatest

ferry ride, perhaps only equalled by a trip across Hong Kong
harbour in a Star ferry. The *Canal Grande* is Venice's main
thoroughfare. It's their own Oxford Street, Champs-Elysees,
Broadway or Fifth all in one. Here the streets are paved with brine.
The New Yorker magazine humorist Robert Benchley once sent a
wire home to his friends in the USA: '*Have arrived ... streets are full
of water ... please advise.*' The great writer Hugh Hefner once
remarked that in Venice the street walkers must first learn how to
swim.

This *vaporetto* is slow and we are overtaken by successive water
taxis, well cared for boats in cream fibreglass or a walnut burl. A
few weeks earlier an Australian tourist abandoned this water bus to
plunge overboard, intending to swim the half kilometre from the
Rialto stop to his hotel in *Piazza San Marco*, even though it was
4am. He wasn't drunk but the police nicked him anyway.
Swimming in the canals is banned. He was possibly inspired by
Lord Byron, the romantic poet who swam the length of the canal
while pissed one night, and who would swim in the nude to the
windows of beautiful Venetian women with a torchlight in his
hand and peep inside their bedchambers, hoping for an invitation
to enter, so to speak — an amorous solitary nocturnal male
practice nowadays most likely to lead to a short stay in a penal
institution.

Looking downwards, I consider the possibility that the
Australian tourist might have died had he not been hauled out by
the police. Venice has no sewerage system. Sewage and waste flow
into the canals and are washed out into the ocean twice a day with
the tides. Another legendary but native Venetian lover was
Giacomo Casanova, the eighteenth century's most famous man
about these canals. He had a private love boat in which to get
about. His memoirs claimed he 'courted' 122 ladies in his life. Sadly
he died from a venereal disease, and possibly also from exhaustion.

I cannot absorb the armada of architectural sights around every
bend: rococo palaces, merchants' mansions, baroque churches,
gilded and golden. Upon close inspection many are damaged by
buffeting, with brickwork exposed, plaster peeling away, cracked
wooden beams and green lichens not letting go. In other places

along the canal bank wizened gardeners tend blooming geraniums, staff clean tall arched windows and trusted housekeepers hang out colourful laundry on lines in this living, breathing nautical city.

Each *vaporetto* can take 229 passengers, that's forty more than a Boeing 737, and cheaper at €10 for all day travel. Everyone has their own boat except me. The laundryman has a boat, so do *Carbinieri* and firemen, the builders have one with cranes inside, the fruit and veg. men pile theirs high. Even the task of removing garbage in green metal containers by boat becomes exceedingly glamorous. And when it all gets too much a black and gold death boat will whisk you away to the nearby San Michele graveyard.

I see my first black *gondole*, tied up at barber pole moorings, prancing up and down like eager stallions ready for the off. Their *gondoliers* sport the traditional uniform of straw boater, black and white striped shirts, black trousers and Nike sneakers, the latter I assume for grip. Parties of the world's wealthiest Japanese tourists provide the valuable custom.

The *Rialto* Bridge was built to link two sides of the canal at the oldest site of commercial activity and remains Venice's own waterlogged answer to Wall Street. Some commuters alight at *Rialto* with briefcases and newspapers, being the luckiest commuters in the world. This is where Shakespeare's Shylock once asked 'What news on the *Rialto*?' which is still taken to mean 'How is the stock market doing these days?' Up close the marble and stone work is smooth to the touch, worn by generations of admirers. The bridge is achingly picturesque and large enough for rows of shops, like the *Ponte Vecchio* in Florence. The shops sell everything from Venetian face masks, glass beads from Murano, lace napkins, to the strip of the Italian national soccer team, even that of Allessandro del Piero who has suffered the longest goal drought of all.

After forty minutes and ten canal-side stops, I disembark at the floating jetty of San Marco. St Mark's Square is the touristic hub, being the size of several football fields. I should visit the Doge's Palace or the Basilica but the history is initially overpowering, too much to imbibe in a few days. I would need weeks to do this justice. So instead I walk around while string quartets play light classical music in the side arcades. Thousands of tourists pass me by, led by guides with microphones with speakers, in competition with each other. Visitors coming and going pull suitcases about the square, there being no way to hail a cab like back home. Grown men feed pigeons with bird food on sale at one euro a shot until grown women burst into tears and run in fear across the piazza, closely pursued by several hundred ravenous Hitchkovian birds.

There's a crowd stopped on the *Ponte della Paglia*, taking photographs of the Bridge of Sighs, so called because it ran between the justice courts and the prison. But what a wonderful city in which to serve your sentence. I step back to the edge of the piazza where the water ebbs and flows to lap up over the steps with alarming eagerness and determination. A section of the waterfront is cordoned off with building works and signs for the preservation of San Marco. Already I am getting that sinking feeling.

If I had been standing in this spot on 31 October 2004, I'd now be rooted in sixteen inches of salty seawater. When Venice was founded in 421 AD, long oak pilings were driven into the clay, wooden planks were placed on top and then layers of Istrian stone were laid, upon which the buildings were constructed. Wooden pilings lying underwater are ideal, since in the absence of oxygen, they do not decay. At that time the level of the Adriatic Sea was five metres lower than what it is today. In 1900 the city was flooded about six times a year but now the city is flooded about 100 times per year because the sea level around Venice has risen by about four and a half inches and the land base has subsided by eight inches in a century.

Venetians are familiar with *acqua alta*, meaning high water, a polite term for bad flooding. They are prepared: sirens sound a warning and raised plywood boards are laid out to walk upon. They keep one set of rubber waders at home and another set in the office. They monitor the tide and can call flood helplines. In some old houses prone to flooding, the ground floors remain permanently unoccupied. On 3 November 1966 the city was under six foot of water, damaging much art. But there is long-term damage as salt water from the Adriatic soaks into the soft permeable brickwork that lies above these foundations. The evidence is before my eyes as workmen on their knees replace brittle paving stones in Piazza San Marco.

Project Mose is designed to protect the three entrances to the lagoon that surrounds Venice with 79 movable barriers. The barriers remain below the surface of the sea when tides are low but can be raised when tides are high, blocking the sea from entering the lagoon. MOSE stands for *Modulo Sperimentale Elettromeccanico* which translates for me as a modular electrical Meccano experiment, so it should work. Note that this is an Italian government construction project. Approval for the €4 billion project was given in a 1973 law, the design was finished in 1989 and the project received government approval in 2001 for completion in 2011. There is no guarantee the project will be completed since the government changes in Italy more often than the guard at Buckingham Palace. Italy has enjoyed sixty governments since 1945.

The majority of visitors arrive here by bus for a day trip, smash and grab and leave at dusk. I have to constantly remind myself that this city has a real population of 63,000, sadly a huge reduction from a population of 184,000 as recently as 1950. Occasionally a mother and child will stop up ahead in a narrow street by house 7866L with their daily shopping, open a hall door with a key and disappear inside a dark and cool ground floor. I step back to allow them their privacy, aware that I too am one of the space invaders.

It is a hazard of modern tourism that often we exhaust the must-see global destinations. A decade ago I took a trip with some friends to see Egypt. It was at the time of the Gulf War when terrified Americans on vacation were a rare species. In Cairo we stayed at the optimistically named *Chateau des Pyramides* hotel after a late-night flight arrival. Next morning a friend woke first and pulled back the curtains to reveal the three Pyramids of Giza at the foot of the back garden of the hotel. Stunning. In the next two weeks we overdosed, went inside the Pyramid of Cheops, visited the Step Pyramid at Saqqara, the sights at Abu Simbel,

Luxor, Karnak and Aswan and even took in the *Pyramid That Was Merely A Glint in the Architect's Eye And Never Made it Off the Draft Plans*. On the last day we overnighted at the same hotel before flying back on Air Gippy to London Heathrow. My friend was up first for the early flight and he pulled back the same curtains, turned to me and uttered the immortal words, 'If I ever see one more fucking pyramid ...'

There is a dead calm in the northern *Campo San Margherita*, a square with bars and restaurants and not a canal in sight. Ancient trees, quite a rarity in Venice, provide shade and aged church bells chime authentically on the hour as pizza, macaroni, tiramisu and beer flow into the early evening, courtesy of model waitresses in white aprons and Armani jeans. Children play, diners shift tables to converse and a bloke on his own scribbles notes for a travel book. I settle my bill early so I can find my hotel while there are still a few hours of light to be had. I could provide the directions to this square but I'd be wasting my time. I stumbled upon it and could never find it again without the use of a high-resolution satellite photograph.

My final thoughts are of these peaceful streets and deserted canals at this late hour, the locals at ease in their community in spite of the relentless waves that pound this island daily, the tidal onslaught and churning volumes threatening to drown them all and sink this special place for ever. Bloody tourists. Fifteen million of them come here every year, that's 40,000 people every day evacuating onto one small island, using the toilets, buying Cokes and pizza and pointing at things.

Next morning I make the trip home on Ruinair because they are so cheap and also they are big in Italy. Mick was here when he dressed up as Caesar to launch some new routes in Italy: *'They're not used to someone going down and making a complete tit of himself. You've got to keep people interested. We specialize in cheap publicity stunts. As long as it's not safety-related, there's no such thing as bad publicity. If you have low fares, you have to shout your mouth off a lot more. I'm not doing something new as Richard Branson did it for years. If you make a lot of noise and fight with a lot of people you generate a lot of cheap publicity. All we do is go around, create a bit of controversy, do silly things, get your photograph taken in silly places and reduce the advertising money — and like that we can afford to keep the prices down.'* And Mick was in Rome where he dressed as the Pope, declaring: *'Habemus lowest fares.'*

Speaking of the Pope, the Vatican has started an airline to fly pilgrims to destinations such as the shrine of Fatima in Portugal and Santiago de Compostela in Spain. The seat headrests have the message: 'I search for your face, oh Lord'. But passengers from Lourdes were told they could not take on board any of the holy water they had bought due to EU regulations on liquids. One passenger was so distraught at having to hand over his holy water that he drank it on the spot. While not representing real competition, a Ruinair spokesman felt obliged to comment: *'Ruinair already performs miracles that even the Pope's boss can't rival, by delivering pilgrims to Santiago de Compostela for the heavenly price of ten euros.'*

It's a 6am start, a one-hour bus excursion to Treviso, a two-hour wait in a veritable dive of an airport at departure gate 1 (of two), a long standing queue in a tunnel, a mad rush for seats, the hard commercial sell, the disgusting yellow aircraft interior (the same shade as cowardice or custard), the seats without pockets which don't recline, the hostile crew with unpronounceable first names and poor diction who don't have the confidence to answer simple passenger enquiries, don't know the price of a sandwich and don't have the maturity to overcome a collective fit of contagious giggles when delivering the safety demonstration before our on-time departure.

In 1984 the BBC TV newsreader Michael Buerk filed an earth-shattering report on a famine in Ethiopia, where he stood before a mass of suffering humanity in tattered rags with bloated stomachs and uttered the immortal words, 'If there is a hell on earth, then this is it.' Evidently he had not been to Treviso airport. And if it's true that every aircraft flight shortens your life span, then I am surely going to hell soon. I have taken nine flights within the past thirteen days. I am not sure I can take much more of this. In the words of Seal's 1990 song 'Crazy' … *in a world full of people, only some want to fly.* This is *Cryin'Air.*

There are few things more unpleasant in life than flying with Ruinair. But I keep doing it. Why do I keep doing it? Because it is cheap and even though after each flight I'm raging and angry, I always forget it after a few weeks and book another flight. Something or someone needs to stop me doing this. Soon.

Customer Service
Ruinair Ltd
Dublin Airport

Dear Sirs,

I had the great misfortune to travel on FR793 from Venice Treviso airport and found it to be a disgusting airport. In the words perhaps of your Chief Executive, it could best be described as, and please excuse the Italian, a 'shit hole'. It's less of an airport, more of a bus station. I would like to advise you of the following.

We sat in a filthy departures lounge with bad lighting, torn floors and broken seats. Several of the rows of seats have missing seats. Where do they go? Are these the same seats which your airline famously sells for as little as 1 cent? Two of the four urinals in the Gents toilets are out of order. There are several telephone booths on the walls but the telephones have been removed. This is the only 'airport' in Europe which does not sell newspapers, magazines or books airside. I purchased a coffee from the small bar area but only after the girl who served me got down on her hands and knees, picked up dirty towels from the floor which were sodden with water, wrung them out and replaced them below the leaking refrigerator units with a practised ease to suggest that she does it every day. I don't object to the specifics above but if those who manage the airport cannot fix a completely fucked fridge what chance do they have of safely receiving and despatching a Boeing B737-800 aircraft with 189 passengers on board? I am aware that a new airport terminal is under construction. Whatever you now pay in landing charges at Treviso, you are being significantly overcharged. I would like to know why you subject your passengers to these dire conditions and please do not try to blame the airport authority since your jolly Ruinair signs are all over the airport. 'Vola Ruinair. Volare a Prezzi Bassi.'

Yours etc,
Disgusted of Dublin

Two days later … (they are getting slow) …

Dear Mr Kilduff,

I acknowledge receipt of your letter.

Please note that I have forwarded a copy of your correspondence to our commercial department.

Please accept our apologies for the inconvenience caused during your departure from Treviso Airport.

Unfortunately you will need to contact the Italian Airport Authorities, regarding your complaint. It is the Italian Airport Authorities who are authorised to maintain the Italian Airports.

Once again please accept our apologies for any inconvenience caused.

Yours sincerely
For and on Behalf of
RUINAIR LIMITED

More bolloxology.

San Marino

I almost forgot that I visited another country. *TrenItalia* from Venice takes three and a half hours to reach Rimini on the Adriatic coast, where I make a connection with an international bus service. Along the way I pass another Ruinair destination, Bologna-Forli airport, albeit 84 km from Bologna itself. In Rimini I learn I must buy a bus ticket at the bus stop from an aged, aggressive lady on a moped unless I am a good-looking Russian lady tourist in see-through jeans and a bikini top, in which case the bus driver is only too happy to assist. I am the only person on the Bonelli bus with any overnight luggage. Forty-five minutes later the gradient becomes almost vertical. There are neither customs posts, border controls nor even a frontier as we drive under a foot-bridge which proudly proclaims '*Welcome to the Ancient Land of Liberty*'.

At 61 square km, the Most Serene Republic of San Marino is the third smallest nation in Europe (making the Vatican and Monaco look teeny) and it is the oldest constitutional republic in the world. In 301 AD a Christian stonemason from Dalmatia called Marinus sought refuge here from religious persecution and began a community which later became a free city. Marinus was so popular that he was venerated as St Marinus, and gave the nation its name. San Marino survived the centuries thanks to its rugged terrain, lack of natural resources, isolation and the fact that most people prefer, like Andorra, to circumnavigate it.

San Marino has only been occupied by foreigners twice. In 1503, the Borgias took over for a few months and two hundred years later, Cardinal Alberoni invaded the country but the Pope told him to give it back and he did. In World War Two the nation's population swelled to 100,000 in this eternally neutral republic, so if war breaks out in Italy again the best thing for any Italian with sense is to head for the hills of San Marino. The centre was heavily bombed in WWII but you would not know it from the pristine buildings and streets.

San Marino is not one of the world's great sporting nations. They possess a modest football team, for which the eleven players are chosen with some difficulty from the nation's population of 30,000. They have only won one match and that was versus Liechtenstein (see earlier chapter). They were beaten 13-0 by Germany. Our Republic of Ireland team thrashed them 2-1 with the decisive winner coming in the 95th minute. Let's face up to sporting reality. We are never going to see San Marino playing in the World Cup finals. And the San Marino Formula One Grand Prix is not even held here, but 80 km away in Imola, Italy.

Their capital is also called San Marino, where 5,000 Sanmarinese live on the rugged western slopes of Monte Titano, a giant, craggy, limestone rock looming out of a heat haze. It is the only mountain peak for miles and looks like a wandering offspring from the much greater nearby Apennine range. Three magnificent turreted fortresses perch on the pinnacle of the sheer cliffs, la Guaita, la Cesta and Montale, each representing one of the nine towns which make up the republic. The towers are connected by castellated walls and winding pathways. Monte Titano is 740 metres high and is not for those with vertigo. The view at the top is special because it is not often you can see an entire country from one vantage point.

My earliest memory of San Marino was thirty years ago as a junior philatelist. I joined the Stanley Gibbons *Stamp Collecting Club* for a tenner since I was promised a bumper first delivery of 1,000 stamps. The press advertisement promised me unsorted random stamps and it included a picture of a rare Penny Black, so I expected to receive some valuable stamps, possibly even another Penny Black upon which I could retire for a life of leisure at the age of twelve. As it happened 500 of the 1,000 stamps were from San Marino and were crap. I could never figure out how such a small nation needed to send so much mail. The shops in this postcard republic still sell pages of stamps commemorating every event that ever happened. They affix two stamps into my passport when I ask for a tourist visa — on the same page as Liechtenstein.

Three million tourists visit San Marino annually, mostly for three hours because that is all the time that is required, and they are all here today. Tourism generates half the nation's revenue and it places the population amongst the most affluent on earth. And a different kind of invasion has been taking place; gold-digging women travel to San Marino to marry rich old men, and so many have been picked off by their employees that San Marino passed a law prohibiting foreign domestic servants under the age of fifty. San Marino suffers from a loss of population and the Museum of Emigration confirms that most Sanmarinese emigrated to, of all places, Detroit, Michigan. This is surprising since the locals are not poor. Income tax is capped at 25 per cent, unemployment is nil, Italians commute to work and there are Ferraris to be seen, but the latter is due to the fact that Maranello Rosso and its exhibition of twenty-five Ferraris dating back to 1951 is only forty miles away. That's five minutes in a Ferrari. Enzo Ferrari once said of San Marino: 'Looking back at the mountain peak, I see the crowds and names that accompanied my career' — proof that he was better at fast corners than eloquent literary quotes.

I skip the Torture Museum with its 100 plus instruments used to inflict pain and death, mainly because there is an iron chair with spikes, leather straps and a stiff metal back which reminds me of a seat I will sit in for three hours soon on Ruinair. The Museum of Curiosities houses a unique collection of incredible facts, objects and personalities that are strange but true. The exhibits are seedy, ghoulish and freakish, not unlike a poor man's *Guinness World Records*. The interior here reminds me of a sex museum I once visited in Amsterdam (for research purposes) with black floors,

wall mirrors, spotlight bulbs and red railings. Today I see the man
with the world's longest fingernails at 135 inches and the man with
the world's longest hair at 311 inches, neither of which are curious
but represent poor basic hygiene. There's the world's heaviest man
at 1,399 pounds, and naturally enough he's from the USA. There's
waxy Saint Simeon le Jeune who spent the last forty-five years of
his life living on the top of a stone column. He certainly needed to
get out more often but he lived in Syria in 390 AD before the advent
of low fares airlines. And I wonder how they knew that he had
died? Did they leave him up on the column for a few more weeks
to see if he moved much? All in all it's not very entertaining, except
for the howling spelling mistakes in the English descriptions of the
exhibits. I leave aware that the Museum of Curiosities is only
missing one curious local exhibit not seen anywhere else in the
world: the Republic of San Marino itself.

There is a distinctly medieval air to the capital; a time when men
lived by the sword and women were chaste. A lot. I am very
fortunate to accidentally arrive here during the *Giornate
Medioevali* festival. For a whole week the many districts of the
historic capital are transformed by over five hundred performers
in period costumes with picturesque retinues, colourful standards,
swirling banners and booming trumpets. They offer a *Ye Golden
Olde Days* spectacle in the impressive setting of the town's streets
and squares. Musicians, actors, jugglers and acrobats involve the
public in living theatre shows. Serving wenches wander about
wearing super-tight boned corsets. Open-air restaurants recreate
medieval fare and offer menus and food from a thousand years
ago. Ugh. A medieval market lit by twinkling lanterns is the
backdrop as master craftsmen in costume demonstrate bygone
arts and crafts. There is probably a fair bit of pillaging and
ravishing going on behind the scenes too but I don't know how to
get any for myself.

The mood in this capital is amazingly welcoming. Two
comedians dressed as monks perform a routine to turn Campari
into lemonade and it's all in Italian and I cannot understand a
word of it but the humour is infectious. A bevy of harpists play
classical airs on the steps of the cathedral. Groups of knights in full

metal jacket with tall pikes parade through the darkening streets and scare me shitless. Twenty-foot-high giant caricatures dance in unison in the *Palazzo Publico.* A mad fool of a lady in white clothes and skullcap strides about the streets chasing a piece of bread on string hanging from a stick on her head, sadly destined never to catch it. A tight-rope walker wobbles over a low-slung rope but really he's very skilled and will never fall. Star troopers hurl giant furling flags way up into the air, five at a time, and catch them all. Archers in natty Robin Hood outfits use crossbows to knock plates off targets with alarming accuracy. Radio San Marino is here to broadcast to the nation, which is unnecessary because all of the nation are here. Elderly ladies appear on high Juliet balconies of terracotta and geraniums to observe the entertainment. I am the only person not in medieval costume since I am in my Nike, Gant and K-Swiss.

I retire to take a late evening meal at the open-air *La Capanna* restaurant. Nearby church bells toll 9pm and it is still 30 degrees Celsius. Tourists stand up to take photographs of the setting ochre sun over Monte Carpegna. Way below across the plains of Emilia Romagna I see Rimini and the Adriatic coastline only 10 km away. On a clear day, some can see Croatia. I down *picolas* of *birra,* and *gelato. Summertime* by the Fresh Prince wafts on the speaker system. A hum of lazy conversation permeates the still air. I don't think there can be a better place to be in all of Europe than San Marino on the last day of Medieval Week.

I wonder why does San Marino exist? I assume the answer lies in the nation's tourist industry. San Marino primarily exists to offer another country to Italians to visit without having to go too far and it exists to give American tourists something medieval and curious to tell the folks back home about. *Believe it or Not.*

The Low Fares
Airline (4)

THE TRAIN FARES AIRLINE

A group of Scots stranded by Ruinair in Germany arrived home yesterday after a gruelling 36-hour road and rail journey across Europe and said they would never again use the budget airline. Faced with the prospect of having to wait days for the next available flight and having been offered a refund of £5 each, the 38-strong church group defiantly made their own arrangements to travel the 1,000 miles home. They were among 180 passengers with the Irish no-frills carrier whose Prestwick-bound flight from Hamburg-Lubeck was cancelled due to 'technical problems'. The airline's apologies failed to satisfy the group, and it may have breached European legislation by refusing to offer hotel accommodation or any meals. The group from Muirkirk, Ayrshire, who had been on a shopping trip to the German Christmas markets, jumped on a service bus into Hamburg city centre. There they boarded a train to Brussels, transferred to the Eurostar train to Euston and then took a Virgin train to Glasgow Central. Rae Howat, a pensioner, said: 'They completely abandoned us. No-one showed any concern about us whatsoever. They wouldn't give us a penny for meals or anything. No-one representing Ruinair came to see us or talk to us. So we just decided to make our own way home.' The St Thomas's Church group, among them many elderly people who did not have credit cards, had to pay out more than £300 each for their train journey back to Scotland. There to greet the party at the station was David Loy whose mother, Theresa, 72, and 82-year-old aunt Mary Murray, were among the passengers. Hugging his mother, a relieved Mr Loy said: 'It is an absolute disgrace what these people have been put through. My mother has a heart condition and is waiting for a hip replacement.' Members of the group also revealed how they had to sit in the departure lounge at Hamburg for five hours with no information, and with only a 'delayed' sign showing against their flight. They only found out the flight was cancelled when one passenger's husband phoned from Scotland, telling her that the message was on Ruinair's website.

THE HERALD

THE BUS FARES AIRLINE

Ruinair passengers have 'flown' from Paris to Madrid by bus. Some 50 travellers have demanded compensation after their flight was cancelled last Sunday, after they arrived at Barajas airport in Madrid yesterday afternoon after the 18-hour bus trip. Ruinair says the flight was cancelled because of adverse weather conditions at the Paris Beauvais airport. The passengers were refunded their money and offered the coach, or the alternative of waiting until Thursday for another flight. The deal was done after three people from the Spanish Consul in Paris went to the airport to mediate.

TYPICALLY SPANISH

THE LOW FERRY AIRLINE

What should have been a 40-minute flight for 47 students ended up in a marathon 22-hour bus and ferry journey as they desperately tried to get home. The group of teenagers were left stranded in London after they claimed that Ruinair staff would not let them board their flight home because they were just two minutes late. The soccer players, aged between 12 and 16, made it home after a 460km drive across England, an early-morning ferry back to Dublin and a three-hour coach trip back to Galway. Organisers of the trip say the missed flight cost them over €3,700 in coach hire, food and the ferry *home. Vice-president of Mervue United George Guest said the group of soccer players were attending the Allborg Youth Games in Denmark, where they won a number of medals. They flew out Dublin-Stansted-Aarhus with Ruinair and were due to travel home from Denmark to Dublin with the low-cost airline but a technical fault at Aarhus airport delayed them for over five hours. When they arrived in Stansted for their connecting flight back to Dublin, they were told they were too late to board the plane. 'Ruinair said if we could find the internet we could see about getting flights home for a penny. The pilot was helpful — he rang London on his own mobile phone to tip them off that we'd be late,' club president Peter Long said. 'We're pissed off with Ruinair. Fair enough if it was adults, but it was 47 kids. Ruinair gave us a voucher for 35 kroner, which was enough to buy a bag of chips. We're all-Ireland champions, and we're treated like this by Ruinair, and it's shitty.' The low-cost airline has lost out on future business from the young players. Asked if they would travel with Ruinair again, there was a resounding 'No' from all of them. The airline said that it was 'unfortunate' that the Danish leg of the trip was delayed by five hours.*

IRISH INDEPENDENT

THE LOW FEAR AIRLINE

After a nightmare flight with budget airline Ruinair, Mr John Wilkie found himself the unlikely leader of a passenger revolt when a terror alert caused their flight to be grounded. His family were forced to spend nearly six hours on the plane without food or drink. Unable to get water for his wife and two children and frustrated at the lack of information from staff, Mr Wilkie tried to disembark, followed by 30 fellow passengers. After being persuaded to stay, however, the rebels were stunned when police arrived and arrested their 'ringleader' for causing a security alert on a flight. In court, Mr Wilkie, 36, admitted the charge. But a Scottish sheriff refused to punish him after receiving dozens of letters from passengers supporting him. Instead, the sheriff called on Ruinair to apologise for its 'ridiculous' behaviour. Elected the passengers' spokesman, Mr Wilkie told the crew he was taking his family off the plane. Staff called the pilot, who Mr Wilkie claims told him: 'On you go then, get off.' With his wife and children, Mr Wilkie stepped out of the open aircraft door, followed by dozens of other fed-up passengers, only to be met at the foot of steps by airport staff who persuaded them it was in everyone's interests to reboard the plane. Mr Wilkie reluctantly agreed, but was shocked to see police later walk on to the plane and arrest him despite the protests of passengers. At Edinburgh Sheriff Court Sheriff Andrew Lothian decided simply to admonish him: 'It is ridiculous that this has been taken so far. I feel you are due an apology.'

LONDON EVENING STANDARD

THE LOW LIFE AIRLINE

Ruinair did nothing for its public relations when angry passengers staged a revolt after a 17 hour delay waiting at Valencia airport for a flight to Rome. According to one of the passengers, just as they were ready to board the plane, an Italian woman asked an attendant about the delay, and the employee gave a curt reply in Spanish. The Italian woman said she found this attitude 'unprofessional' to which the flight attendant reportedly said 'You goddamned Italian, I speak Spanish here.' The Italian replied with 'And you're a bitch.' The attendant then pulled the boarding pass from the Italian's hand, upon which an Italian man lunged at the attendant and grabbed the boarding pass back. Just as passengers were on the minibus to the plane, the police showed up to arrest the Italian man for assaulting the attendant, but the other passengers prevented them, chanting 'No, you will not take him!' A lawyer who was present convinced police that the man could legally only be interrogated, not arrested. Unfortunately for Ruinair, a journalist was on board and the whole incident appeared in the Spanish daily El Pais.

EXPATICA

THE SO LOW FARES AIRLINE

A Ruinair advertisement depicting Sinn Féin politician Martin McGuinness claiming its flights are so low even the British Army 'flew *home' from Northern Ireland has been branded 'crass' and 'deliberately provocative'. Michael Copeland, Ulster Unionist Party East Belfast representative, has blasted the airline for the press campaign. Copeland says: 'The Ruinair marketing department is clearly stupid if they think that an advertisement like this is going to endear their company to a large chunk of the Northern Ireland travelling public.' He adds that the advertisement 'makes a clear political statement on the part of Ruinair'. But a Ruinair spokeswoman has made light of the politician's concerns. 'Michael Copeland should book one of our cheap flights. Maybe he needs a break — he certainly needs a sense of humour.'*

MARKETING WEEK

THE NO! FARES AIRLINE

Ulster rugby fans are up in arms after no-frills airline Ruinair cancelled their France-bound flight without any warning. The supporters had booked return flights from Dublin to Grenoble with Ruinair for Ulster's Heineken Cup encounter with Bourgoin. But now they have been told by the airline that the only alternative flight is to the coastal city of Nice — some 250 miles away, and across the Alps. One fan, Iain Thompson, said he had been sent an e-mail informing him of the dramatic change in his travel plans and denounced Ruinair's offer to the fans as simply not good enough. 'We were told we could have our money back or be transferred to Nice,' he explained. 'But Nice is 250 miles away from Bourgoin, so it would take around five hours to get there by car. The flight back from Nice to Dublin is around 8.30am the next day, so we would have to leave Bourgoin around 2am to get to the airport. It's just ridiculous.' With his hopes of seeing the Heineken Cup clash in France dashed, Mr Thompson said he would be wary of travelling with Ruinair in future. 'Michael O'Leery was in Belfast a couple of weeks ago to promote Ruinair and he had a banner that read "Ulster says Yes",' added Mr Thompson. 'Well, my attitude would be that Ulster rugby supporters say No to Ruinair.'

BELFAST TELEGRAPH

THE LOW CARES AIRLINE (1)

A pensioner said today she had to drag herself up the steps to a plane after flight staff failed to help her get on board. Judith Dutton, 66, who has steel rods in her spine and a paralysed left leg, claims Ruinair staff told her that unless she boarded the plane without a disabled lift, it would take off without her. Special equipment is hired by Ruinair at Nottingham East Midlands Airport to allow wheelchair-users to board planes. However, Mrs Dutton said staff at the airline told her they had not been told in advance that she was disabled and the equipment needed was not available. She said they told her it was too expensive to hire at the last minute for just one person. To board the plane, she had to sit at the bottom of the metal stairs, pushing herself up step-by-step. Her 66-year-old husband Eric, who was ordered by doctors not to do strenuous activity after a heart attack last year, had to help. Mrs Dutton said she was still aching from the ordeal days later. She said: 'It was just so humiliating. Everyone on the plane was looking at me.'

LEICESTER MERCURY

THE LOW CARES AIRLINE (2)

A disabled granny was left abandoned on a holiday jet by its crew, cleaners and even the pilot. Ellen Cummings was then ignored by staff who boarded the Ruinair plane at Stansted to prepare for its next flight. The 63-year-old paraplegic claimed one even barked at her: 'Can't you get off, we're already 30 minutes late?' Ellen was rescued after her wheelchair was spotted in an inch of snow on the ground and workers finally brought specialist lifting equipment. The furious pensioner, who claimed she was trapped for an hour, said: 'I have never been so humiliated. It's a disgrace, no one should be treated like that.'

THE MIRROR

THE LOW CARES AIRLINE (3)

A boy of 14 in a plaster cast from his ankle to his thigh was forced to stand for nearly two hours on a Ruinair jet. Tom Cannon could not bend his leg but cabin crew refused to give him an extra seat so he could sit down. Adults who were with Tom claimed staff were 'rude and offensive'. His parents have complained to the budget airline about its 'inhumane' treatment of the boy. Tom's ordeal began when he was playing for a Hertfordshire youth team at an international football tournament in Milan. He was stretchered off the pitch with a knee injury and was taken to hospital for emergency treatment. He then travelled to the airport to fly home. One of the team organisers, Chris Hollands, said: 'Tom was in a significant amount of pain so we sat him in the first available seats on the plane, in the first row, whilst we herded the rest of the boys on to the aircraft. A stewardess said, "He cannot sit there. Move him now", without any further explanation. She did not speak directly to any particular person but shouted this as an order. She was extremely rude. She said, "If you wanted an extra seat, you should have paid for it." It was astounding and I could not believe what I had heard. She was unsympathetic, arrogant, rude and unaccommodating, even after hearing the story of our plight.' Matters got even worse when the flight captain intervened. Mr Hollands said: 'I explained that I was trying to arrange for the boy to be as comfortable as possible, but he cut me off midsentence and told me to "stop it" and to "shut up". He told me that if I did not stop I would be removed from the plane. I was flabbergasted.' During take-off and landing, staff insisted Tom was strapped precariously upright with a seat-belt. He stood for the rest of the one hour 40 minute flight back to Luton. He said there were at least three or four spare places on the 189-seat Boeing 737-800 which, with juggling, could have given Tom the extra room he needed. Tom, a pupil at Verulam School in St Albans, said: 'I just had to stand for the whole flight. It was very uncomfortable.'

LONDON EVENING STANDARD

THE LOW VISIBILITY AIRLINE

A Caribbean steel band was thrown off a Ruinair flight after passengers feared they were dangerous terrorists intent on bringing the plane down. The mix-up started when blind drummer from the Caribbean Steel International group Michael Toussaint was reported to the pilot for 'acting suspiciously' on the flight. Mr Toussaint had been led to his seat by his friends and another band member read football scores aloud to him from a newspaper. Italian military police then took the band off the plane. Mr Toussaint presented his disability card and removed his sunglasses to prove he was blind yet even after he was cleared by the airport authorities Ruinair still refused to let him, or the group, re-board the plane.

METRO

Most Definitely ... 'Not Ruinair'

A short cartoon not about Ruinair, as viewed 12,000 times on www.YouTube.com

Scene 1
A field with many wandering cattle and one blue, white and yellow Boeing aircraft.

Ruinair check-in girl behind wooden desk, with strong Irish rural accent: 'Hello. Welcome to Ruinair. Here is your boarding pass. Please proceed through the gap in the hedge to your aircraft. Next!'

Scene 2
An underground cave somewhere on the Pakistan/Afghanistan border. Ominous music plays.

Osama: 'Hah hah hah. The city of London is our next target, oh soldiers of Islam. We will punish the infidel.'

Gang of excitable sabre-rattling bearded men in long robes and turbans: 'These are wise words, Osama.'

Osama: 'We will turn this filthy city into a raging inferno. We will conjure up a conflagration that will burn for centuries. We will toast them in a holy fire. Who will sign up for this great mission?'

Men in turbans: 'Choose me, Osama, choose me. I would happily die on this glorious and holy adventure.'

Osama: 'I am glad to see so many willing warriors of Allah. We will hijack ten Ruinair planes in Dublin and smash them into London's more sacrilegious centres of sin.'

Men in turbans: 'Not Ruinair, Osama, not Ruinair. Those are the most dangerous airplanes in the world.'

Osama: 'But you are all suicide bombers. You are going to die anyway.'

Man in turban #1: 'Yes but on a Ruinair plane they are flying so crazy that we will get lost on our way to the Kingdom of Allah.'

Man in turban #2: 'We will be stuck for all eternity in a dirty cabin being given out to by air hostesses from Leeds and Glasgow.'

Norway

Ruinair Flights FR206 & FR2254 – Tuesday @ 8.10am
– DUB-STN-HAU-STN-DUB

Fare €0.04 plus taxes, fees and charges €88

Some brave travellers scale Everest or cross the Atlantic in a dinghy but nothing compares to the courage required to alight from a Ruinair aircraft at Stansted, walk through Arrivals, past immigration, customs and the inviting exit, to cross the concourse and check in to an immediate second Ruinair flight to Haugesund. I took out insurance for the return flight but not the usual sort which Ruinair sell. With a connection time of two hours I bought a seat on a later flight in case I miss the first flight. The second flight cost 49 pence. *'Ruinair is strictly a 'point-to-point' airline. We therefore cannot facilitate the transfer of passengers or their baggage to other flights. You should not book onward flights with Ruinair or with any other air or surface carrier.'* But I did.

We are easy prey for the obsequious grease-monkey MBNA salesmen contracted by this airline who scour the tail-end of the check-in queues looking for easy pickings. I am amazed they approach me today since they usually only speak to single girls going to Girona (see Barcelona) or to Ciampino (see Rome).

'Hello sir, do you travel much with this airline?'

If only they knew. 'I do.'

'We are offering a free flight for every five flights you take with this airline.'

'Is there a catch?' I ask.

'You only have to sign up for a new credit card,' he smiles.

I already have four credit cards but I play along for the hell of it. 'Wow, I get a free flight?'

'You certainly do, sir.'

'Does that include the taxes, fees and charges?' I hazard.

'No.'

'Today's flight from Dublin cost me one cent. So you're offering me one cent to take a credit card?'

'Not exactly, sir.'

'Exactly.'

He regroups with colleagues on spare seats near the check-in desks and they compare successes. 'I got to speak to two blondes, a brunette, one with legs, a big busty one and one difficult Irish bastard.'

In a taxi this morning the driver asked me where I was flying, so I told him and he asked why, but I wasn't sure. Why does this airline fly to my destination? Here's why. Businessmen in Haugesund were jealous of the success of Oslo (Torp) airport, two hours from Oslo. So they contacted Ruinair, told them about their cosmopolitan fishing port, despatched their mayor to Ireland to meet the airline, invited executives back on a freebie trip, and worked with the Norwegian airport authorities to satisfy Ruinair's twin demands: a longer runway and little or no landing fees. All around Europe regional hamlets are coming to this dominant airline with their continental cap in hand, begging them to connect the dots and put their town on the Ruinair map. Some people say that the world is getting smaller but I'm convinced that it's still the same size as ever.

In this check-in queue I am the only person not wearing five layers of clothing, a Berghaus fleece, combat trousers and mountaineering boots, nor carrying crampons, carabiners, ice-picks and fifty foot of nylon rope. Unsurprisingly I am the only non-Norwegian on the aircraft. Few Londoners would wake up one morning with a sudden burning desire to visit my destination. I suspect more Norwegians wish to escape.

Olga strides through the cabin with a smile and a sparkle, counting us off. I am impressed. There is no way I could count past one hundred in Serbo-Croat. I almost know the pseudo-semaphore signalling system used by the crew when dispensing food and drink. Flapping your arms by your side means we need chicken sandwiches. Circling your finger about means we need a wrap. Waving your hand up and down like a fish in the sea means tuna. Waving a hand by your nose means we need hot ciabatta. Making a cube with thumb and index finger means we're okay or maybe we need ice. Pointing at your eyes either means we need glasses or we need ice, the latter delivered in the film-developing envelope which doubles as a sick bag. Holding your clenched fists out wide means that a passenger wishes to purchase a newspaper. Moving one clenched fist with an extended thumb repeatedly up and down means we need a bag.

We descend through the clouds and over a churning bottle-green sea towards a craggy granite coastline. Vanessa announces in error we will be shortly landing at *Stansted* airport (again?) which would be a serious disappointment. We land twenty minutes ahead of schedule, another staggering display of punctuality.

It's important to get on the right bus since some buses go to Stavanger (two hours) and Bergen (three and a half hours.) The *Nor-Way* (ho ho) *Bussekspress* service takes me the eight miles to town in twenty minutes. The countryside is sparsely populated. On the nearby island of Utsira, 240 inhabitants are outnumbered by 310 species of bird. The landscape here is blighted by rows of motor home rentals. The Norwegians like nothing better than to rent a camper and head off for weeks in the wilderness, speaking to no one else. We cross the span of Karmsund Bridge, meant for a much larger city, and this journey is suddenly worthwhile. Below in the harbour is a genuine hulking North Sea oil rig. Now you don't see those on every holiday.

Haugesund is the largest town in Haugalandet, perched on the western coast. Population 31,000. This port is blessed with a sound through which ships pass safely. A nearby strait is called *Nordvegen*, meaning 'the way north', and it's where the country's name originates. It is considered to be Norway's birthplace since the first king of Norway, *Harald Fairhair Head & Shoulders*, came from near Haugesund. Don't attempt to learn Norwegian because it makes learning Dutch look easy. Don't bother trying to remember the essential words for the international traveller such as hello, goodbye, thanks and beer. There is only one word you will ever need to know when holidaying here in Haugesund. *Sild.* Meaning ... herring.

The town centre consists of a few parallel streets, so few that it would be embarrassing to get lost. *Haraldsgaten* is the longest pedestrian street in Norway. In August the locals bring out tables from their homes to make a single table stretching for two streets. The *Cooks Guild* pile on 101 varieties of cooked herring on what is the longest herring table in the world, and also most likely the only such table. The town holds a simultaneous jazz festival called *Sildajazz*, because jazz is so meaningless without ... herring.

There is some excellent shopping here, if you wish to stock up on oilskins, souwesters and waders, cleats, winches and pulleys, general chandlery, GPS navigational aids, fluorescent life jackets for dogs and nets for catching mackerel, crab and ... herring. I almost tumble over a canoe outside a shop on the main street. In the town centre square there's a statue of two fishermen on the lookout for ... herring.

Everyone fishing for bargains on the main street wears bright red jackets and coats. I guess it's in case they fall in later, to make it easier for others to spot them. The Norwegians are an outdoor nation and like nothing better than to head off on a ten-mile ski trip on flat ground with a rifle on their back, stop at a range to shoot a few red plastic dots and then race off for another ten miles. They are so keen that Norwegian TV features some lunatics doing orienteering at 3am by the light of only miners' tin helmets. However, the Norwegians do have a great story-telling tradition because half the year it's too bloody cold to go outside. In Norway going out often means staying inside (bars and restaurants) in the absence of beach parties.

There are two famous sons of Haugesund and even then they're not that famous. One is a Mr Mortensen who emigrated to the US and changed his surname to that of his chosen profession, a baker. His daughter was Norma Jean. So there's a statue of Marilyn along the waterfront and it's an impressive bust. Mr Moritz Rabinowitz was a Polish Jew who moved here in 1911, set up a clothing company and became one of the wealthiest and most prominent citizens in the town, and the lone Jew. Everyone had a wooden hanger with his name. His wife's favourite pastime was sitting at the cash register receiving money from customers. But the insular locals never warmed to him and the Nazis took him in 1940. In the war 90 per cent of Jews in Denmark survived but fewer than 50 per cent in Norway survived. A film about Mr Rabinowitz was called *The Man Who Loved Haugesund*. There won't be a sequel and sadly I won't be in it.

The *Smedasundet* harbour reminds me of a nineteenth-century Arctic whaling station, only without the excitement of all that blubber. The berths are empty, the wooden buildings are shut ... and this is the summer season. It's the sort of isolated spot where even the likes of Captain Oates would never have ventured out.

The *Folkemuseum* on *Skargaten* displays life in Haugesund over the past 150 years. There are all sorts of fishing nets. There's a slide show called *Silda E Kommen*. It's particularly brutal stuff to witness. What with all those men, boats and nets, the poor defenceless little herring never stood a chance. Otherwise it's not that busy around these parts. The local TV channel shows pictures of rush-hour traffic over the Karmsund Bridge and occasionally a car hoves into view. Other shots of the town centre might be stills or live shots. I cannot tell which. The local paper has a two-page spread on Anita who works at the airport duty-free shop.

Dolly Dimple's is Norway's largest pizza chain and is the ideal place for a bite, primarily because it's the only open restaurant I can locate. There are two groups eating inside who are most probably closely related, given the size of this town, but they don't seem to converse in public. The waitress who takes my order disappears into the kitchen. '*We have another one of those Ruinair people who came here by accident.*' Eating out, or doing anything apart from solo line fishing from the harbour wall, is not cheap in

Norway. The small pizza costs NOK 190 (€25) and 400 ml of Hansa draught beer costs NOK 52 (€7). Having telephoned my bank manager and broken the sad news to him, I settle the bill and bid goodnight to the multi-millionaires who dare to order dessert and coffee. Dolly's does not offer pizza with herring.

Norway has a zero national debt. Norwegians arguably have the highest quality of life worldwide, but they worry about the time in the next two decades when the oil and gas begins to run out. Norway has been saving its budget surpluses in a Government Petroleum Fund, which is invested abroad and is valued at more than $150 billion. But they may soon have to get those boats out again and go fishin'.

Next day the bus takes me back to Haugesund Lufthavn. The *Sild & Jazz* café serves decent food under a giant shoal of silver three-dimensional … herring. I see Anita in the duty-free and learn this A-list celebrity is block-booked on Norwegian chat shows for months. Once we take off, the Norwegians start spending money on food and drink as if there's a famine back home, such is the perceived cheapness. Down below, the heathery slopes give way to crested sea foam. The occasional boat ploughs through the choppy waters. There's not much to do in Haugesund unless you can skipper a North Sea fishing trawler.

Customer Service
Ruinair Ltd
Dublin Airport

Dear Sirs,
   Please treat this letter as a genuine complaint about your airline.

- *On 14 June I flew from Dublin to Stansted for a fare of 1 cent*
- *On 14 June I flew from Stansted to Haugesund for a fare of 1 penny*
- *On 15 June I flew from Haugesund to Stansted for a fare of 1 penny*

- *On 15 June I flew from Stansted to Dublin for a fare of 1 cent*

My complaint is that these fares are too low. Frankly, I find it embarrassing to have to pay so little. I am concerned that your little airline may become commercially unviable and may go out of business. Can you please provide me with some assurance that you will charge higher fares to passengers in the future?

Yours etc,

Disgusted of Dublin

I wait a few days but nothing arrives as usual by email. So this is proof they do not reply to 100 per cent of customer complaints within seven days as per the claims on their website. Then a letter arrives at home.

Dear Paul,

I thank you for your letter.

I fully share your view that fares of 1 cent or 1 penny are much too low, but if that is what we have to do to fill our aircraft, then that's what we have to do. As our recent financial results demonstrate, we remain Europe's biggest, lowest fare, most profitable airline.

The only airlines in danger of going out of business are those that are charging high fares, with high costs, such as British Airways, Alitalia etc. because they can't compete with our prices or our costs.

Unfortunately I can't give you any assurance that we will charge higher fares in the future, as it is our intention to charge even lower fares, or rather offer more seats available at these ridiculously low prices, because that is what our customers want.

Thanks for the support.

Best wishes.

Mick O'Leery

Chief Executive

Ruinair Ltd

Signed personally. In black ink pen. Honest. They gave Him my letter and He bothered to reply.

After months of travelling, finally, I have arrived. I think now I will go and see Mick.

Annual General Meeting

Is that Mick? I stare around the small room. Others spot him too and peer over. It looks like Mick. He wears dark trousers and a blue striped Gant shirt, with the buttons undone, much like a *Chippendale* performer about to go on stage. Since the last time I saw him he has invested in a smart navy blazer. He is active andagitated. So it must be Mick. I have never sat so close to a man worth six hundred million euro who doesn't possess a tie. Mick once told an interviewer, '*Don't make me look like a boring bastard in a suit.*'

Irish public companies prefer to hold their Annual General Meetings for shareholders in plush five-star hotels in the Dublin 4 embassy belt. Not so with Ruinair. We are in a conference room in a Dublin airport hotel, minutes away from the silvery hangar of their head office, which is known within the airline as the White House. The invitation specified the Holiday Inn but the hotel has been renamed as The Clarion Hotel to confuse us.

The annual report stated the meeting was at 11am but the invite stated it was at 10am so I take the necessary Ruinair precautions. I arrive in plenty of time because there is always a scrum for the best seats. They will check my identity carefully so I carry my Shareholder Attendance Card and the girl who makes me sign my card speaks fluent Serbo-Croat. No passport is required. There are six rows each of ten seats in the Fitzmaurice Suite and we can sit anywhere. The seats don't recline. I take an aisle seat.

One director of the company greets a few of the poverty-stricken shareholders. James is the legal expert and was a big-shot lawyer with Ireland's leading law practice. He owns fifty thousand Ruinair shares so naturally he is in a jovial mood today, as he always is, I suspect. 'Good to see you here. Do have tea or coffee, and biscuits. You don't often get those free from us. But of course, you have to buy a share.' As an aside, and this is conclusive proof that it is a small world, a few months later one Sunday morning I walk out to play a tennis doubles against Carrickmines to find myself playing against the same James. We lose 6-7 4-6 but I must admit I was intimidated because his holding is so much larger than mine. Another shareholder at the meeting makes a jibe. 'I only came for the tea … and perhaps some dividends some day.' There are free *Kit-Kats* on offer. These cost €1.50 on board so I take two for later and I save three euros.

Mick is an expert on press conferences. On being told once there were no women present at a male-dominated press conference, he replied, *'I wouldn't be too sure. There's someone here from* The Guardian *and you can never tell with them.'* And once at an over-hyped press conference he was heard to utter: *'I'm a bit disturbed the rumour went round we would announce my resignation and the share price rose three per cent.'* He once used the F-word (not flying) fourteen times at a press conference: *'I am in the first year of marriage.'*

I am impressed as Mick works the room, walking about, shaking hands and using the F-word with one elderly shareholder. Most of the attendees are pensioners, country gents, *Stockbroker Suit* types and other loonies like myself. An old lady privately asks Mick if there is going to be a rights issue, something a company does to raise extra cash. *'We have €2.2 billion in cash. We won't be having a rights issue, dear.'*

We are content shareholders. Mick has made us some money since the share price is up by 50 per cent in a year. It's enough for me to finance a trip to every country in Europe, several times over. It is poetic justice. It's fortunate too since Mick doesn't worry about the share price. *'Screw the share price. We're in a fares war. We're going to see the bloodbath to end all bloodbaths.'* J&E Davy are one of Ruinair's stockbrokers and they provide advisory services to Ruinair. Kyran is the Deputy Chairman of J&E Davy and he is a director of Ruinair, having advised them on the 1997 flotation, and he sits here at the top table.

The other directors arrive one by one, many of them with tin suitcases on wheels since they will fly home afterwards. These suited directors look more BA, Lufty, Iberia and Air France types than any low fares carrier. Ray is a former European Commissioner whom I have seen on Aer Lingus and he wears the most expensive suit of all the directors present. There is an Italian called Paolo, a Frenchman called Emmanuel and a German called Klaus who I assume have the required local knowledge of the continent. The US based chairman called David sends his apologies because he has better things to do back at home in California. This Board are old and all male so that the top table looks like a quango of elder statesmen with Junior in the middle. Often youth defers to age and wisdom but not today. The scene is somewhat reminiscent of Da Vinci's *The Last Supper* with Jesus seated in the midst of his disciples, this time wearing an open-neck shirt and blazer. Peter is their hyper-active corporate communications guru, wearing a pair of jeans lent to him by Mick, and he eyes the room's audience nervously. Well he might. I'm here and no one knows it.

At precisely ten o'clock, Mick takes his centre seat at the green baize table. Everything about this airline runs on time. They don't wait for anyone, whether it's a flight or the annual shareholder fest. I suspect 85 per cent of their AGMs start on time, as measured officially by the Civil Aviation Authority. Punctuality is a primary measure of their customer service. Of Ruinair's 320,000 annual flights, 85 per cent arrive within fifteen minutes of the scheduled arrival time. But this is because the airports are in the middle of nowhere. It's our choice. We can be thirty minutes late at Frankfurt-am-Main International or on time at Frankfurt-Ryahn.

Mick sits ten feet from me but my view is obscured by the ranks of press photographers. There is an RTE camera crew taking shots of the room and that night I am on the news, looking shifty. Each time Mick looks up, a barrage of flashlights explode, like an Oscar premiere red-carpet trip. He obliges by picking up a model Boeing, making an eye-popping contorted face, the photograph to be in the *Business*. The foot-long branded jet is the only corporate icon on display, no posters nor logos, no expense not spared. *'I tell the staff not to buy pens to save money. Just to pick them up from hotels, legal offices, wherever. That's what I do.'*

James, the legal expert, summarises the financial year as we peruse the almost humorous annual report. Ruinair has annual revenue of a €2,237 million and profit of €400 million. So with 42 million passengers they make ten euros profit each time we fly.

Mick has sounded some timely words of warning: *'The airline industry is going to suffer a downturn. Every six to seven years, the backside falls out of it, we've had six years of record profits, so we are due one in the next three to six months. Sky Europe will probably go bust. Wizz Air, it's harder to say. Historically, the downturns have usually come after British Airways and Aer Lingus order new jets, which they have both just done, so we're battening down the hatches in readiness for the shit to hit the fan.'*

Revenue includes €362 million from rail and bus ticket sales, hotel reservations, car hire, insurance, priority boarding fees and excess baggage charges. Mick plans to earn more such ancillary revenues by renting in-flight hand-held personal videos to passengers: *'We expect it to make enormous sums of money. We wouldn't do it otherwise'* and by in-flight mobile telephones. *'People tend to not want to get into long mobile phone discussions with people sitting around them so I think it will be more people sending texts. Why should I care if it is generating some money? If you want a quiet flight, use another airline. Our flights are noisy, full and we are always trying to sell you something.'* Mick takes a swipe at Bertie. *'Unlike Irish politicians, we don't accept cash — only credit cards.'*

Here is the reality. Ruinair fly 320,000 flights each year and with an annual profit of €400 million, they make on average a profit of €1,250 per flight. Their average fare is €44 so it's only the last twenty-eight passengers on every flight which allows this airline to make a profit. A few less passengers and they are at breakeven.

They tell us that their criteria for selecting new bases and new routes are threefold: cost, cost and cost.

In terms of profitability Ruinair are alone in the airline industry, which despite 2 billion passengers in 2006, has collectively lost 40 billion US dollars since 2001 and has $200 billion of debt. A journalist once asked Mick how he does it, how they make so much money in such a tough business and Mick replied that the secret of success is that passengers get on their aircraft in one airport, are flown to another and then they get off the aircraft.

The biggest dent in profitability comes from spending €693 million on jet kerosene. They operate 133 thirsty Boeings which burn an amazing 250 million gallons of the stuff per annum. No wonder they watch the price of Brent crude oil with so much trepidation and hedge like a City of London oil trader. They cut the fuel bill by 4 per cent per aircraft by fitting those curvy, bendy winglets to the end of the wings. Amazingly, airlines don't pay tax or VAT on fuel, a nonsensical anomaly dating back to a Second World War agreement called the Chicago Convention, which was established to foster harmonious international relations that would likely ensue from developing the then fledgling aviation industry. We motorists pay around one euro a litre but airlines pay around a fifth of that per litre. Mick is modest about his fuel hedging strategy, such as when Ruinair hedged at $73 when the oil price was at $60. *'Jesus, we don't look bright. If we were bright we wouldn't be working for airlines. We're no experts on oil here. Frankly, we'll never get it right.'*

I have a terrible admission to make, worse than being cabin crew. I am a chartered accountant, so I have a burning urge to see how they do it. There are copies here of the *Annual Report & Financial Statements* and I have my sharpened HB pencil and trusty calculator. Their publication has insightful information but it's not exactly a riveting read and doesn't have a twist at the end, nor even a plot. It tells us how they do it. No sales force is required as 98 per cent of tickets are booked on the internet. Use secondary airports with lower costs and fewer delays. Fly direct point-to-point routes and avoid complexity. Twenty-five minute turnarounds with higher punctuality. Sell us lots of ancillary services so we can choose our extras but we pay for them. Use new B737-800 aircraft with a lower fuel burn and better efficiency. Word is that Ruinair can now sell on its old 737-800s at higher prices than the cost of acquisition from Boeing, and Mick confirms this to the attendees: *'What I am about to tell you is confidential, so please do not repeat this outside this room.'*

Ruinair's average fare in 1997 was six euros more at €50, so they are getting cheaper year by year. *'People look at 20 per cent profit margins in the airline business and they assume you are smuggling drugs.'* Other alleged low fares airlines like EzJet have an average fare of €62 and Herr Berlin's is €87. Aer Lingus is €88. Mick has a jibe at Aer Lingus and their slogan of *Low Fares, Way Better*. He refuses to refer to the airline by name but instead calls them the *High Fares, Way Worse* airline. *'Ruinair is now Ireland's national airline,'* he announces. I have doubts about the fare comparisons. The average fare in BA is a whopping €268 but that's because they fly to exotic places like Rio, Sydney, Hong Kong and Edinburgh.

Ruinair make an 18% profit. BA make 4%. Alitalia (which according to industry sources stands for Always late in takeoff, Always late in arrival) have a negative 11% margin and have not made an annual profit since 2002. Mick hates Alitalia. *'Alitalia? I would not want it if it were given to me as a present. Alitalia could have a future, but only if it is free from political influence and union pressures.'*

The payroll bill is €227m. There's 4,500 staff so the average pay is €50,000 which they claim is the best in the industry but here's how. The two professionals in the cockpit in the nice shiny uniforms are employed by Ruinair on €100k plus per annum. The lead cabin crew member is employed by the airline on £25k per annum. *'Cabin crew are at the lower end of the earnings spectrum.'* But half the cabin crew will be contractors and they don't work for Ruinair and are not part of the staffing or average pay, and the Crewlink.ie website says they take home £1,100 per month — they're the staff you will see on board wearing the airport access ID badges with the word 'Contractor' in red capital letters. Staff are updated on corporate news in a company newsletter called *The Limited Release*. There are no trade unions in Ruinair. *'We do not have any hard and fast rules on employing new staff on the same terms as existing staff. We do not do any union demarcation bullshit here. We have never had a strike in twenty years because we don't have somebody in the middle telling us lies.'*

Ruinair train staff at zero cost since they make the new hires pay for their training, plus uniforms and airport ID badge. They have a target to have 50 per cent of the cabin crew as contractors. Mick, the one and only executive director, earned €992,000 which somewhat distorts the figures for lesser mortals in the company. The biggest Ruinair shareholder is the unknown Capital Group with 12 per cent of the company. Other institutional big boys own large chunks. Mick owns sixty-five million shares so he's not so poor. Mick regularly sells his shares for the security of cash. *'I'm not going to be like those dotcom gobshites.'*

I read the customer service statistics, or at least how they measure service. They only lose 0.4 bags per thousand passengers, which is one bag too many as far as I'm concerned, especially when it's mine. British Airways manage to lose 28 bags per thousand passengers (*'On BA your bag will travel further than you will'*) but the numbers are a confidence trick because it's not a like for like comparison. Ruinair operate short-haul flights where the average passenger is away for two days so they prefer carry-on luggage rather than paying excess baggage charges. BA operates long-haul flights where passengers have a suitcase or two for the hold. Statistics don't lie but liars can use statistics.

Ruinair only receive one customer complaint per thousand passengers but that's because they only accept complaints in writing and there's no point in writing to them about any complaint. I doubt they even possess a cheque book to write refunds to customers. Please refer to chapter one, *Spain...not quite*. I feel guilty about these complaint statistics because I have personally contributed greatly to these complaints.

Some annual general meetings are over in five minutes as resolutions are nodded through, but not here. We pass a series of company resolutions at alarming speed. One is to re-elect Mick as a director. There are no dissenters at this fan club. They are obliged to read out the proxy votes, those votes cast by large shareholders

in absentia. Four hundred million shares are cast in favour of
Mick. Twenty-five million shares are cast against Mick being
elected as a director. The latter are investors of the lemming
variety. There are fifty of us in the room and our votes are not
going to overturn a four hundred million majority. James finally
announces, *'And now for the Mick O'Leery show.'*

This is a PR opportunity so Mick delivers a Power Point
presentation largely on the merits of Ruinair versus Aer Lingus. He
says with 50 million passengers Ruinair are now the World's
Favourite Airline, which is odd because Southwest Airlines fly 96
million passengers annually, and the IATA press clipping in the
annual report to support this claim neatly excludes Southwest.
Mick says Ruinair will fly 80 million passengers by 2012 and will be
twice as big as Lufty. Ruinair have 142 new aircraft on the way, a
terrifying prospect. They promise us the joys of in-flight gambling.
We learn that *'Shannon is dead in the winter. Shannon is not the
centre of the universe. It may be so in Irish rugby, but not in world
aviation.'* Mick soon feels he has said enough soundbites for today.
'We prefer to dole out bon mots at regular weekly intervals.'

The first question for Mick is from a shareholder with an
English accent. 'I live by Stansted airport. There are planes flying
over my house all day. Can you assure me your airline won't start
flying at night?'

'We have no plans to fly at night,' Mick replies. *Firstly, our aircraft
are in the air from 6.30am to 11pm at night, they fly on average eight
flights per day, that's two sectors of four flights each, and we change
the crews after a sector. More importantly we need the aircraft to be
maintained during the night-time and safety is our top priority. Not
so recently people had to fly on charter flights at night-time to get
cheap fares. Now with our airline you can get cheap fares all day long.
And there's no fare cheaper than a free fare.'*

His next question from the floor is to explain the staff
productivity number to a baffled shareholder. Ruinair have a
sizeable competitive advantage that each employee gets through
far more passengers than any other airline each year. They measure
staff productivity by the passengers per employee ratio.

'Each of our employees looks after 10,000 passengers per year. In

contrast each EzJet employee looks after 6,000 passengers. Each Southwest employee looks after 2,220 passengers. In flag carriers like Aer Lingus and BA each employee looks after 800 passengers. But we sub-contract work like baggage handling and our standard aircraft size is bigger than our competitors, so our staff don't work that hard.'

Next a question about whether they might serve meals like the hot breakfast offered by Aer Lingus. *'We don't have such plans. We are happy to see families opening up tin-foil packs of sandwiches.'*

A lady wants to know if the airline plans to fly from Dublin to Athens because it's 'inconvenient' having to fly via London. *'We are in discussion with seventy airports about new routes. The problem with Athens is that it's a four-hour flight from Dublin. Passengers are now accustomed to very cheap fares and expect similar rates for flights lasting three hours or longer, which is something we could not afford. Athens airport is expensive in terms of landing charges. And of course Dublin is very expensive for landing charges.'*

Someone wants to know if the thirty-minute flight from Dublin to Cork will successfully compete against the established *Irish Rail* train service. Mick is confident. *'At least with us we guarantee each passenger a seat. You won't have to stand in an aisle or sit on a toilet seat on an overcrowded train carriage.'* Mick is not a fan of Cork airport. *'Cork is Mickey Mouse stuff. Do we care about Cork? Frankly, no. Bristol is bigger than Cork, nearly everything is bigger than Cork. The reality for Cork airport is they put up costs and they lost passengers, and that will cost them. Get them to explain how that makes fucking business sense.'*

One elderly gentleman complains about the company share split effected during the year when shareholders received two new shares for every one existing share, and consequently the share price halved on the day. 'You did not send us out any formal notification about the share split. I opened up *The Irish Times* one morning over me breakfast and I saw that the share price had fallen by one half. I almost had a heart attack over me cornflakes.'

Another man asks if the Ruinair share price is now behaving like an oil stock? *'High oil prices are good for us and they are bad for competitors. It doesn't affect us. We are fully hedged. We are delighted with the rise. It's great as it will knock the crap out of most rival* airlines. *It will hasten the demise of the basket cases. The sooner they go to the wall the better. If oil goes to $75 a barrel we'll still be the only break-even airline in Europe, but at that stage we'll probably be the only airline in Europe still flying.'*

There's a question about government proposals for a new airport terminal in Dublin. *'The Department of Transport didn't have the vision to create a low-cost terminal. They gave us the M50 where the cars don't fit, the port tunnel where the trucks don't fit and an airport where the passengers don't fit.'*

Another shareholder complains that the 15 kg excess baggage is too low. *'Half of our passengers don't check in any luggage. Packing luggage into aircraft takes time. When I travel I take only 2 or 3 kg.'*

The same shareholder won't give up. 'Has getting married changed your view?'

Finally an admission from Mick. *'My wife always takes more than 15 kg. I don't know why she needs to pack so much. In fact on our last flight together, I too was a victim of our excess baggage charge.'*

I have to ask a question but I do not offer my name as others do. I raise my hand and Mick gives me the nod. 'What do you plan to do with the two billion euros of cash in the company?'

I know what the answer will be. Mick never wishes to pay cash dividends: *'We are never paying a dividend as long as I live and breathe and as long as I'm the largest individual shareholder. If you are stupid enough to invest in an airline for its dividend flow you should be put back in the loony bin where you came from ... We plan to pay ourselves a huge management bonus.'* Serious. There's much laughter in the room.

Mick likes to joke. I take the bait. 'Perhaps you might give it back to shareholders via scratch cards.'

Mick is still game. *'If so, we would require you to buy the cards for two euros.'* He gives a decent genuine answer about dividends and share buy-backs. Mick, however, fails to advise me that in ten days' time he will spend our cash buying up 25 per cent of Aer Lingus.

The AGM breaks up after forty entertaining minutes. On the way out I overhear a retired couple in the hotel lobby. 'That was great, wasn't it? Sure, Mick gets better every year.'

Figures quoted above are as per the most recent Ruinair annual accounts at the time of writing. For annual passenger numbers since, add 8 million additional passengers to number above per annum ad infinitum.

Some Appreciation

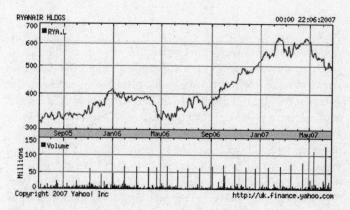

Cost of 1,000 Ruinair shares purchased solely to
attend the AGM in person   = €3,000

Value of 1,000 Ruinair shares two years later
upon completion of this book   = €6,000

Value of 1,000 Ruinair shares one year later upon publication of
this book   = €3,000

P.S. A devilish fact: Since my purchase the shares were split on a 1
for 2 basis but before that, on the 6th day of the 6th month 2006,
the Ruinair share price closed at €6.66. Is this an Omen?

Aero-Naughty-Cal-Endar

I do a lot of good work for charity so I am one of the first to purchase the *Girls of Ruinair Charity Calendar*. Fortunately it arrives at my home address in a sealed plain brown envelope.

January features Julia of Dusseldorf Weeze inside a Boeing cockpit in a bikini. February features Jaroslava of Rome Ciampino inside a jet engine in a bikini. March features Karolina of Liverpool holding a refuelling hose, in heels and a bikini. April features Nicola of London Stansted wearing little more than a life-jacket and sucking suggestively on its mouth piece. May features Olga of Frankfurt Hahn standing on an aircraft wing in gold heels and a leopardskin bikini. June features Magda (my favourite) of Brussels Charleroi perched upon a suitcase, in cowboy boots and bikini. July features Edita of Marseille lying over an aircraft wheel, her torso smeared with axle grease and a monkey wrench in hand. August features Vera of Barcelona Girona directing aircraft, in yellow heels and a bikini. September features Iris of Milan Bergamo sprawled on another wing in cool shades and a black bikini. October features Joanna of Dublin lathering her bikini with a soapy sponge under the nose of a Boeing 737-800. November features Ingrid of Stockholm Skavsta posing on a baggage trolley in a pink bikini (the baggage being tagged CRL for Charleroi so it might be lost). December features

Dominika of Madrid on the runway in a seasonal Christmas red bikini.

But on the last page, entitled 'Sneak Preview of the Aer Lingus Cabin Crew Calendar' is a picture of a matronly stewardess in a green swimsuit wielding a giant porcelain teapot with a painted shamrock and matching cup. 'Fly with Bridget from Dublin', it says, with a thought-bubble from the lady's head declaring: 'They'll have me selling scratch cards next.' Why would Ruinair humiliate an airline in which they own 29 per cent shareholding and which they want to buy? How low.

It's all been done before forty years ago by Pirelli. Scantily clad women don't do much for the image of female cabin crew, nor of this airline, but it will provide much encouragement to stag parties on their next flight. I am glad that I forked out seven euros (plus two euros of taxes, fees and charges) since I hope to encounter some of these lovely ladies in the flesh on my travels.

Cockpit

JUNE
MAGDA – BRUSSELS CHARLEROI

Excess Baggage

Well, Mick? *'Passengers will be able to bring a dozen of Europe's most stunning cabin crew home for just €7. We are seriously considering making this the new in-flight uniform.'*

Denmark (and Sweden)

Ruinair Flights FR258 & FR296 – Wednesday @ 9.05am
– DUB-STN-MMX-STN-DUB

Fare €28 plus taxes, fees and charges €88

It is one of the most illogical aspects of Ruinair's network. If you wish to visit the capital of Denmark, this airline flies you to an airport called Copenhagen (Malmo). When I last looked, Malmo was in Sweden. So in order to visit country A, I fly to country B. And worse still, I don't fly to Malmo, but to a nearby village called Sturup. Mick knows business is good for Ruinair from Denmark to the UK: 'Our best-selling route at Luton is Esbjerg. On these flights, 72 per cent of the passengers are of Danish origin. Passengers are coming over on our flights to watch football — the likes of Arsenal and Chelsea. Not Luton Town, they're a shit team.'

The check-in staff ask me the usual security questions.

'Is this your own bag, sir?'

'No, I found it.'

'Did you pack the bag yourself, sir?'

'No, I employ a full-time professional luggage packer, such is my arduous travel itinerary.'

'Does it contain any sharp items, sir?'

'Nothing as sharp as myself.'

We stand in line like sheep, wondering how it can take a person of presumably average intelligence so much time to distribute pre-printed boarding cards. Behind the desks eager revenue collectors hover like avaricious vultures to ensure no modicum of mercy is shown to those who arrive with excess baggage. A fire alarm suddenly sounds and we are repeatedly told by loudspeaker 'A fire alarm has activated in another part of the building' but no one budges because we've been queuing for thirty minutes and are only feet from check-in and we're not losing our place, even if we do burn to death in a fiery inferno.

I can now gauge national characteristics from check-in queues. Swedes queue but unlike other nations they stand to face others behind to show others how attractive they are. However, if everyone turns around, it become a rather pointless exercise. Swedish youth travel in minimum groups of fifteen and are more in tune with their iPod than with any social order. They like to spike their hair with gel to achieve what is known as the wind tunnel effect. Ahead of me a group of teenage Ice Maidens compare passport photographs excitedly; the least attractive would likely be short-listed for the Miss World contest.

We have reason to be grateful to the Swedes. They gave us bits of IKEA (I Keep Every Alunkey) furniture plus tasty meatballs in the restaurant afterwards. They gave us the *Ryvita* biscuit, which is particularly nutritious as one approaches old age. They gave us ABBA, particularly the blonde one with the steely blue eyes, rather than the two beardy trolls who penned the songs. It's a little-known fact there were three married couples in ABBA; the blonde and a troll, the brunette and a troll, and the two trolls. They also gave us the peroxide screeching of Roxette.

The Swedes are exacting revenge. In the newspaper the Swedish prime minister Göran Persson and foreign minister Laila Freivalds are suing Ruinair over an advertisement mocking them. The advert for low fares shows an unflattering picture of their faces with the slogan 'Time to flee the country?' and the publication of the advert in a Swedish newspaper coincides with heavy media scrutiny of both leaders. The lawsuit says the advertisement is offensive to the leaders and a government spokesman says the images were used without permission. A Ruinair spokeswoman says the lawsuit is a waste of taxpayers' money. 'This must be the first time that a politician has objected to their image being published in a newspaper.'

There is a minor distraction in the air when a small boy begins to walk up and down the aisle in an increasingly distressed state, tears visibly welling up and his face red with anxiety. I think he is lost. I am about to assist because there is no apparent sign that the crew are either interested, or even aware, of his predicament, when a kindly lady takes him back up along the aisle, hand in hand. She stops beside me and asks me if I am the boy's father. I look at him for a moment and decline. The lady continues searching up the aisle. I am optimistic she will locate his real father. I mean he is unlikely to have gone anywhere.

There's an Englishman in the row behind who seems to be a greater expert than I on this airline, which is no mean feat. I hear him telling other passengers about his experiences with this airline. His worst story is the time he saw a middle-aged couple run up to the departure gate in Stansted just as the Ruinair staff ceased boarding. The couple pleaded to be allowed to board because they were going to a funeral in Ireland but it was to no avail. They asked about the alternatives and were told to buy tickets for the next flight. The wife was in tears because they couldn't afford the huge fares. The Ruinair staff member replied, 'There's always the boat.'

I wish to reconsider customer service on airlines. Jan Carlzon was chairman of one of Europe's most poorly rated airlines, Scandinavian Airline Systems (SAS). Carlzon wrote a book entitled *Moments of Truth*, in which he said, 'Last year, each of our ten million customers came in contact with approximately five SAS employees, and this contact lasted an average of fifteen seconds each time. Thus, SAS is "created" in the minds of our customers fifty million times a year, fifteen seconds at a time. These fifty million "moments of truth" are the moments that determine whether SAS will succeed or fail as a company.' SAS may now have taken customer service too far. Last time I flew on SAS, cabin crew had name tags saying 'Air Host'.

I do not understand customer service as defined by Ruinair and measured by timeliness, numbers of complaints, lost baggage and replies to complaints. I expect an airline to get me there on time and not to send my baggage somewhere else. It's what they do. It's not customer service. It's the basics. It's like my bank who send me a statement of my current account a few days after each month end. I expect it to arrive and for it to correctly add up. But my bank manager and his staff do not run around their branch office whooping and hollering and giving each other high-fives because my bank statement is correct.

Customer service is about warmth, amenability, compassion, flexibility and fairness but most of all it's about the people who deliver it. I have met five people today who work for Ruinair, a check-in girl, boarding staff and cabin crew, and all five appear on the verge of a serious mental breakdown. I know why they are this way. The cabin crew training includes modules such as '*The Linguaphone Beginner's Guide to Basic Spanglish*', '*How To Be Assertive When You're Not*' and '*How to Frighten Small Children*'. Those who graduate pass '*Laying Down the Law*' and '*Personal Grooming — What You Can Omit.*' Dale Carnegie's course on '*How to Make Friends and Influence People*' remains an optional extra on their training. Ruinair remains the only airline where I have ever seen staff remonstrating, and almost fighting, with passengers.

Ruinair have twelve Dublin customer service staff and in one six-month period they received 6,000 written complaints, 52 per cent of which were from passengers looking for a refund due to a schedule change, the weather, or an illness or a death. Mick? '*We don't fall over ourselves if you say "My granny fell ill". What part of "No Refund" don't you understand? You're not getting a refund so fuck off.*'

A further 18 per cent of complaints were from passengers looking for compensation under the EU Directive on Passenger Compensation. '*We will be complying with European legislation pledging compensation for passenger delays but not embracing them. It's a lot of rubbish. They will get overturned in the end. It's stupid legislation but that is what Brussels does. Most claims will be met with "not our fault, go away."*'

Mick does not entertain complaints about damage to baggage. '*Passengers are carrying baggage which is clearly inappropriate.*' Or that checking-in luggage is necessary. '*It's a throwback to the era of ocean liners. I'd stand on my head if I could fly with an airline and avoid standing in a check-in queue.'*

Sturup airport is a low-rise, corrugated, bright yellow metal fabrication, adjacent to a large car park brimming with families in Volvo estates but there's not a flat-pack seat in sight. The Ice Maidens jump into Daddy's car and zoom off. He parked like many others in the Disabled spaces. I like the Swedes already. Not being a fan of bus excursions to foreign countries, I first catch an airport bus to Malmo city centre. Along the road are forests of pine, beech and spruce. Now I know why the Swedes are so good at making furniture. The traffic comprises Volvo after Volvo after Volvo, interspersed with an occasional Saab.

The bus terminates at the Central Rail station where the signs offer *Hotel Boknings* (one typo away from an irresistible offer). The station bar is called *O'Leary's Bar.* I bet he loves that when he comes here to do his mega-deals. I stay at the Elite Savoy Hotel, a grand, stylish, four-star place where I am surprised they allow someone like me, with white sneakers, a back-pack and a Ruinair boarding card stub, to check-in.

I remain significantly mathematically challenged by the *Krone* currency, which has a huge exchange rate versus the euro. Everything seems so expensive, yet when I convert it to euros in my head, I realise it *is* expensive. It's not as bad as Turkey where every worker is a millionaire when they get their weekly pay packet, nor like when Italy converted from the lire to euros and old ladies handed over €5,000 for a coffee in Milan. Paying at reception after one night's stay in Sweden makes you feel like an investor buying the hotel for cash, rather than settling an account. And don't ever look at the mini-bar prices. I don't know why guide books to Sweden list galleries, museums, hotels, bars and cafés. They should only list bank ATMs.

Sweden has always been an expensive destination and particularly for someone as tight as myself. I think I was separated at birth from Ernie Wise since I too have a decent lock on my wallet. I was once in Stockholm and a ticket cashier in the *Tunnelbanan* subway tried to charge me SEK 40 (about 5 euros) to travel from the City Terminal station to the old town, Gamla Stan. I explained to him in pidgin English that I was only going to the next stop on the line. He explained to me in pidgin Swedish that the ticket allowed me to travel anywhere on the subway in the next hour. I didn't know how to tell him that I had no desire to visit all 100 (exactly) stations on the subway network in the next sixty minutes, so I acquiesced and unlocked my wallet. On the upside the female voice announcing the station names onboard was wonderfully sexy.

Southern Sweden, including Malmo, was part of Denmark until 1658 when the Danes obligingly handed back this part of the country to the Swedes, without a substantial land war. Malmo, population 250,000, is Sweden's third largest city and Southern Sweden's commercial capital. It is suitably pedestrianised yet traffic moves freely. The ample seating in the expansive city squares of *Stortorget* and *Gustav Adolfs Torg* invite me to linger. Near the latter a gracious old cemetery has been transformed into a peaceful park, with godly monuments and historic tombstones, all dead quiet. These are the parks where secretaries sunbathe topless in high summer but I am alas too early.

The city has a colourful mix of Gothic and Dutch Renaissance architecture. Window shopping on *Södergatan* is a social joy. *Lilla Torg* is a restored cobbled square with outside cafés where the patrons are provided with blankets to keep them warm as they look cool. There are three kilometres of sandy beaches within walking distance of the city centre. There's an IKEA store too. Malmo is urban, yet urbane.

The city is very walkable but immediately I am distracted by how beautiful everyone is. The Swedish government must pay citizens to walk around their cities looking cool and attractive. Everyone here strolls. No one is in a hurry. No one needs to wear a suit. No one has a meeting to get to. No one seems to have to work. Many Swedes retire at the age of twenty-five to work full-time on their personal image and grooming. The only street beggar I see even has distressed clothing and three days of designer stubble.

There's a canal trip around the city and we are provided with more blankets for our nether regions. Blankets are big in Malmo. Tomas the excellent guide tells us that the first building we see used to be a women's prison but sadly there are no longer sufficient loose women, Malmo means sand heap, Malmo has the best soccer team in Sweden, and if we buy an apartment in the spectacular 58-storey Turning Torso flagship building, the whopping price fortuitously includes regular external window cleaning. Most of the others on the boat are from Minnesota so everything we see is either pretty, neat or awesome. The captain of the boat follows the Ruinair model with low fares, unassigned seating, 10-minute turnaround times, 82 per cent passenger loads and we can buy our coffee with cake on the dockside and bring it on board.

Getting from Malmo to Copenhagen was ferry difficult until 2000 when the Oresund Bridge opened. An express train from Malmo takes ten minutes via an immersed tunnel to reach an artificial island before floating for ten miles over the world's longest cable-stayed bridge. No passports are required. The day before the bridge opened, 80,000 lunatics ran a half-marathon across its international span without paying the toll.

Kobenhavn: capital of Denmark, home to 1.7 million. First impressions matter; a smoky central train station, litter outside, Burger King, McDonald's and KFC (several), neon and billboards, jostling crowds, Inca pipers, winos, wasters, druggies, hippies, buskers, boy racers in souped-up Gti's, motorcyclists laying rubber on the streets, Harley easy riders revving to the max, yobs scaling regal monuments, twelve-year-olds chucking beer bottles at each other, food stalls, pigeons, more litter, tourist traps and trapped tourists.

Stroget: five connected streets of the best shops. Gant opposite the *Chinabox* takeaway selling egg fried rice in cardboard boxes. Louis Vuitton luggage opposite the vagrant on the bench with the pit-bull. Boarded up shops and scaffolding. The *Viking Gift Shop*. The waft of freshly carved kebab. The *€1 Shop* where, much like Ruinair, everything sells for one euro but instead the secret of commercial retail success for the owner is to purchase as much crap as possible for twenty cents or less wholesale. People ahead of me get hustled so they check that their wallets remain in their back pocket. It's a drag in every sense. *Stroget* is the longest pedestrian shopping street in the world, but who would want to walk along its thoroughfare twice?

Kongen Nytorv: a square at the eastern end where I pause for respite amidst vicious traffic. The grass is railed off. A local cycles up, leans his bicycle against a railing, unzips, produces his member and urinates over the railing. Nearby women and children look away, while gentlemen frown but say nothing.

Nyhavn: a wonderfully picturesque canal-side street with multi-coloured bars and restaurants and outdoor seating amidst nautical charm. Only it's not. The usual photographs of this small street were taken with a wide-angle lens and depict one side. The other side of the canal is derelict, blighted by rusty tugs going nowhere. I sit at the canal-side and watch the Tuborg cans, wine bottles and cigarette butts float by.

The Little Mermaid: she sits naked on a rock in the windy harbour, photographed daily by punters and manhandled in the most appalling fashion. She's ninety years old and has endured much: decapitated, amputated, doused in red paint and worst of all having a bra and panties painted on her slim body. She's not the first one to sit here. Her predecessor was stolen and they made another from the same mould. Up close she is nonchalant, maybe also bored. I think she wishes she lived somewhere else. Nicer. Dublin?

Amalienborg Palace: the Danish Army's finest guard this royal residence. The square is vast and empty; its centrepiece is a figure on horseback with two sets of railings. No seats. Five soldiers in black and blue uniforms move in unison and outnumber the viewers. They don't march, rather they stroll, with arms folded. Under the beefeaters they are boys not men. If you harbour a desire to commence a land war against Denmark, based upon my brief observation, you'd be safe in launching a pre-emptive strike now.

Radhuspladsen: this could be a great square with an imposing town hall, red brick and shining gilt, but in front the city fathers have created a barren paved wasteland for hot dog vendors, with not a blade of grass in sight. At the other end lies a squat municipal building. Dirty brown offices surround the square, all plastered with corporate logos. On one façade there are 29 logos. Mutant pigeons crap. Eight flags are in view; six Danish national flags and two with the Golden Arches. It's the sort of square where it only takes a minute to rest upon a bench before a beardy local with a bottle of beer and plastic bags sits alongside me.

The Tivoli Gardens: Copenhagen's famous amusement park, which was essentially the world's first Disneyland, and like all great theme parks it should be an inaccessible fifty miles plus out of town, as in Paris or Tokyo. The park is small, surrounded by high metal railings and with bouncers on the doors. Inside the pen, visitors are screaming and not only at the prices. A day's admission is called an *Arskort*. Danish is a mouthful. The bus company is called *Hovedstadsomradets Trafikselskab*. Or HT for short.

Christianshavn: along the canals hangs a giant wall poster. '*I left Copenhagen for Berlin.*' A bunch of arty squatters live in a rent- and tax-free commune called Christiania. They call it power to the people. I call it weak government. You'll often see riots in Copenhagen on TV. One of the streets on the map of Christiania is called Pusher Street. There's a boat trip of the harbour and canals but now I am in Denmark our commentary is delivered without an iota of humour. They spent 2 billion krone on a protruding glass spaceship in the docks which now masquerades as an Opera House. The Maersk shipping line head office resembles a stack of their own ship containers.

You'll never get lost in Copenhagen since the city tourist folks have kindly painted pairs of white footprints on the pavements to guide us daft tourists. Has any city ever stooped so low? The footprints are twelve paces apart so they figure we are blind too. The footprints have an annoying downside. When I find myself on a street without these footprints, I know I am in a dead-end cul de sac of zero interest. When the footprints face the opposite direction, I battle against oncoming groups with maps and back-packs, feeling like someone trying to leave Harrods as they open the front doors at 9am for the manic Boxing Day sale.

All this in a country that has, not one, but two national anthems. The first anthem, 'King Christian Stood by the Lofty Mast', celebrates Denmark's glorious military and nautical past. The second anthem focuses on the beautiful scenery and character of the people, called 'There is a Lovely Country'. Where?

I check out of my hotel. The lady at reception has taken the liberty of adding thirty-five krone per night to the agreed room rate. Thirty-five krone is a lot of money. I inquire what this charge represents.

'That's the *Environmental Fee* for every night a tourist spends in the city,' she explains.

'What do you spend the money on?' I ask.

She is puzzled. 'I'm not sure.' They certainly don't spend it on parks, toilets or street cleaning.

I walk along Hans Christian Andersens Blvd, dedicated to Denmark's greatest contribution to literature; the ultimate, and possibly only, *Great Dane*. He's a hero around these parts and has sold more books than that lady who writes those boy wizard books. It's two hundred years since Hans' birth so there's a new museum on *Vester Voldgade* but it's grossly commercial, so much so that it shares a building with *Ripley's Believe It or Not!* (That's their exclamation mark, not mine.) Posters outside invite me to *Come and Meet the Author*, which is unlikely since he has been dead for one hundred and thirty years.

Instead here are the directions to visit the attic in which Hans resided for one year in 1827. Walk down *Vingardstrasse* until you come to the *Magasin* department store on the corner. Enter the store and take the escalators to the third floor, avoiding the temptation of fragrances on the ground floor. Head past homewares and china, past linens and bedware but hang a right before bathware and you are there.

The minimalist ante-room offers a summary of Hans' life. Like every great writer except me, he was a pauper's son. Hans had phobias. He was afraid of being buried alive so he requested to have a hole in his coffin to provide oxygen. He often went to bed with a note saying he was only sleeping, in case there was any doubt. He was afraid of a fire so he travelled with a rope in his luggage in case he needed to make a speedy exit via an open window. Hans travelled extensively, although not on low fares airlines. He went to England and made the acquaintance of Charles Dickens and was invited to stay with Dickens at Gad's Hill. Dickens grew so tired of Hans' hypochondriac moaning that he left his house whenever Hans came. Hans' timing was poor since Dickens' marriage was on the verge of collapse. When Hans left, Dickens placed a sign on his guest room door: 'Hans Christian Anderson slept in this room for five weeks which seemed to us ages.'

Hans was vain and wished only to be photographed in profile, which he regarded as most flattering. He was not at all a handsome man. Take a look at any picture. He was endowed with a huge snozzer. The pianist Clare Schumann told her husband Hans was the ugliest man she had ever laid eyes upon. Yet Hans was obsessed with being photographed daily. This is his diary for a week in October 1867:

Thursday the 10th. ... Sat for Miss Hallager. Friday the 11th. Rain; not very well. Sat for a cabinet portrait for Hansen ... Saturday the 12th. Sat for a cabinet portrait for Budtz Müller, but the weather was too bad ... Sunday the 13th. Beautiful sunny weather, sat for Budtz Müller ... Monday the 14th. ... Went to Voss about my teeth ... Tuesday the 15th. Beautiful weather, ate at a restaurant. Visited Israel Melchior and Watt. Wednesday the 16th. Sunshine ... Sat for Miss Hallager. Again ate at a restaurant ... Thursday the 17th. Rain; not really well, head heavy and legs weak. Nevertheless, went out to the photographer Hansen, but the weather was too dark ... Friday the 18th. Sat for a cabinet picture with photographer Hansen ... Saturday the 19th. Sat an hour for dentist Voss.

And for such a great writer, doesn't he go on a lot about the bloody weather?

The attic is a tiny, low-ceilinged, bare room with a cot and a wood-burning stove. There's a cupboard in which Hans kept bread, butter and sausage. Most importantly the attic has a small window which looks out over the city. He drew inspiration from the bustle of the city but success did not come easy for Hans. His early books were torn up and were used to wrap goods in shops.

There's no one else here, no tourists, nor a curator. It's my first moment of peace and relaxation in this city. I pull up an old chair, take out pen and paper, look out of Hans' window and scribble a few words. Copenhagen: a city of fly-posters, Carlsberg, takeaways, grunge, fringes, litter; faded and jaded. *Probably not the best city in the world.*

www.airlinemeals.net

The world's first and leading website about nothing but airline food

Route: Girona–Eindhoven
Airline: Ruinair
Ticket price: € very cheap
Flight duration: 1 hour and 40 minutes
Aircraft type and class: Boeing 737-800, Economy Class (standard)

Business or leisure trip: Leisure
Meal: Nothing
Drink: Nothing
Comments: If you want to eat something you have to pay for it
Rating 1-10 (worst-best): 0 for food, 10 for ticket price

The Only Official Ruinair Joke in the Universe

Bloke sits on a barstool, drinking a pint, at an airport, when a really beautiful woman sits down next to him.

Bloke thinks to himself, 'Wow, she is gorgeous, she must be a flight attendant, but I wonder which airline does she work for?'

Being a bit of an aviation know-all and hoping to chat her up, he leans towards her and utters, 'Love to fly and it shows?'

She gives him a blank, confused stare, and bloke immediately thinks to himself, 'Damn, she doesn't work for Delta'.

A moment later, another slogan pops into his head. He leans towards her again, 'A great way to fly?'

She gives him the same confused look. He mentally scratches Singapore Airlines off the list.

Next he tries 'Going beyond expectations?'

Not Malaysia Airlines either.

This time the woman turns on him, 'What the fuck do you want?'

Bloke smiles, and says, 'Ah, Ruinair.'

Bus Excursions from Airports Ruinair fly to

Destination	Distance from city centre
Dublin	10 km from Dublin
Venice (Treviso)	30 km from Venice
London Stansted	40 km from London
Brussels (Charleroi)	46 km from Brussels
London Gatwick	48 km from London
London Lootin'	48 km from London
Glasgow Prestwick	51 km from Glasgow
Hamburg (Lubeck)	65 km from Hamburg
Leipzig (Altenburg)	75 km from Leipzig
Dusseldorf (Weeze)	78 km from Dusseldorf
Paris (Beauvais)	80 km from Paris
Pisa (Florence)	80 km from Florence
Bologna (Forli)	84 km from Bologna
Stockholm (Skavsta)	100 km from Stockholm
Stockholm (Vasteras)	120 km from Stockholm
Frankfurt (Ryahn)	124 km from Frankfurt

And the winner is ...

Oslo (Torp)	140 km from Oslo

Source: Ruinair.com

Finland

Ruinair Flights FR216 & FR2194 – Thursday @ 1.40pm
– DUB-STN-TMP-STN-DUB

Fare €0.04 plus taxes, fees and charges €88

For the first time I use the web *Check N' Pray* facility. Like a Doubting Thomas I check in online and on the next day pray that security control personnel in one of the world's leading airports will permit me to go airside solely based on an A4 page I printed off on my home computer. But they do so. It works.

Today's flight costs 1 penny for the two and a half-hour trip so on this basis flights to the USA should cost 3 pence. It's my longest flight on this airline and by the end I'm manic, agitated and restless to be confined in such a small space, empathising fully with the lifers at any maximum security prison. The flight is uneventful except for a screaming child in row 7, sadly within earshot. I am reminded of the scene in the movie *The Battle of the Bulge* where a boy takes a pot-shot at Robert Shaw but misses. The boy is caught but his father pleads for forgiveness. Shaw pronounces: 'Release ze boy. Shoot ze father.'

On board a male crew member walks the aisle and counts us off. '166', he says to a fellow member.

'165', she replies, then shrugs her shoulders. 'I don't care.'

The catering trolley stops by me and I can read some scribbled writing on the white sticker on the side and I can categorically confirm that today on catering trolley 1518, above the printed city names, someone has written in small black ink: '*Fuck O'Leery.*'

Hard to say if it's penned by staff or passengers.

An eager, experienced passenger stops a crew member: 'Are you doing a second service today?'

She shrugs. 'I dunno.'

Over the aisle a family begins an afternoon meal; bread, ham and cheese, a tub of Flora plus a plastic knife. I could be impressed at their economy and self-sufficiency but I am not because three ladies in front have all this plus *Tuc* biscuits, garnishing and condiments, salt and pepper sachets, and the *piéce de résistance* of chicken drumsticks with napkins and a mayo dip. Did I mention that in Tampere Pirkkala duty-free airport shop, using the last word very loosely, one can purchase *Reindeer Paté?*

By now I have a copy of each of the first ten editions of the Ruinair magazine and they are for sale to the highest bidder — see eBay. I stop a crew member in her tracks. 'Do you have the Ruinair magazine?'

'No, we don't have it today.'

Soon she makes a cabin announcement. 'Ladies and gentlemen, due to a *catering* discrepancy we do not have the in-flight magazine onboard today.' Eh? I only wish to read it, dear. I don't wish to eat it.

I spend the flight staring up at the luggage bins, which, for the first time, have advertising emblazoned on them at a cost to the advertiser of €4,000 per plane per month. Ruinair claim the adverts will be seen by 50 million people annually, although this will be achieved in increments of a maximum of 189 people, so it will be a long haul to get there.

At the hotel reception I am greeted warmly. 'Mr Kilduff, we have been expecting you.' Such is the price of fame, plus the fact that I made a reservation. I am disappointed to learn there are no messages waiting alongside dangling keys in the numbered pigeon holes, nor is there a hand-written note inviting me to attend a local casino in a tuxedo with a stunning lady in order to win millions at roulette. You see, spies and agents are big in Tampere.

So once inside an apparently normal hotel room, I check behind the doors, shift pictures hiding wall-safes, stare into double-sided mirrors and examine bedside lights for hidden microphones, tape recorders and bristling antennae. Sad to say there is no sleeping beauty in my king-size bed, no cobra slithering inside the shower and no book of nightclub matches with a telephone number scribbled inside the cover.

The Finns are not the chattiest of nationalities. I first observe this in the queue at the departure gate and its veritable communal silence. They look an odd sort: pixie faces, albino blondes, pale complexions, bad fringes in a nation where hair salons oversell the merits of bright colours. Later in a taxi-cab the driver makes zero effort at conversation but insists on showing me the city map on his *SatNav* screen, to prove he knows the location of the only four-star hotel. When I see Finns meeting English businessmen in the hotel lobby, the English want a handshake but the Finns' body language is saying: *Stay the Hell Away from Me.* It is said that the further north one goes in Europe, the more distant people become. Spaniards and Italians like to hug and kiss each other often. Finns prefer to keep a suitable distance, usually upwards of one mile.

In compensation, the Finns are a wonderfully nosy nation. It is considered very vulgar to ask someone their salary in Finland but there is an alternative. Every November the Finnish tax authorities make public the prior year's tax returns of every citizen. Newspapers are crammed with the incomes of the wealthiest in the nation. Tabloids carry 24-page supplements of the incomes of the celebrities. And if you don't wish to ask your neighbour, a private firm will text your mobile telephone with his annual income.

Tampere is the largest inland city in the Nordic countries, and may in fact also be the only inland city in the Nordic countries. If Finland is a country of 180,000 lakes, Tampere is a city of hundreds of lakes, most of which are in the city centre. Imagine a sartorial bow-tie of freshwater lakes with a narrow isthmus of land between both sides. The city's red-bricked industrial past has been transformed into apartments, cafés and studios. It's not famous yet but it is a candidate city for European Capital of Culture in 2011.

The nearest town lies a few miles to the west, with a population of 28,000. Here a mining engineer, Knut Fredrik Idestam, established a wood mill in the 1860s and used local water power to manufacture quality loo roll and rubber boots, which were to be found in every Finnish home. Later Knut's company made a few billion mobile telephones. Now every third mobile telephone sold in the world originates from there. The town is called Nokia.

Finland is the second most northerly country in the world, and also one with more saunas than homes. Finns are so obsessed with saunas that they hold the Sauna World Championships annually in a town called Heinola, where competitors fly in to sit in a sauna in temperatures of 110 degrees Celsius, and where the rules say that half a litre of water must be chucked on the stove every thirty seconds. Last year's winner managed a miserable 12 minutes 21 seconds. The other competitors presumably simply expired.

I will now break the golden rule; not to write about the weather. Tampere is the furthest north I have been in my life, three hundred miles from the Arctic Circle. It's November and the day's high will be zero. Here the brass monkeys stay at home. The last time I was this cold was when I went from Toronto to see Niagara Falls in January in a trenchcoat. The visiting Americans were huge. I assumed they were obese but not so. They wore six layers of clothing. The sun is contrary in these parts. In the summer it appears at 4am and hangs around until 11pm. At this time of the year it is lethargic, not rising until 10am and going off for a kip as early as 3pm. I am not even sure the sun came up when I was visiting. I am in the dark.

The locals endure the snow. In Ireland if there's a rumour of snow, we all ring in sick to work, sit in ten-mile tail-backs and stockpile food and water. In Finland when there's two foot of snow, they hop into their cars and do ninety miles an hour down the motorway on snow chains to purchase a pint of milk. I couldn't reside around these parts. I mean, there are locals doing their shopping carrying ski poles. At Tampere airport you know the incoming flight will arrive when the yellow snow-ploughs head off to clear the runway.

The Finnish language fairly trips off the tongue. I exit my hotel on *Yliopistonkatu*, turn left on *Itsenalsyydenkatu* and onto *Hameenkatu*. Finnish, like the main shopping thoroughfare, is excessively long, and sadly often makes more sense when read backwards. While the rest of Europe refers to their currency as the euro, the Finns call it the *eurollar*. I am ashamed to say I don't know even the most basic of phrases, such as Hello, Goodbye, Thank You and Jesus, is that more snow? On the way to my rendezvous I pass the giant statue of the Tax Collector on the Hameensilta Bridge. Legend has it that my wish will come true if I rub the base of the Tax Collector. I polish his golden big toe like many others and mumble, *I wish that the Irish tax authorities maintain the tax-exemption on royalties from writing for ever.*

The blue *Tokee* airport bus departs the railway station, its destination displayed on the front in yellow fluorescent letters. It's not going to the *Airport*. It's going to *Ruinair*. Amidst the barren tundra of Finland's frozen interior, there is some corner of a foreign airfield that is forever Ireland. Seeing this magical bus lifts the local spirits, knowing if you can collect one cent, then you can leave. Flying to London, Frankfurt or Riga is exciting, particularly if you live in Tampere. There is a common misconception that Finland has the highest suicide rate in Europe but that's utter rubbish. Hungary has the highest. Finland is only second.

Tampere is a museum city gone mad. The *Coffee Cup Museum* has a display of 1,300 different cups manufactured by the Arabia factory over a 100-year period. The *Finnish Refrigeration Museum* addresses the history of refrigeration, a must-see for all fridge fans plus there's a café. I suspect the *Finnish Boxing Museum* does not draw hordes of overseas visitors. The *Shoe Museum* includes birch bark shoes, bowed shoes, slippers and pumps; Tampere is Finland's former shoe capital. Outside the city there is the Teisko *Milk Churn Platform Museum* but it is only open in the summer alas. Lastly the *Chain & Handcuffs Museum* claims to the biggest such museum in Europe — is there another? The collection includes handcuffs owned by Harry Houdini and Idi Amin, one pair of which was easy to get out of.

The opposition have a sacred site. I dare to visit. Finland borders Russia but it's still a surprise that Vladimir Ilyitch Ulyanov lived in Tampere in 1905 and 1906. Aka Lenin. The Workers' Hall contains history and his story, memorabilia and photographs of his fairly horrendous close relatives. Lenin hid in homes of twenty different supporters and friends in Finland, making him not only one of the world's greatest political revolutionaries, but also the world's greatest freeloading lodger. Reading his political pamphlets and seeing what later happened to the USSR, reduced now to a mere souvenir, I cannot help thinking he was wrong.

Later Finland became so anti-Soviet that for three years in WWII it sided with the Germans. Despite the subsequent cessation of the Cold War, I am in a surprisingly well-militarised city. Many hostile, spotty youths in khaki trousers and flak jackets wolf hamburgers and slug Cokes but there is some consolation. All Finnish males are liable for military service with the usual call-up age being twenty. Conscription rules.

Through driving blizzards and true grit, I struggle to Findlayson, an old factory built by James, a Scot who harnessed the water power in this rapid city. Now it's a trendy eating and hanging out mall favoured by the Bright Young Finns. Inside is Europe's largest, and only, *Spy Museum*. Here it's quiet, maybe too quiet. These are my kind of people, those who continually traverse the globe, visit glamorous places and spy on others to eke out a living.

John le Carré said that a spy, like a writer, lives outside the mainstream population, steals his experience and reconstructs it. The world's greatest spies reside here. Sydney Reilly was the role model used by Ian Fleming. Mata Hari used her poisonous charms. The very first spy was from the fourth century BC when Histaius wrote secret messages against the Persian king on the shaven head of a subject, waited for his hair to re-grow and sent him on his way, secret message and all, hoping the ink wouldn't run if there was rain. Top US agent Richard Sorge opined that 'Women and espionage don't mix well together', before he was caught, with the help of a female agent. I learn about cryptography, bugging, reconnaissance, wirelesses, gadgets and cameras. There is the lethal umbrella that was used in London on the Bulgarian Georgi Markov, who died from a small prick. There is a map from the US Air Force, to be used by downed pilots marooned in the USSR with words of comfort for the terrified pilots: '*Don't worry, every day on the run is a day of freedom.*' The map is plastic and the optimistic instructions advise the plastic may be used to shelter from the rain, to carry food or water, to collect rainwater, as a wash basin, as a protective quilt or rain-gear, as a floating device when packed full of hay, and to staunch an open chest wound. Yeah, right.

I sit at a table and they connect the electrodes to my tense body. I watch the dial swing about and anticipate the worst. I ask myself the first question. Can I endure more flights on this airline? Maybe, I tell myself. Can I suffer the hostility they throw at me? Yes, I scream. The dial swings to the right. There is no avoiding the truth. I am almost a broken man. This lie detector test works well. Finish.

| Wheel Share

Mr Bob Ross, from Islington in north London, travelled frequently with Ruinair from Stansted to Perpignan in France, and he is not untypical of frequent travellers, except that he has cerebral palsy and arthritis. Due to his illness he was unable to stand for very long, and had to pay Ruinair £18 each way to use a wheelchair when moving through the crowds and queues at Stansted. '*Unlike other airlines, I get charged £18 each way by Ruinair for the right to access the airport's wheelchairs. Given my painful arthritis, I simply must have a wheelchair at the airport. But every time I have taken a return flight with Ruinair from Stansted, it has cost me £36 more than other passengers. It is unfair and discriminatory to charge disabled people more to travel.*' Bob took Ruinair and the British Airports Authority (BAA) to court.

In the Central London County Court, Judge Crawford Lindsay ruled that Ruinair acted unlawfully by not ensuring that a wheelchair was provided free of charge for Bob to use at Stansted and that the £18 wheelchair charge levied on Ruinair's disabled passengers was unlawful. The Judge said that Ruinair were under a duty under the Disability Discrimination Act to make what is legally termed '*a reasonable adjustment*' for Bob, by providing him with a free wheelchair so that he could get to the plane.

The court awarded Bob £1,336 in compensation to cover the

original cost of hiring a wheelchair (£36), the purchase of a wheelchair by Mr Ross (£300) and injury to his feelings (£1,000). Bob said: '*It was blatantly unfair that I should pay more to fly simply because of my disability. Ruinair were operating a two-tier fares system — a cheap deal for non-disabled passengers but a raw deal for disabled travellers.*'

Bert Massie, Chairman of the Disability Rights Commission, said: '*Ruinair's wheelchair charge was a slap in the face to disabled people wanting to take advantage of low cost air travel. All right-thinking people knew that the charge was grossly unfair. It beggars belief that a company with £165 million annual profits last year should quibble over meeting the cost of providing disabled people with a wheelchair.*'

Counsel for Bob said that in the past year, Ruinair carried 6.6 million passengers of whom 7,296 requested a wheelchair. Had the wheelchair costs been shared across all passengers, it would have added 2p to each fare. He told the court that Ruinair, when first presented with Mr Ross's claim, tried to categorise use of a wheelchair as a 'frill'. '*Ruinair adopted a position suggesting the use of a wheelchair was a matter of choice, a frill akin to sandwiches and newspapers — and Ruinair does not provide that frill.*'

So Ruinair introduced a levy for the provision of wheelchairs for disabled passengers. '*Wheelchair Levy — This charge apportions the cost of airport assistance for reduced mobility passengers across all travelling passengers. This charge is 35p/50cent per passenger/per flight.*' Fifty million passengers per annum at 50 cents each equals €25 million revenue equals a lot of wheelchairs.

The Disability Rights Commission, a body set up by the UK Parliament to stop discrimination and promote equality, thinks that the levy should be no more than 2p. It bases this on its own analysis of the cost to airlines at Stansted to take disabled passengers from the check-in to the aircraft.

What does Mick think? '*The Disability Rights Commission wouldn't fucking know how much it costs if it jumped up and bit them. We estimate it costs £25 per person to transport disabled passengers, and we carry 1.5 million such passengers every year. Prior to the Bob Ross case we absorbed these costs. We would rather not charge the levy, but we kept getting people who just didn't fancy the long walk to the plane and declared themselves to be in need of assistance. You don't expect to turn up at Bluewater shopping centre on the bus and expect the driver to wheel you round the shops.'*

France ... encore

Ruinair Flight FR1984 – Sunday @ 9.40am
– DUB-CCF-DUB

Fare €15 plus taxes, fees and charges €46

I am flying to a remote French airport and I am worried. I learnt fifty stranded Ruinair passengers were forced to hire a bus here and drive 600 miles home after their flight was cancelled and they were told that the next aircraft out would be in ten days' time. The holidaymakers, led by a Belgian window cleaner, clubbed together to rent a vehicle for €4,000 after Ruinair announced that their flight from Carcassonne to Charleroi would not be replaced. The passengers were told upon arriving at the airport that their flight home had been cancelled due to bad weather. 'They abandoned us there as if we were dogs,' said Gauthier Renders, the 28-year-old window cleaner from Brussels. 'There were children and an old woman with a walking stick. They didn't even give us a glass of water. They said they wouldn't pay for us to get there. So I looked for a bus in the Yellow Pages and we were on the road by 9pm.'

If flying on Ruinair in August 2001 to Carcassonne was good enough for Tony Blair plus his family, then it's good enough for me. I wonder did Tony queue at check-in and did they ask him for his passport? In the Year of Our Lord 1998 BR (before Ruinair) the aerodrome of *Carcassonne en Pays Cathare* had only one daily flight, being northwards on TAP/Air Liberté *à Paris*. Along came Ruinair and now Carcassonne is the largest regional airport in

Languedoc. In 2002, the airport handled 215,200 passengers but it plans to reach 600,000 passengers soon. Settlers follow where tourists lead. The *Aude* was a rural patch of southern France in gentle decline until the British came *en masse* and stayed. They bought property and wine and sent their children to the local schools. *Aude* property prices rose by 28 per cent in 2003. Ruined farmhouses became *chic* but no longer cheap. Estate agents worked overtime. C'est la '*Ruinair Effect.*'

Mick has an opinion on ending flights on routes used by those travelling to holiday homes abroad: '*We don't have any obligation to second home owners that we are always going to carry you there for ever and a day. Please don't ask me to feel sorry for rich people with second homes in France.*'

Judging by the faces and baggage tags, all eight passengers on the airport shuttle bus were on my Dublin flight. Without Ruinair this bus driver would not have gainful employment. Seen first from the bus, the city, set high on a hill-top promontory on the right bank of the River Aude, is breathtaking. The nineteenth-century French songwriter Gustave Nadaud advised, 'You should not die without seeing Carcassonne.' The only reason I would leave this city in a hurry would be to stop immediately and look back in awe.

I vaguely recognise Carcassonne from one of those medieval backdrops often seen in Sunday afternoon BBC2 1960s Technicolour movies, the sort featuring jousting tournaments where gallant knights fight for the hand of a fair maiden with a tight bodice, flaxen hair and a strong American studio accent. Mr Walt Disney used this fortified town as inspiration for the design of his theme parks and the castle in *Sleeping Beauty* and the location also featured in *Robin Hood: Prince of Thieves.* Below the city the Canal du Midi snakes past the lower environs on its leisurely amble to the Med. Carcassonne is the oldest walled city in Europe and is a UNESCO World Heritage Site. It has become something of a tourist trap with shops selling plastic armour and replica swords but the welcome from locals is genuine, from the girl on the airport tarmac who utters a friendly *Bonjour* to the under-worked immigration staff. This is the second most visited

place in France after Paris, frequented by three million tourists
annually. Ruinair did their sums.

Aside from its stunning scenery, Carcassonne pulls in the
tourists because it is the capital of Cathar country. The Cathars
were a medieval dissident heretical sect which featured in some
religious code book. It is rumoured that Mary Magdalene stayed
nearby at Rennes le Chateau and the Holy Grail is hidden here. Yes,
it's here too. There were some fairly gruesome events in these parts
such as when the Cathar stronghold of Montsegur fell and 200
Cathars were burned alive in a pyre. I visit the Basilica of Saint
Nazaire in the darkened heart of the old *Cité* where the tombstone
of the Crusader Simon de Montfort rests. It was best not to shoot
the breeze with Simon nor utter your fave religious jokes. He
believed in the following maxim: 'Slay them all. God will recognise
his own people.' On one occasion Simon chopped off the ears,
noses and lips of a group of prisoners and gouged their eyes out
before sending them on their way to warn others, but left one
prisoner with one eye intact to guide them along. I cannot help
thinking he would have made an excellent cabin supervisor.

The invitingly named *Hotel Le Donjon* is possibly one of the
safest hotels in the world. It lies within the twin concentric city
walls that make up two miles of crenellated battlements topped by
fifty-two pointed turrets, and is accessible only by walking over a
bridge across a moat. Inside the walls 120 loyal citizens reside,
being shopkeepers, bar owners, restaurateurs and of course the
odd inevitable revolting peasant. Many an army laid siege to this
prized city unsuccessfully, except perhaps with the compromise
reached by the Crusaders in 1218, who permitted the inhabitants to
go free provided they left the town naked, which they did, allowing
the city's booty to be preserved intact and the populace to carry
away nothing but their sins.

The least successful defender was Ramon-Roger Trencavel,
Viscount of Carcassonne in the thirteenth century, who, when
besieged, rather stupidly went out to have a chat with the besiegers
during a truce period, where he was promptly seized and later died
in a cell in his own prison at the age of twenty-four. Another
legend has it that when Charlemagne besieged the town and as the

food was running out, a cunning townswoman named Dame
Carcas fed the town's last ears of grain to the last pig and tossed
him over the wall. Splat went the entrails. Charlemagne's restless
forces, amazed that the town still had enough food to throw fat
party pigs over the wall, decided they'd never succeed in starving
the people out and ended their siege. The inhabitants celebrated
wildly by blowing trumpets. *Carcas sounds.* Carcassonne. On the
little train ride around the walls, two Australian ladies in sensible
shoes enjoy the story. 'Ah, so the woman had the idea?'

The hotel's owner is the head of the hotelier's organisation in
the Aude. She advises that the concept of a tourist season is rapidly
disappearing. Now the tourist season spreads to nine months of
the year. 'My hotel rooms are taken throughout the year. It's due to
Ruinair.' Later in the tourist office the two ladies behind the
counter provide me with a schedule of the airport shuttle bus.
There are only six trips per day and each trip meets a Ruinair
flight. Without Ruinair, they would not need to operate an airport
shuttle bus.

That evening I dine al fresco in a small, dappled and authentic
square in the old *Cité*. Around me are the happy voices of English
and Irish couples in love. The couple at the next table will appear
in the check-in queue for my return flight. Without Ruinair, the
Brasserie Marcou would be empty tonight.

Later I stay at a converted manor house in the village of Pomas
(population 709, one baker, one grocer, one butcher, one post
office). The owners are a welcoming Belgian couple, from near
Brussels South International. No prizes for guessing how they
came to this part of France. Eric is a fan, as is I suspect his bank
manager, who financed the conversion. 'Sixty per cent of my guests
come here on Ruinair. I fly home six or seven times a year for only
one euro … but the taxes, fees and charges cost so much more.
There is an English family in the village and the father flies to work
in London on Monday and he returns home on Friday. There are
many English and Irish people buying property around here. It's
great for the area.'

Not everyone in France is as keen on having Ruinair. With its
film festival, racetrack and casino, the French seaside town of

Deauville is the height of chic, so its fashionable residents don't want planeloads of visitors arriving from Essex on low-cost flights. A 'No Budget Flights' association campaigned to prevent Ruinair operating flights from Stansted. Christiane Célice, who runs the association, said: *'It's not snobbery but it is not the clientele we want. Deauville doesn't want that sort of crowd. We are particularly against people who wear T-shirts and bring their own sandwiches to eat outside the casino. The English do not spend much money, that is well known.'*

Deauville is in Normandy, the only region without a low-cost air link to Britain, even though thousands of Britons buy homes and live there. The recent property boom has prompted complaints about 'Anglo-Saxon culture' in the shape of pubs, TV satellite dishes, football hooligans and even fish and chip shops, replacing the traditional French way of life. Deauville agreed to foot the advertising bill for the Ruinair route, estimated at £114,000 a year. *'Why should our taxes be used to boost Ruinair and pay for something that will massacre our countryside and cheapen our image?'* said Mrs Célice who shuddered at the idea. *'We have nothing against the English, quite the opposite. We want the English to come, but we ask them not to come on Ruinair. Ruinair does not bring high-quality tourists.'* Low-cost travel in general seems to fill her with horror. *'I hear that you even have to pay for your coffee if you are lucky enough to be offered any.'* The head of corporate communications for Ruinair said: *'The idea that hordes of Brits will arrive in Deauville wearing napkins on their heads is not real'.*

There is an Irish couple staying here who flew on Aer Lingus from Dublin to Bordeaux but they are going back on the same Ruinair flight as me from Carcassonne. She is worried and asks me, 'Do you know where Carcassonne airport is?' I advise that it's ten minutes from the town centre. She is hugely relieved. 'You never know with Ruinair where their little airports might be. I'm amazed that Carcassonne airport is actually near Carcassonne.'

The airport provides 180 direct full-time jobs and an estimated 3,000 other jobs locally in tourism, hospitality, retail, transport and leisure, injecting an estimated €415 million into the local economy annually. But this prosperity and development comes at a price. The airport is owned by the Carcassonne Chamber of Commerce and a *faux pas* by the President of the Chamber at a press conference revealed that they pay Ruinair €1.75 for each of the first 110,000 passengers, €2.25 each up to 250,000 passengers and €5 each for every passenger in excess of 250,000 per annum. This is 'marketing assistance', the sort of illegal subsidy that ended Ruinair flights to Strasbourg in 2003 following a case of sour grapes by the state monopoly that is Air France and subsequent EU intervention.

The Chamber has little choice but to pay for us to fly here. Their official airport guide has a schedule of all flights to and from the little Aude airport. There are six daily flights to Stansted, Charleroi, Dublin, Shannon, Liverpool and Snottingham. Every flight is a Ruinair flight. No other aircraft use this airport, save for the odd private Cessna or a lost pilot. When I arrived the only other flying machine I could spy was an air ambulance helicopter. Locals cannot even fly north to their national capital.

The Carcassonne arrangement epitomises everything about the success of Ruinair. I cannot imagine that legions of French people living in the Languedoc region harbour a secret desire to fly to Dublin, nor can I imagine that most Dubliners could find Carcassonne on a map of France. Yet the route is successful and the planes are 83 per cent full. *Vive la difference. Vive la Ruinair. Bon Voyage. Merci d'Avoir Choisi Ruinair. Volez Moins Cher.*

Taxes, Fees and Charges

Ruinair were once fined £24,000 by a UK court for misleading customers about the cost of flights. A jury found them guilty of six breaches of the Consumer Protection Act by omitting the words 'excluding taxes' from their website adverts. The Act 'prohibits a business giving a misleading price indication'. Ruinair denied any offence and claimed the omission was accidental. Essex Trading Standards told Chelmsford Crown Court: '*The price you see should be the price you pay — pure and simple. The case we encountered here with Ruinair was akin to going to a petrol station advertising fuel at 29p and then being billed an extra 60p in tax at the till not to mention an extra sum for short term car parking.*' Another Ruinair advertisement which offered seats for £0 was grounded by advertising watchdogs. The fare failed to include extra taxes and charges. Ruinair said, '*14 million people viewed the advert and not one passenger had complained.*'

The taxes, fees and charges quoted by various low fares airlines on their websites during the booking process include items such as air passenger duty, local airport taxes, passenger service charges, fuel surcharges, insurance charges, credit card charges and even wheelchair surcharges. These are usually quoted separate to the 'low' fare and are seen in the final stages of the online booking process. It is a feat of Cana wedding proportions for Ruinair to transform a 1p fare into a sixty euro final price.

	€
Fare	0.01
Using a check-in desk	3.00
Travel Insurance	5.00
Taxes, fees and charges	16.95
Aviation / Wheelchair Levy	5.54
Credit card handling fee	3.00
One item of baggage	6.00
One coffee	2.75
One sandwich	5.00
One bottle of water	2.50
Bus excursion from middle of nowhere airport	10.00
Total	€59.75

When customers reach the point of paying, Ruinair adds on an 'aviation levy' to cover insurance of £3.15 per traveller. The airline has carried fifty million passengers over the past year, which means the surcharge raises £157 million on an annualised basis. Inquiries by *The Guardian* established that Ruinair pays only a fraction of this in aircraft insurance. Ruinair declined to disclose its exact outlay on insurance. When pressed on the point, he advised *The Guardian* to '*stick to reading and writing because the sums clearly aren't your strong point*'.

An industry-wide report on low fares airlines' ancillary revenue was prepared by London stockbrokers ABN Amro and co-authored by Andrew Lobbenberg, one of the most respected analysts in the aviation sector. ABN argue that ancillary revenues can be divided into 'genuine' ancillaries and 'hidden fares'. 'Genuine ancillaries are those that earn revenue from offering the customer a useful service or product related to air travel, and hidden fare increases are taxes, fees and charges introduced for something which was previously free.' 'Hidden fares' swelled Ruinair's coffers by €109 million as the airline charged passengers for everything from handling credit cards to carrying luggage. Credit and debit card fees were the key earner, being €76 million. A spokesman for Ruinair said he could not comment on the report beyond saying '*Andrew Lobbenberg is a clown.*'

It is easier to understand the Ruinair approach to taxes, fees and charges if you imagine for example that *O'Brien's Irish Sandwich Shops* adopted the same pricing approach. Firstly O'Brien's would advertise their sandwiches in the shop window at a price of 1 cent each. But when you went inside to buy a sandwich, they would charge you €6.41. When you asked why, they'd tell you that it's comprised of: bread 1 cent, butter 20 cents, fillings €1.50, paper bag 30 cents, government tax 60 cents, disabled seating fee 30 cents, public liability insurance 50 cents, labour €1, VAT €1 and a cutting and handling fee of €1. So it's €6.41. You would try to pay with cash but they only take credit cards. 'That's another €3.'

After paying up, you would stand in a long queue for an hour and then suddenly race across the sandwich shop to fight with the other customers for the very best sandwiches. It's first come, first served. After selecting a sandwich of your own choosing you then ask for a seat where you can eat your sandwich in peace. "That'll be €3 extra but if you'd ordered the seat at the same time as the sandwich, it would only be €2."

The worst part is that you return to work and tell your colleagues about the amazing sandwich which only cost 1 cent. And now they all want one.

Customer Service Dept
Ruinair Ltd
Dublin Airport

Dear Sirs,

  I recently took advantage of a 'free' seat sale and purchased a return Dublin - Lootin' flight for a fare of only 1 cent each way. While 1 cent is not exactly 'free', it nevertheless represents excellent value for money.

  However imagine my shock and horror when I came to pay online with my credit card to discover the total cost for this 'free' seat came to the whopping amount of €50. I have my emailed itinerary / receipt but it is certainly not clear from this what these additional monies represent. This is the nature of my complaint. Can you please explain what comprises the €35.25 of 'taxes, fees & charges'? Also could your email itinerary clearly explain these components as other airlines do? I had a look at your website which says, 'Taxes, fees and charges refers to that portion of the total air fare payable by each passenger' which doesn't make any sense in English since the passenger will always pay ALL of the total air fare? Also can you please explain what comprises the €8.98 of 'aviation / WCHR Levy'? In the absence of psychic powers I am unable to determine what the initials WCHR stand for? We Charge Highest Rates?

* Yours etc,*
* Disgusted of Dublin*

Four days later they deliver the goods by email.

Dear Mr Kilduff,

* I acknowledge receipt of your letter. I wish to confirm that the free flights are called same because the fare is "free", however passengers must pay taxes, fees and charges. Taxes, fees and charges refers to that portion of the total air fare payable by each passenger. It is calculated by reference to the Government taxes and airport charges payable by Ruinair in respect of passengers travelling on a particular route on that particular itinerary. These may include Government taxes, airport taxes, passenger service charges, insurance surcharges and in some cases passenger security charges as well.*

* Yours sincerely*
* Ruinair Ltd*

Another cut and paste reply which fails to answer my questions. *Bolloxology.*

Ruinair also make money from taxes, fees and charges levied on passengers who book tickets but who do not fly with the airline. Ruinair refuses to refund these charges. *'All monies paid are paid on a non-refundable basis,'* says Mick. Ruinair do not reveal how much they make from these particular taxes and charges which they take in but do not pass on to national exchequers and airports.

However, the figure was included in a regulatory filing made to the US Securities and Exchange Commission: 27,593,923 flights were booked in one financial year, but only 25,641,508 of these were actually flown, earning a cool €39 million in taxes. Passengers can claim a refund of the taxes but Ruinair charge an administration fee to make it difficult.

> *Customer Service Dept*
> *Ruinair Ltd*
> *Dublin Airport*
>
> *Dear Sirs,*
> *I recently booked a flight from Dublin to Oslo-Torp but I was unable to travel due to other commitments. I read on your website that you refund government taxes to passengers who do not travel and I believe that you charge an administration fee of €20 to process a refund. I therefore hereby request a refund of the government taxes on the above unused reservation. Please find enclosed my cheque for €20.*
> *Yours etc.*
> *Disgusted of Dublin*
>
> *Dear Mr Kilduff,*
> *Following your recent request for a refund of the taxes paid on your unused booking.*
> *Applications for tax refunds are subject to an administration charge per passenger. Please note that all other fees and charges, such as the passenger service charge, aviation insurance and credit & debit card handling fees are non refundable as per our General Conditions of Carriage.*
> *Unfortunately, no refund is due in this instance as the administration charge exceeds the tax refund amount.*
> *Yours sincerely,*
> *Ruinair Customer Services*

They did not return my cheque but neither did they cash my cheque. Yet.

Taxes, fees and charges remain another mystery, like why do geriatric doctors look so young, why does Jamiroquai release the same single every year, why does Mariah Carey bother to wear any clothes at all in her videos, why do dishwashers need regular supplies of salt, why do mothers buy lower-sugar *Sugar Puffs* for their children, why do the Poles always matter so much in general elections, why does Prince Charles keeps a private diary so that disgruntled ex-employees can leak it to the tabloid press, and who does Condoleezza Rice's hair?

Portugal

Ruinair Flights FR216 & FR8347 – Tuesday @ 1.40pm
– DUB-STN-OPO-STN-DUB

Fare €6 plus taxes, fees and charges €88

As I book my final flight online, I imagine the corporate voice of Ruinair advising me in no uncertain terms of what I should be aware of. It goes something like this:

So before you fly with us for the last time let's ensure you understand the exact conditions by which we will fly you from Dublin via Stansted to Porto. The fare will be low but let's see how low we can go.

We make it easy for you to book your flight online but once we have your money, the gloves are off. When you book, do check the check boxes and ensure you don't insure. See if you can book your flight without paying for insurance because we made it difficult to do so. You can change the time and date of your flight but only if you pay us twenty-five euros extra and you must pay the latest fare available at the time of any change. You can change the name on any ticket but you must pay one hundred euros extra. We can change your flight times whenever we like and if so we will send you an email and you can take it or leave it and make any alternative arrangements. We only do refunds if you certify someone has died.

We will fly you to many destinations in Europe. They may not be the most desirable destinations but we fly there because these small regional airports offer us the best financial deals. Every year in a blaze of free publicity we will open new bases and launch new routes, primarily designed for commuting Polish plumbers and other jobbing rural migrants, but we will quietly close unprofitable routes and tell no one. Do not buy property near one of our regional European destinations because we might not fly there next year.

We open our check-in desks two hours before departure. That will cost you three euros. We close our check-in desk forty minutes before departure time. If you don't arrive on time, then tough. We don't want to hear any of your excuses, particularly ones about going to the funeral of a loved one. We don't want to hear about traffic tailbacks on the motorway. We are not responsible for connecting buses, neither are we responsible for grim conditions in any regional airport. That's the job of the airport authority.

We are not bothered if you don't turn up to fly because 10 per cent of our passengers never even show. Although you have paid government taxes and airport charges we will not refund your money if you don't show and we won't pass it over to governments or airports, so it's a nice little annual multi-million earner.

We wish to see your passport or national identity card at check-in. We do not wish to see your credit card, work ID, driver's licence, bingo card, library card, student card, Blockbuster membership or John Lewis store card.

Our check-in staff will allow you to check in 15 kg of luggage for the hold. Going out is easy but we weigh your luggage very carefully on your return flight because you will usually have more and you will not leave it behind. The majority of our passengers make trips of only two days' duration so we don't know why you want to put that bloody big suitcase into our hold causing our aircraft to burn so much aviation fuel. It is best not to worry or to make any preparations regarding your luggage because either way we will get you.

Our crew may assist you, and if you speak Spanglish, then all the better. We don't hand out free sweets, we don't lift baggage, we don't help old dears but we do charge for wheelchairs. We don't tolerate complaints about our cabin crew. The reason they look so miserable is because they are new to the job, are a long way from home, are paid a pittance and must rise and shine at 4am. The crew will look scruffy and unkempt but that's because it's always very dark in the bathroom at 4am. Do not worry that some of the crew may have recently had a close family bereavement. They have not. They always look that way.

When you arrive at the departure gate you should immediately join one of the two queues. One queue is *Sad Bastards Who Like to Pay to Stand in a Queue in Case They Don't get a Seat On board* and the other queue is for people who like to sit down and couldn't give a flying fuck about the departure time.

We guarantee you a seat on the flight because unlike other airlines we do not overbook our flights. Our average load factor of 83 per cent means there are thirty-two empty seats on each flight. You may sit anywhere in our aircraft provided you can do a four-minute mile whilst shoulder-charging fellow passengers. You may sit in any row except the rows in the front and rear of the aircraft, which we often block off so we don't have to look at you up close. Your seatbelt will not be neatly folded on your seat because that takes us time.

The seats are cheap vinyl because vinyl is easier to clean than cloth. Our seats do not recline because people like you break them and Boeing charge money to repair such extras. There is no safety card in the pocket on your seat because we don't have seat pockets since they take our staff time to empty. Instead the safety instructions will be spot-welded to the back of the seat in front, and appropriately enough, are in your face.

We deliver our safety demonstrations in a variety of languages, simultaneously. We won't laugh. Much. Don't stare at the cabin crew whilst they deliver these announcements because most of them don't have much self-confidence or suffer from low self-esteem and staring makes them even more nervous. We know they can appear to be unprofessional and immature, but they will be great in an emergency.

While on our aircraft we will try to sell you everything we can. We will wheel the food and drink trolley up and down the aisle twice on longer flights. We will sell you cuddly toys, rail tickets and telephone cards because 10 per cent of our annual revenue comes from such ancillary services. The only thing we don't sell is the bottled oxygen you breathe on our flights, but give us time. And have you considered that some day soon we might charge you 50p to take a pee in the wc? You are not going anywhere while confined for two hours in a Boeing at 36,000 feet. You are fair game. Now anyone for scratch cards?

If you feel nauseous during the flight you may be staring too much at the vomit-yellow interior of our aircraft and their wall-to-wall advertisements. You may use a sick bag upon request. If you do not feel nauseous you may use the sick bag to despatch your photographs to *Klick Photopoint* who will process a roll of film for only 95p, plus you receive a free film with every order. We call them *dual-purpose bags*.

You will arrive on time because we fly to airports which no other airlines use. We won't lose your luggage because you usually carry it on board or they are the only pieces of luggage the baggage handlers see all day. We will not cancel your flight unless there is bad weather or a technical fault, the latter being suitably vague. Some of our flights might be late because of a late incoming flight, in which case we are late because we are late. This is how we define and measure customer service. We don't do smiles.

If you are unhappy with any aspect of our service you may write us a letter. We don't accept emailed or telephone complaints. We guarantee you a reply within seven days and also guarantee to agree or concede nothing. We will reply to you by email but don't reply to our email because it disappears into a black hole. You are not a person, nor even a passenger. You are a six-character alpha-numeric booking reference. And we won't speak to you unless you pay us up to 80 cents per minute on our premium telephone line.

We don't really care if you have a pleasant flight, or not. We know you will fly again with us because we are cheap. It's the same as finding a pair of jeans in Tesco for a fiver, a CD in HMV for a quid or a Tommy Hilfiger shirt for ten bucks in a bargain bucket in

Century 21 in Manhattan. And the beauty is that the more awful we make the flying experience, the more of you want to see how bad it can get. We may piss off 189 passengers on any one flight daily when we cancel or re-route flights but there are 700 million potential passengers in Europe so we have a very long way to go before we run out of paying customers.

I am not disappointed on today's flight but something is different. The cabin crew seem ... happy. A female cabin crew member helps a lady with air sickness and checks back on the passenger a few times. A male cabin crew member shares in the excitement of those buying scratch cards and watches them win nothing. Several crew are well-groomed. I know what has happened. Ruinair sent me an invitation to participate in an online customer service survey a few months ago. I scored them low but they are already acting on the narrative comment I made at the end of the survey. I wrote '*Hire Less Miserable Staff.*'

Next up is the bus ride from hell. There is meant to be an *Aerobus* direct to Porto city centre but no such bus shows for thirty minutes. A last 606 *Local* bus arrives at 10pm. The driver is a Snr Grumpy who hasn't a word of English and doesn't have change of a ten euro note. I should have offered a hundred euro note. We take off but instead of using the obvious motorway we circumnavigate the suburbs of Porto at speed, hurtling through one-way streets inches from the residents' living rooms and claiming the odd wing mirror. The driver may be slumped dead at the wheel. It's hard to tell. Or Sandra Bullock may be driving.

Some passengers alight into a black void at bus stops in the midst of fields. We crane our necks at the gritty port area and pass truck stops with working ladies in search of a ride. On occasion we stop dead in our tracks as eighteen-wheel juggernauts come in the opposite direction. The roads are unfinished because the city has spent its money on incredibly ugly public art for the roundabouts. We do U-turns and slalom courses at speed for fifty minutes and passengers are hurled about in the bus like Lotto balls in the drum on a Saturday night until we are finally collectively spewed out in the main square of *Avenida dos Aliados*.

Porto is Portugal's second city; a city of 350,000 inhabitants clustered around the Douro River. The *Barredo*, the old town centre, is another ruddy UNESCO World Heritage Site. A dense amalgam of houses and churches cling to the steep riverbanks. Narrow streets of almost tenemental residential dwellings wind their way up the hills like a South American *favela* on the wrong side of the building laws, tiered and layered upon each other in the style of a giant wedding cake about to topple over and slide into the waters. Their finest laundry proudly hangs on display from balconies, fluttering away in sweet surrender. This is a positive statement about any city. These citizens are prepared to wash their dirty laundry in public.

On the opposite side of the river in *Gaia* are the old Port wineries and related company logos. The banks of signs for Crofts, Taylors, Sandeman and Dow remind me to add another question to the list of those most easily answered, such as *Is the Pope a Catholic? Does Judith Chalmers have a passport? Did Fred West own a shovel?* Now we can add *Can you buy Port wine in the Porto Airport Duty Free shop?*

Do not visit Porto solely for the gastronomic experience. The inhabitants are known as *tripeiros* (tripe eaters), due to their sacrifice made to help their army that conquered Africa in 1415 when they offered all their good meat to the expeditionary forces and kept only tripe for themselves. Hence the city's most traditional dish is *tripas à moda do Porto,* which alas I do not have time to sample. Yet the dish of veal tripe, sausages and beans still symbolises hospitality, self-sacrifice and altruism. Much like the duck at *Fawlty Towers* I suspect one can have tripe with orange sauce, tripe with cherry sauce, or tripe surprise. Do visit Porto if you like touring 500-year-old baroque churches. Porto's tourist office provides me with a free map of twenty churches which are worth a visit. This remains a deeply spiritual city but twenty places of worship is a lot to see. I doubt even an omniscient Jesus Christ could pack them all into a day.

I climb from the riverfront *Cais da Ribeira,* with its bobbing port transport boats, towards the city centre. Overhead the giant *Ponte D. Luis I* coat-hanger of a bridge traverses the gorge. It's steep around these parts. Porto is bloody hilly. If you ever get lost and are in doubt where to go, the best thing to do is to start climbing any street or some steps. There are no gyms in Porto. It's better to go for a walk outside.

Along the streets are the most amazing shops; window displays of pink hot water bottles and plastic kitchen bins, newsagents of a thousand magazines hanging on bulldog clips but they don't sell postcards, and religious shops selling Baby Jesus for €26.50 but his ruby blanket costs €20 extra. Old Romany wenches smoke chestnuts at street stalls and blind accordion players sell lottery tickets. Further up the vertical steppes, I stumble upon the faded *Sao Bento* train station from 1916, peeling and unappealing.

This is a generalisation but the inhabitants of Porto appear a little odd. It may be their swashbuckling nautical past but they have the look of hunted desperados, with furtive glances and dark sunken eyes. I am not tall but they are tiny. For some reason many walk with a pronounced limp, which might be something to do with all that struggling up and down these hills over the years. After twenty-four hours I too develop a slight teeter in sympathy. I try to recall those many famous Portuguese celebrities but all I can think of is Vasco da Gama and he died in 1524. Where are all the *Beautiful People* in Porto? The answer may be … Lisbon.

In the Middle Ages, before the discovery of the New World, Porto was balanced upon the edge of the world. One wrong move and you fell off the edge. Later travellers came here to admire the architecture, the river views and to visit the wineries but now there is a new attraction in town. I catch the spanking new metro northwards. On the official metro map of the city there are only two images and both are football stadia.

The 52,000 seater, €95 million *Estadio de Dragao* stadium perches high on a hill to the north of the city, like some giant *Close Encounters* spaceship sent to observe the citizens from a safe distance. Here lies the field of dreams where José Mário dos Santos Mourinho Félix became another cult, much like Mick O'Leary. Little José was the son of goalkeeper Felix Mourinho, who played for their home town Setubal and the national team, but José never had enough skill to play soccer professionally. So instead he wrote match reports for Dad. His mother sent him to business school but he only lasted one day, quitting to join a sports college.

He earned the nickname *Tradutor*, the translator, when working as an interpreter for Robby Bobson. José worked at Barcelona and Benfica before getting the chance to manage Porto. There he resurrected a team and won the League, the Cup, the UEFA Cup and the ultimate prize of the Champions League within two years. He was awarded Portugal's highest civilian honour, *The Order of Infante Dom Henrique*. As the late Brian Clough once remarked of him, '*That Portuguese bloke. He's got a lot to say.*'

Ruinair's CEO and the world's greatest, or at least best paid, football coach were separated at birth. They share a streak of modest confidence. '*Please don't call me arrogant, but I'm the European champion and I think I'm a special one. We have top players and, sorry if I'm arrogant, we have a top manager. I am absolutely sure that we will be champions next season. We are on top at the moment but not because of the club's financial power. We are in contention for a lot of trophies because of my hard work.*'

They are both commercially minded. '*I am very happy because the club is beating records with the sales of new shirts. If Roman Abramovich helped me out in training we would be bottom of the league and if I had to work in his world of big business, we would be bankrupt.*'

They are both leaders. '*There is no pressure at the top. The pressure is being second or third. There is no pressure even in football. Pressure is the millions of parents in the world who can't get food for their children.*'

They are both ambitious. '*If I wanted to have an easy job, I would have stayed at Porto with a beautiful blue chair, the UEFA Champions League trophy, God, and after God, me. So do not tell me your movie. I am in a movie of my own.*'

I climb more damn steps to the official fan store of *Futebol Clube do Porto*. Inside they sell branded kiddies' place mats, shower gel, fluffy slippers, boxer shorts, inflatable sofas, downy pillows, cuddly toys, snooker cues (?) and official bottles of FC Porto Port, but there's no sign of José, even in the display of souvenirs from the glorious victories over Celtic in Seville and Valencia in Monaco. José has been erased.

There is an official tour of the stadium which includes the pitch, dressing room, media centre, press box, conference room, the Hall of Fame and the *glazed tile painting*. I will be able to walk on the grass that José paced upon, maybe sit in his seat in the home team dugout. The tour costs one euro more than my return air fare. They charge visitors €5 per each photograph they take but I don't know if it applies to my mobile telephone camera. They do not offer tours on match days but I have checked that this is not a match day. I enter by gate 2 and immediately a female security guard in khaki uniform rushes towards me.

'I'm here for the tour,' I advise.

'No tour,' she advises.

'There is a tour. It's on the club website.'

'Tomorrow.' She points to a sign in the lobby with the tour details. There are tours on Thursday and Friday. Even on Saturday and Sunday. But today is Wednesday and I fly home later today.

'I have come a very long way for the tour. From Ireland. I'm a huge fan of Porto FC.' Blatant lie.

'Tomorrow.'

'But I won't be in Porto tomorrow.' She is unmoved. 'It's Ruinair's fault. I can't afford to fly on a Thursday or Friday because their fares are too high. And I can only dream of travelling at the weekend.'

'Tomorrow.'

Behind her is a sheer plate glass wall which opens out on the stadium. I see the sponsors' logos, the TV commentary boxes, the banked seating, the cantilevered roof supports. I can't see the bloody grass.

'Can I have a look?' I ask, moving closer.

She stands in my way. 'Tomorrow.'

It's a visitors' centre for the football club alright. It's just that they don't like visitors much. Later Ruinair depart Porto on time and I eventually see below the grass of the *Dragao* stadium. I am reminded of the time ITV football commentator Clive Tyldesley rhetorically asked the nation a question during a live broadcast. 'You wonder where José Mourinho would be if Porto had lost that Champions League final?'

To which football pundit Andy Townsend sitting alongside expertly replied, 'At Porto, probably.'

Caught Napping

I watched a scary documentary programme tonight on TV, so scary it should have been on after the 9pm watershed. The Channel 4 *Dispatches* team sent Mary Nash and Charlotte Smith to work undercover for five months with an airline at Stansted to investigate the real cost of flying on low fares airlines. Channel 4 promoted the programme with full-page newspaper advertisements picturing a sleeping flight attendant and said they would expose the airline's 'cynical attitude among staff towards passengers and their welfare'. The airline is Ruinair. Is this really a revelation? Have they ever flown on this airline?

The programme was loaded with sound bites from their jaded staff. *'Passengers don't matter.' 'I'm not bothered about the passengers.' 'The aircraft doesn't get cleaned between flights.' 'If you pay only one penny for your ticket, then don't expect a life jacket under your seat.' 'You can check the life jackets if you like, hah hah.' 'You pay nothing for your ticket so you get nothing.' 'Ruinair take everything and give nothing.' 'All I do is work and sleep.' 'They are killing me.'* Now I know why their cabin crew never smile. Come to think of it now in retrospect after so many flights, the passengers don't smile that much either.

One cabin crew member was filmed catching a nap at the back of the aircraft on one flight. She lay with her arm up against the

exit door. Another guy nodded off. It's not surprising that people
are tired at work. Like I get tired sometimes in the day and snooze
but I'm not looking after 189 people at 33,000 feet going 500 mph.
But I learned a few things I never knew despite a year of flying back
and forth on this airline. After-shave is great for masking the smell
of vomit. Cabin crew earn a mere £14 per short sector flight.

Ruinair is a *Teflon* brand. The next day they launch another one
of those never to be repeated three million seats sale. This time it's a
zero fare offer because low fares are no longer enough. Bookings rose
15 per cent after this TV documentary. They place advertisements
headlined 'An apology from Ruinair' and 'Sorry' in newspapers, not
apologising for allegations about their safety standards or service,
but to say sorry to competing airlines because they are stealing their
customers. 'It is going to make it very difficult for other airlines to
sell seats.'

They place eleven glowing letters from satisfied customers on
their website in the following week, which is an impressive enough
number of raving fans, considering they fly fifty million passengers
annually.

Mick held his own *Oscars* on the same night when he invited
Ruinair staff to watch the programme at the Stansted base. Mick
allegedly presented awards to staff captured on camera by
Dispatches. The prizes included a weekend for two in Barcelona
with £300 spending money for the staff member who tells the
biggest whopper on air. Of course there are probably additional
taxes, fees and charges to pay and the destination will not be
Barcelona's *El Prat* airport, but places like Reus or Girona. There
was also a £200 contribution towards the cost of divorce
proceedings for the staff member who delivered the best chat-up
line to one of *Dispatches* 'undercover investigative dollies', as Mick
dubbed the two Channel 4 reporters.

Mick wasn't impressed. *'This is not a documentary. It's more like
a soap. The public have more common sense than a sensationalised
TV programme. If that's the best they can do after five months, then
they should give up filming. Channel 4 can shove this programme up
its jacksie, there's nothing in it. We got the rosters for the two
journalists who'd been working for the three months. One averaged 36*

hours a week, one 28 hours. They filmed one in her flat late at night who, crying and whispering, claimed to have been at work since 4am and just got back at 8pm. Rubbish. We have maximum duty days of 14 hours. She never did it. What you're left with is two journalists, one of whom was working a four-day week and the other working a 3½ day week — which I accept for journalists is a very busy week.'

The strangest aspect of this programme was that Ruinair didn't deduce that Mary Nash and Charlotte Smith were not genuine Ruinair staff. It was obvious to me. They both spoke perfect English.

Ireland ...again

Section 482 of the Irish Finance Act provides tax relief to the owner of an approved building in respect of expenditure incurred on the repair, maintenance or restoration of the approved building. The building must be determined by the Minister for Environment, Heritage and Local Government to be one which is intrinsically of significant scientific, historical, architectural or aesthetic interest. One of the conditions which entitles owners of 'significant' houses to full tax relief on any building work is that they must open their property to the dreaded general public on at least sixty days of the year and they are obliged to provide the Irish Tourist Board with the dates and times of these openings.

Mick owns and lives in a splendid Georgian mansion which received a favourable determination for Section 482 tax relief. The government's tax website shows the property is open from 9am to 1pm Monday to Friday each week from 26 February to 5 July. All visitors are required to produce photographic ID, much like check-in, and no photography is permitted, much like any airport security area. A tour guide is on hand to show visitors around sections of the house and surrounding gardens. Admission is £2.50 for an adult, £1.00 for a child, in old money. That's expensive enough considering the price of air fares these days. So I am off to look inside Mick's home and he can't stop me.

Our routing takes us in a north-westerly direction along the M50 and M4 towards Mullingar airport, if Mullingar had an airport. I am pleasantly surprised to find the motorway network now extends beyond County Dublin. However, I must pay a €2.50 toll on the M4 despite the fact that I also pay 42 per cent of my annual income to the Irish government so that they can spend my money on matters for the greater good, like roads. A few miles along the road from Delvin to Collinstown, I hang a left to the windswept hilltop church of St Livinius in the parish of Killulagh. This church is hard to locate so it was ideal for Mick's wedding in 2003. Today there are two Travellers' caravans, a few mongrels on the end of some string and a beat-up Ford Escort but I suspect it was different when Ireland's tenth richest man surrendered his status here as the country's most eligible bachelor to a Citibanker from Blackrock named Anita. Anita's mum Kathleen was once in charge of cabin crew training for Aer Lingus. A one hundred-strong crowd of locals gathered on the manicured grassy slopes, where I now stand, to see their famous neighbour. The bride wore a traditional Vera Wang off-white scoop-neck gown and full-length veil and the groom swapped jeans and open shirt for a black morning suit with smart wine-coloured waistcoat. Mick arrived a typical ten minutes before schedule with his best man and brother Eddie, joking it was the most nervous moment of his life, but his bride arrived with her Dad thirty-eight minutes late in an old Bentley. Mick quipped, 'She's flying here with Aer Lingus. The reception is going to be cheap but the honeymoon is going to kill me.'

Afterwards, back at Mick's estate, three hundred guests including Tony Ruin, the Tánaiste, an EU commissioner and government ministers attended the wedding reception, plus a twenty-person private security team. Guests indulged in pink champagne and a four-course meal of two starters of fresh asparagus and a seafood mix, a main course of steak, followed by a Bailey's cheesecake for dessert. No warm paninis were on offer, but ice and lemon were. Mick hired a jazz band and a covers group, Fabulous Hit Connection, to play his favourite U2 and Bruce Springsteen songs at the reception. A footbridge over the estate's swimming pool allowed guests entry to three marquees, such as those used at Beauvais airport, and a hundred trees were decorated with fairy-lights. Mick shed his low-cost reputation, splashing out for the event and asking guests to donate money to the North Westmeath hospice in lieu of wedding presents. I mean does a man of Mick's means really need another toaster or cappuccino-making machine? Mick unusually paid €250,000 for a flawless diamond engagement ring, followed by a business class honeymoon to Mauritius, not a low fares destination. *'I'm a fat cat when I fly in business class on long-haul flights. Otherwise I am not a fat cat. I am actually quite a slim cat. But my wife disagrees with that.'*

Attributed to the renowned architect John Skipton-Mulvany, Gigginstown House was built for Elizabeth Busby between 1853 and 1855. Designed in the classical style, it comprises a large neat house, renovated stables and gate lodge, all in pristine condition. The palatial pile is set at the far end of an oak-lined gravel drive amidst 200 acres of grounds and sleepy meadows set behind a stone cut wall. Mick bought the pile, in need of renovation, from a Patsy Farrell in 1993 for approx £580,000. In 2005 Kilroe Developments were paid in excess of five million euros to refurbish and extend the property, and to construct a courtyard, reception area and even a swimming pool. There are nice pictures on their website. *'The house itself isn't massive. It's a very nice family home. I wouldn't want my kids rattling around in a ginormous fucking mansion. If you have kids and the kids are growing up and bringing friends back, you don't want them to think they are arriving in Buckingham Palace.'*

It's not an easy house to locate, and I am not going to spell out the directions because Mick won't want every other loony turning up here, but I find it and it's an extensive, white, two-storey home with a lot of Mercedes parked outside (more taxis?) but in truth it's also a farm. Mick grew up on a farm and maintains a hands-on approach to managing his large estate. *'My hobby is agriculture.'* Farming can be an expensive business, even after Mick realised €40 million from the sale of company shares: *'The money is spread around banks and post offices. I'm using it to staunch my farming losses.'* He remains sanguine about his personal wealth: *'It used to be my motivation. You always want to make the first million. Then*

you get to £10 million and you think about £100 million. But
somewhere in the middle — do not ask me where — you stop
worrying about money.'

Mick established an elite pedigree, the Gigginstown House
Aberdeen Angus herd. Many top heifers in Canada, including
champion and reserve champion show heifers, were imported for
their confirmation and maternal traits. He has supplied herd sires
for some of the top herds in Ireland, Northern Ireland and
Scotland and his bulls are doing a tremendous job in many
commercial herds. And that's a lot of bull.

Gigginstown House Stud is also home to his thoroughbred
horses. *'As a businessman, I can make plans and I can have influence,*
but in jump racing I have to accept that the owner is merely the idiot
at the bottom of the pile. The trainer and the jockeys make all the
important decisions, I just pay the bills. But if you like the people in
jump racing, as I do, then the sport becomes a great social activity —
it's a perfect pursuit, I guess, for stupid rich guys.'

His War of Attrition won the Gold Cup at Cheltenham.
'Unbelievable, I've died and gone to heaven. I thought the finish was
a bit slow — it lasted about two and a half hours there from the last
fence to the line. Tonight we shall have a couple of very quiet drinks
soberly before catching the 9pm Ruinair flight. And we'll be paying
for our luggage.'

Everyone knows about Mick's horses, even the baggage handlers
in Spain. When Spanish airport workers went on strike against
Ruinair, Ingo Marowsky, Aviation Section Secretary of the
International Transport Workers' Federation, said that workers
were receiving support all across Europe and union leaders were in
talks about a Europe-wide strike against Ruinair. *'All Ruinair's*
workers are asking for is that Mick O'Leery treat them with a fraction
of the respect he shows for his racehorses.'

I wish to enter the impressive property but sadly it is impossible.
I learn that Gigginstown House has been removed from the list of
properties that qualify for tax relief. The website is out of date.
More bull.

Financial Ruination

It must be the chartered accountant in me, usually a terminal condition, but I have a burning desire to summarise the cost of travelling to every country in Old Europe. Honestly, I wish I had an Excel file.

Country	Airline	Route	Fare	Taxes Fees & Charges	Total
France	Ruinair	DUB-BVA-DUB	€2	€33	€35
United Kingdom	Ruinair	DUB-STN-DUB	€2	€42	€44
Belgium	Ruinair	DUB-CRL-DUB	€1	€33	€34
Netherlands	Ruinair	DUB-EIN-DUB	€2	€46	€48
Luxembourg	Ruinair	DUB-HHN-DUB	€25	€40	€65
Greece	EzJet	DUB-LTN-ATH-LTN-DUB	€84	€64	€148
Germany	Wings	DUB-CGN-DUS-DUB	€0.01	€23	€23
Austria	Niki/Herr Berlin	NUE-VIE-DUS	€23	€45	€68
Spain	Fueling	BRU-BCN	€30	€29	€59
Switzerland	Barbie	DUB-LTN-ZRH-LTN-DUB	€38	€144	€182
Italy	MyHair	BCN-VCE-TSF-STN	€40	€54	€94

Country	Airline	Route	Fare	Taxes Fees & Charges	Total
Norway	Ruinair	DUB-STN-HAU-STN-DUB	€0.04	€88	€88
Denmark/ Sweden	Ruinair	DUB-STN-MMX-STN-DUB	€28	€88	€116
Finland	Ruinair	DUB-STN-TMP-STN-DUB	€0.04	€88	€88
Portugal	Ruinair	DUB-STN-OPO-STN-DUB	€6	€88	€94
Total			**€281**	**€905**	**€1,186**

With the €19 left in my budget, I bought a Ruinair pen (€7) and a Ruinair model aircraft (€12).

To enjoy the cheapest possible flights: fly on a Tuesday or Wednesday; fly in October, November, February or March; suffer 6am departures and 10pm return flights; book ahead — the best time to book the next trip is upon returning from the last trip; if you see a bargain, book it immediately (remember *Mick's Law* — if you look for that fare tomorrow, it's gone); subscribe to the regular email updates to receive priority news of seat sales and special offers; consider traditional alternatives — on some routes the flag carriers are competitive; if you crave a four-day long weekend break away, travel Saturday to Tuesday, not Thursday to Sunday; be flexible on your departure and return dates — travel on the dates that suit the airline, not that suit you; consider other low fares airlines, not just Ruinair. Use Aer Lingus more!

And the lesson learned above from this continental travelogue is the same as that of life in general.

Without taxes, life would be so much better.

The Low Fares
Airline (5)

NUN BETTER

*An Irish nun from Ballinasloe, Co. Galway, has scooped €100,000.
Sister Kathleen Murphy, of St Catherine's Convent in Edinburgh,
won the huge cash prize after taking a flight with Ruinair. The airline
ran a special promotion to celebrate its historic landmark as the first
European low fares airline to carry 100 million passengers. The 50-
year-old woman, who has been a nun since she was 16, immediately*

said the money would be donated to the convent where she lives. 'On behalf of our congregation, I would like to thank Ruinair for this very generous gift towards enabling us to promote mercy in the UK. This gift will help us enormously and will be donated directly to feeding the hungry and to the service of all of the Corporal Works of Mercy (as in Matthew 25:34-37) — feeding the hungry, sheltering the homeless, clothing the naked, visiting the sick and the imprisoned, burying the dead, and giving alms, and to the spiritual renewal of women. I announced the news at breakfast and there was a tremendous cheer,' Sr. Kathleen said. She said her nun's vow of poverty meant she had to take the cheapest air fare she could find.

RTE NEWS

NONE WORSE

Ruinair has been voted the world's least liked airline because of cramped seating, unfriendly staff and delays. Online travel service TripAdvisor said it polled 4,000 of its users on a range of subjects from airlines and airports, to worries and holiday hotspots. Ruinair countered that it consistently topped customer-service indicators and it expected to carry 50 million people this year, 'so we must be doing something right. Ruinair carries more UK passengers than any other airline. The public votes with its feet.' Ruinair CEO Mick O'Leery said, 'You get some obscure website which claims some 4,000 people participated, when it's more like 400 people, and the reality is that you get more publicity in these kinds of surveys by finishing last than first. The respondents were probably all British Airways employees.'

BBC NEWS

NONE LOWER

'RUINAIR FLIES 150 MILLION PASSENGERS IN THE UK. 250,000 FREE SEAT SALE ACROSS EUROPE TO CELEBRATE. ZILCH, NADA, ZIP, F**K ALL!!!'

RUINAIR.COM NEWS, 11 JULY 2007

Christmas Presence

Hodges Figgis Bookshop, Dublin 2
– December 21st @ 11.10am

Is that Mick again? I stare ahead at the queue. Others spot him too and peer over. It looks like Mick. He wears faded denim jeans, black loafers and a zipped-up blue coat. He is active and agitated. So it must be Mick. I've only stood this close to a man worth six hundred million euro a few times before but it's still a thrill of sorts. Mick remains the closest thing we have to a real cult in Ireland.

I am in the Sports section of Dublin's leading bookshop, looking for a book on tennis for my godchild so that she can play as well as Roger Federer, when I first notice Mick about ten feet away. He is into Sports too and he examines some horse racing books. It must be difficult for Mick to go Christmas shopping in Dublin city centre in the week before Christmas. I don't mean the hassle with sparse parking and all the crowds, nor even the perpetual hazard of being recognised and stalked in public by loonies like myself. I mean imagine being worth six hundred million euro and giving someone a book as a gift. 'You got me a book?'

I text my sister to advise her Mick is standing mere feet away. She texts me back. 'It's a sign.'

Mick has five books in hand and he is sociable with the check-out girl. 'Busy enough here today.'

She nods. 'It's been hectic.' Mick pays up. 'Are you all done then?' she asks.

'Almost got everything.' He certainly has.

Mick hurries off and I decide to leave the man in peace. He doesn't know it yet but next year's Christmas shopping here will be so much easier. He'll be able to buy copies of *Ruinair* for all his family and friends.

Epilogue

When I began this book, Europe represented a smaller, easier proposition but shortly after taking my virginal flight they went and moved the borders. Some sly bureaucrats in a grey building in Brussels, only one hour by convenient shuttle bus from Charleroi aka Brussels South International, added ten new countries to Europe. I have seen Old Europe but now there's New Europe and it's a daunting prospect: Cyprus, the Czech Republic, Estonia, Hungary, Latvia, Lithuania, Malta, Poland, Slovakia and Slovenia. And later they went and added two more impossible-to-get-to-cheaply destinations: Bulgaria and Romania.

Each country in New Europe now must demonstrate their credentials as an independent sovereign nation, not only by winning the Eurovision Song Contest, becoming the Brits' favourite place for buying second homes or by hosting weekend hen and stag parties, but by having its own native low fares airline.

Centralwings fly from Dublin to a few destinations in Poland. I have always wanted to visit the city of Lodz and write a travel article called *Lodz to Do and See,* and I wonder if Mick is correct about the city of Gdansk. *'Who wants to go to Gdansk? There ain't a lot there after you have seen the shipyard wall.'*

Air Baltic fly from Dublin to Estonia.

Smart Wings fly from Paris to the Czech Republic.

SkyEurope fly from Dublin to Slovakia. I hear there is much local beauty in Bratislava.

Wizz Air fly from London Lootin' to Hungary.

Blue Air fly from London Stansted to Romania.

Hemus Air fly to Bulgaria with fares from as low as 149 euros. Right.

No one cheap flies to Cyprus except holiday charters and the UN peace-keeping forces.

And when there is absolutely no choice I will have to fly on Ruinair to Lithuania, Latvia, Slovenia and Malta. *'We'll push the other airlines out to Russia, then to Siberia.'*

I wonder if I could see all twelve countries of New Europe for another measly three hundred euros.

I log on, check a few new websites, book flights, get my backpack and set my alarm clock for 5am.

I'll call the book *Ruinairski*.

*Dublin airport, at the departure gate, getting a flight
to a soccer match.*

*The flight is delayed and the Dublin skangers
start their chanting:*

'Ruinair! Ruinair!'

Sources

The author acknowledges the following various sources of material used in this book:

The Irish Times 30 January 2007

Irish Independent 29 March 2003, 18 March 2006, 18 June 2006, 22 June 2006, 28 June 2007, 7 August 2007

Sunday Independent 10 August 2008

The Guardian 7 January 2002, 16 June 2002, 24 June 2005, 8 May 2006, 18 August 2006, 6 October 2006, 2 November 2006, 5 January 2007, 29 June 2008

The Times 8 February 2004, 20 June 2006, 30 August 2006, 16 March 2007, 10 August 2008

The Daily Telegraph 11 June 2002, 6 August 2003, 26 May 2004, 27 June 2004, 13 September 2004, 14 September 2004, 12 May 2006, 5 October 2006, 8 January 2007, 17 March 2007, 30 August 2007

The Independent 15 May 2001, 23 June 2002, 19 December 2003, 29 January 2004, 31 January 2004, 3 November 2004, 27 July 2006, 19 August 2006, 7 October 2006, 2 November 2006

The Mirror 14 February 2006, 27 March 2006, 16 June2007

Evening Standard 6 December 2006, 20 April 2007, 5 November 2007,

The Herald 29 November 2005

The Belfast Telegraph 4 October 2007

The Sunday Business Post 12 March 2006

Irish Examiner 6 September 2003

Leicester Mercury 29 September 2005

Metro 13 September 2007

The Southern Star 24 May 2008

Financial Times 26 May 2004

The Wall Street Journal 15 September 2007

International Herald Tribune 23 March 2007

The Columbus Dispatch 20 May 2007

Forbes 19 January 2007

Newsweek 24 October 2004

Business Week 27 November 2006

Reuters.com 6 June 2006, 5 September 2007

www.financialnews.com 18 December 2006

BBC News 12 December 2002, 30 January 2004, 29 March 2006,
    5 October 2006, 26 October 2006

BBC Radio 4 Any Questions 23 March 2007

RTE News 14 December 2004

Moneyweek.com 19 October 2006

www.Celebrity-Gossip.net 4 April 2007

www.Seattlepi.com 16 November 2002

Expatica 16 January 2007

Marketing Week 15 August 2007

www.Typicallyspanish.com

www.brownbagfilms.com

www.airlinemeals.net

www.overheardindublin

www.yahoo.com

Channel 4 Dispatches 'Caught Napping' 13 February 2006

Girls of Ryanair Cabin Crew Charity Calendar INK Publishing photography Cameron McNee

Irish Government Dail Joint Committee on Transport 25 March 2003

Ryanair.com

The author welcomes feedback from readers,
particularly those with Ruinair anecdotes.

paulkilduff@eircom.net

or visit www.paulkilduff.com